YANKEES AND SAMURAI

Books by Foster Rhea Dulles

YANKEES AND SAMURAI

THE OLD CHINA TRADE

EASTWARD HO

AMERICA IN THE PACIFIC

LOWERED BOATS

FORTY YEARS OF JAPANESE-AMERICAN RELATIONS

AMERICA LEARNS TO PLAY

THE ROAD TO TEHERAN

TWENTIETH CENTURY AMERICA

CHINA AND AMERICA

LABOR IN AMERICA

THE AMERICAN RED CROSS

AMERICA'S RISE TO WORLD POWER

THE IMPERIAL YEARS

THE UNITED STATES SINCE 1865

AMERICANS ABROAD

PRELUDE TO WORLD POWER

HARPOON *(Juvenile)*

YANKEES
AND SAMURAI

America's Role in the Emergence

of Modern Japan: 1791-1900

FOSTER RHEA DULLES

HARPER & ROW, PUBLISHERS
NEW YORK

For Marion
Remembering Forty Years

Contents

Foreword   ix

1 : *"Red Hairs from America"*   1

2 : *Whalers, Shipwrecks and Iron Cages*   23

3 : *The Discovery of America*   40

4 : *A Treaty Is Signed*   53

5 : *"Nippon and America, All the Same Heart"*   67

6 : *Envoy Extraordinary*   81

7 : *"Hither from Niphon"*   106

8 : *A Time of Turbulence*   126

9 : *The Yankee Invasion*   149

10 : *Experiment in Hokkaido*   174

11 : *The Japanese in America*   190

12 : *Love at First Sight*   214

13 : *Globe-Trotters*   231

14 : *End of an Era*   249

Bibliographical Notes   255

Index   269

Illustrations

These illustrations follow page 84

The ship *Franklin*, which visited Nagasaki in 1799
William Cleveland
Captain James Devereux, of the ship *Franklin*
"Washington greatly defeats the soldiers of England at Saratoga"
Departure of the U.S.S. *Columbus* and *Vincennes* from Yedo Bay
     on July 29, 1846
A daguerreotype of Manjiro
Fairhaven—New Bedford, Massachusetts
"A Black Ship"
First Landing of Americans in Japan—July 14, 1853
Commodore Matthew Calbraith Perry. Contemporary Japanese print
"True Portrait of Perry." From *The Black Ship Scroll*
Matthew Calbraith Perry. From a daguerreotype by P. Haas
Commodore Perry and Color Bearer
File of American Marines
Commodore Perry and a Japanese Wrestler
Public Baths at Shimoda

vii

Illustrations ✻ viii

Commodore Perry Meeting the Japanese Commissioners at Yokohama

Dinner given the Japanese Commissioners aboard the U.S.S. *Powhatan*

Minstrel Show Aboard the U.S.S. *Powhatan*

Sumo Wrestlers at Yokohama

An American Sailor Drinking with a Geisha

American Sailors Photographing a Courtesan

Commodore Perry Paying Farewell Visit to Japanese Commissioners at Shimoda

Townsend Harris

The Temple of Gyokusen-ji

Townsend Harris Meeting with Japanese Officials

The First Japanese Treaty Commission, 1860

"Tommy"—the Favorite of the Ladies

"American Pleasure Riding in Yokohama"

"Some Americans"

Floral Car Carrying the Japanese Treaty Box

"Foreigners Making Merry"

Ernest Fenollosa

Lafcadio Hearn

Train and Waterfront at Yokohama

"Yokohama Dontaku"—The Famous Sunday Parade

For their assistance in collecting these illustrations the author would like to express his appreciation to Tsuneo Tamba, DeWolf Perry, Carl H. Boehringer, Robert A. Wilson, Foy Casper, Jr., John W. Dwyer, M. V. Brewington, E. Taylor Parks, Mrs. Thomas V. Braband, Emily V. Warinner, Mrs. Brenda Byrne and Miss Bessom Harris.

Foreword

AT NO TIME since the peoples of America and Japan first became aware of each other's existence, which may perhaps be set at the close of the eighteenth century, have they been more mutually interested in each other than they are today. This has its ironies. A cruel and bitter war, with its aftermath of the victors' occupation of the vanquished country, ushered in this present-day era of such lively reciprocal interest and cordial goodwill.

In some measure what we are witnessing is a return to conditions and circumstances that prevailed in the nineteenth century. Even before the days of Commodore Perry, there was a keen curiosity about Japan on the part of Americans and, at least in educated circles in Japan, a growing wonder about this new American nation of which the Japanese had only vaguely heard. After Perry's visits in 1853 and 1854—constituting that epochal event that has come down in history as "the opening of Japan"— there was to develop over the next half century a very close accord between the two countries. The United States felt a generous responsibility for the nation which it had somewhat summarily drawn from its historic seclusion; Japan looked upon the United States as her most disinterested friend in the Western world. Americans in Japan and Japanese in America encouraged a spirit of mutual understanding that made for an unexpectedly friendly relationship.

By the close of the century, political developments within both the United States and Japan were to introduce a new distrust on the part of either nation, and in time these developments led to a mounting hostility which in turn caused a weakening of earlier cultural ties. The American and Japanese people—even before the final tragedy of war—lost some of their interest in one another's civilizations as well as that feeling of mutual esteem which had heretofore generally characterized their relations.

This book is an exploration of the contacts between Americans and Japanese during the nineteenth century. It is not primarily concerned with politics, trade or diplomacy. Its major interest is the personal experiences of individuals—both Japanese in the United States and Americans in Japan—who helped to provide a bridge between two such dissimilar cultures as those represented on the one hand by enterprising Yankees and on the other by the feudalistic samurai who were seeking to come to grips with Western civilization.

I would like to express my gratitude for assistance along the way to Miss Naomi Fukuda, librarian of The International House of Japan, and to the staff of the Kokusai Bunka Shinkokai, for their generous help in locating materials; to Miss Kay Nakada, Thomas Shimizu and Masaya Yamamoto (as further explained in the bibliographical notes) for their aid in translations; to Jerome B. Grieder and the late Kazuo Kawai for their helpful reading of the entire text; and to Mrs. Colette Armstrong for her faithful typings of my revised manuscript.

The interest and encouragement, the invaluable editorial assistance of my wife, Marion R. Dulles, make this book, as in the case of my previous historical ventures, almost as much hers as my own.

A Note on Japanese Names

I have followed the traditional practice in the use of Japanese names of placing the surname before the given name—except in the case of those Japanese authors who themselves follow the Westernized style of placing the given name first. The spelling attempts to conform to modern romanized Japanese. In the case of the envoys appointed to meet Commodore Perry and those sent abroad in 1860, I have used the contemporary honorific title; such as Shimmi Buzen-no-Kami, which may be translated, Shimmi, Lord of Buzen.

The Shogun's capital was spelled Yedo by contemporary Americans and I have retained this spelling rather than Edo. On the restoration of the Emperor, the city of course became known as Tokyo.

Yokohama and Kanagawa were adjacent villages in the 1850's. It was the latter which gave its name to the treaty signed by Commodore Perry in 1854 and it was there the first foreign consuls lived, but Kanagawa was soon absorbed by Yokohama. I have used the latter name for the well-known treaty port.

1

"Red Hairs from America"

EARLY IN MAY, 1791, the local Japanese officials of Kashinoura, a small seaport on the Kii Peninsula which reaches southward from the main Japanese island of Honshu, reported a strange foreign vessel off the shore. The authorities charged with the responsibility of safeguarding the coastline hurried to the scene to prevent her possible landing. To their great relief they discovered that she had already sailed away. However, a note had been left behind which stated that the ship belonged to "the Red Hairs from a Land called America."

This note, still extant in its Chinese version in the Japanese archives, had some further details. The ship was said to be on route from the Flower Country to the Skin Grass Country, which may be translated as China and America's Northwest Coast, and had drifted upon the Japanese shore "under stress of wind and wave." She would remain only a few days, departing just as soon as the weather permitted. Having then stated that the ship's cargo consisted only of copper and iron, the note concluded: "The captain's name is Kendrick."

The visit of this ship almost certainly constituted the first direct contact between the United States and Japan. It did not serve to introduce trade, let alone establish official relations between the two countries. Another sixty years were to pass before Commodore Perry, sailing into the Bay of Yedo with his famous "black ships," was able to achieve even the latter goal. In the 1790's, as suggested both by the trepidation of the local Japanese officials over the ship's appearance and her captain's promise to leave as soon as the weather allowed, the laws of Japan forbade all intercourse with unknown foreigners. The call of this American vessel at Kashinoura was nevertheless a harbinger of the future, the first of a succession of fleeting, episodic contacts between Americans and Japanese that were to help pave the way for the negotiations that finally opened up the secluded Japanese empire to the Western world.

Japan had at an earlier time welcomed both traders and missionaries from foreign countries. By the close of the sixteenth century, the Portuguese had developed a considerable commerce and the Jesuits had made so many converts that it appeared that Japan might become a Christian nation; the Dutch began their trade with the opening of the next century, and soon afterward the English, having secured a charter from the great Iyeyasu (it was only six years after the settlement of Jamestown), set up a factory at Hirado. By 1638, however, the rulers of Japan had become so fearful of further foreign encroachments and of what they considered the subversive influence of Christianity that they summarily broke off all relations with the West. They banished the foreigners, proscribed Christianity and prohibited any overseas travel on the part of their own subjects.

The Tokugawa Shoguns, who were to govern Japan until the revolution of 1868 restored the ancient power of the Emperor, rigidly enforced this policy of seclusion. They permitted a limited trade with China and kept one small window open to the West by allowing the Dutch to retain a trading post on the little island of Deshima, in the Bay of Nagasaki, and to send there two ships from Holland (later reduced to one) every year. Otherwise there was to be no intercourse whatsoever with the Western barbarians. For more than two centuries the Japanese lived almost completely unto themselves behind the forbidding walls of their self-imposed isolation. All that Japan knew of the West, or that the West knew of Japan, was filtered through the medium of the handful of Dutch traders living their own isolated life at Deshima.

In the face of these restrictive circumstances the first contacts between Americans and Japanese remained few and far between. But the American people were to become increasingly interested in this distant island empire on the Pacific's farther shore, and however reluctant they were to welcome foreigners, the Japanese were by the 1850's convinced that if it were necessary to do so, the Americans represented less of a threat to their security than any European nation. It was inevitable that sooner or later Japan would be compelled to abandon her isolation, but that she finally did so at the bidding of the United States was at least in part a consequence of a series of casual visits by Americans beginning with that of Captain Kendrick in 1791.

There could not possibly have been any greater contrast in background or outlook than that which set apart the adventurous, enterprising, acquisitive Yankees who first visited Japan and the proud, conservative, sword-bearing samurai of that mysterious country. Distrust and suspicion on either side warred against the establishment of mutual confidence on official levels, and yet at the same time there was from the very start of their association, as all the early records testify, an instinctive friendliness between the Japanese people and their American visitors.

"The captain's name is Kendrick."

Whatever the vagaries of the Japanese records, contemporary American sources definitely identify this first American visitor to Japan. He was John Kendrick, of Wareham, Massachusetts, one of the best known of those intrepid Yankee seamen who at the close of the eighteenth century sailed recklessly the length and breadth of the Pacific, their ships no larger than modern yachts, in ceaseless pursuit of new opportunities for trade.

Three years before his adventures in Japan, Kendrick had commanded the first American expedition to the Northwest Coast and opened up the lucrative commerce in furs between the Oregon country and the Chinese port of Canton. On that voyage he was master of the ship *Columbia*, outfitted by a group of Boston merchants, and her companion vessel, the little ninety-ton sloop *Lady Washington*, was commanded by Captain Robert Gray, of Tiverton, Rhode Island. While off the Oregon coast the two men exchanged commands. Captain Gray sailed to Canton in the *Colum-*

bia with a cargo of sea otter skins obtained from trading with the Indians, went on from there around the world (the first American circumnavigation of the globe), and on later returning to the Northwest Coast, discovered the great river to which the *Columbia* gave her name. Captain Kendrick had meanwhile remained on the coast for a time with the *Lady Washington*, and then after visiting the Hawaiian Islands, sailed in turn for Canton, where he arrived in January, 1790, with a cargo of furs and sandalwood.

Kendrick was at this time a man of about fifty, powerfully built, somewhat quick of temper and absolutely fearless. No Yankee seaman in the China trade was more enterprising and ambitious, or readier to follow up any possibility for commerce. He was not always too scrupulous in the methods he employed, and sometimes let himself be carried away by grandiose schemes that were the product of a very lively imagination rather than sober common sense. He was perhaps not cut out to command such an expedition as that which first took him to the Northwest Coast ("not a nimble leader," as one of his crew wrote), and he showed up to much greater advantage as master of a single vessel. The supercargo of the *Columbia*, one John Howel, was in many ways highly critical of Kendrick, but concluded in a later letter to the ship's owners that "with all his fooleries he was a wonderful man and worthy to be remembered beyond the Gliding hours of the present generation."

On reaching Canton in the *Lady Washington*, Captain Kendrick appears to have rather blithely disregarded the interests of her owners and acted as if ship and cargo were his own. Moreover, he got in trouble with the Chinese port authorities, under the most complicated circumstances, for trying to avoid payment of duties on his sea otter skins. While the record of his stay in Canton is thus anything but clear, we do know definitely that he left China— as reported by a fellow sea captain, Amasa Delano, of Duxbury, Massachusetts—at the end of March, 1791. He was bound once again for the Northwest Coast with some two hundred sea otter pelts aboard ship that he had been unable to sell in Canton, and the *Lady Washington*, which had been re-outfitted as a brigantine, was now accompanied by the sloop *Grace*, Captain James Douglas, of New York.

There is no suggestion in Captain Delano's report that Kendrick planned on his way to Oregon to seek out a market for his remaining furs in the forbidden ports of Japan, but there would appear to be little question that this was his intention. It was altogether in character, a project that would appeal alike to his sense of adventure and his commercial instincts. The allegation that his cargo consisted of copper and iron is inexplicable, but the further statement in the note he sent ashore at Kashinoura to the effect that his ships had drifted upon the coast "under stress of wind and wave" was probably designed to lull Japanese suspicions while he explored the possibilities of trade.

Contemporary American sources, if not the old Japanese records, bear out such an interpretation of his plans. Captain Kendrick's old ship, the *Columbia*, was once again on the Northwest Coast when the *Lady Washington* and the *Grace* arrived there after their call at Kashinoura. The *Columbia*'s first mate, John Hoskins, recorded the arrival of the two vessels on June 13, 1791. Noting that they had stopped at a port in southern Japan on their voyage from Canton, he further wrote that while their crews reported they had been hospitably received by the natives, it had proved impossible to sell any furs because "the Japanese knew not the use of them." So also another of the *Columbia*'s crew, Robert Haswell, noted in his journal that the *Lady Washington* and the *Grace* had visited Japan but "not finding a good sale port for their furs made but a short tarry."

The contradictions between the letter Kendrick sent ashore at Kashinoura and the reports made to his former shipmates aboard the *Columbia* shroud this first episode in American-Japanese relations in an engaging mystery. It can never be wholly cleared up. Kendrick did not himself leave any record of his experiences, and apparently he made no further attempts to trade with the Japanese. Three years after returning to the Northwest Coast he was accidentally killed while visiting Honolulu. Another American ship in the harbor, firing a salute with a supposedly unloaded cannon, crashed a shot into the *Lady Washington* which struck her captain as he was sitting in his cabin.

Kendrick had failed to open up commerce with Japan—and there may be some doubt as to his actual reception at Kashinoura —but he has a distinctive place in any history of Japanese-American relations. As John Hoskins concluded his account of the *Lady*

Washington's visit in Japanese waters, "Here Captain Kendrick displayed the American flag which is probably the first ever seen in that quarter."

The next visits by Americans to Japan were made under quite different circumstances. Between 1797 and 1807 eight different ships whose home ports were in the United States called at Nagasaki, but the flags at their mastheads as they entered the harbor were Dutch rather than American. In these perilous years of the French Revolutionary wars, the Dutch East India Company had chartered the American vessels to avoid possible enemy capture of their own ships in making the annual visit to Nagasaki permitted by the Japanese authorities. Normally engaged in the tea trade with Canton, the American merchantmen jumped at the profitable chance to sail under contract between Batavia, the Dutch East India Company's headquarters in Java, and the fabled Japanese port from which they were in their own right barred.

The first of these chartered ships was the *Eliza*, originally hailing from New York, under the command of Captain William Robert Stewart, and the last was the *Mount Vernon*, Captain J. Davidson, whose home port was Philadelphia. Two years after the *Mount Vernon*'s visit, in 1809, the Dutch East India Company chartered the *Rebecca*, Captain James Deal, a Baltimore ship which had once before called at Nagasaki, but she was captured by the British and taken to Calcutta as a prize of war. The expedient of employing American ships was thereafter abandoned.

Although the Japanese allowed the American merchantmen flying the Dutch flag to enter Nagasaki Harbor in accordance with their agreements with the Dutch East India Company, there was at first considerable confusion when the authorities discovered that the crews aboard them were English-speaking. However, when assured that these newcomers were the "Red Hairs from America" rather than Englishmen, they made no further difficulties over their presence in Nagasaki. For while the English were still suspect in Japanese eyes because of their association with the foreign troubles of the seventeenth century, it was already known through the Dutch that the Americans were a people who had risen in revolt against British rule. The Japanese did not believe that they were likely to have any ulterior purpose in coming to Nagasaki.

The Dutch-chartered American ships, as we very specifically know from the log of the *Franklin,* Captain James Devereux, of Boston, which visited Nagasaki in 1799, carried cargoes largely made up of cloves, sugar, pepper and cotton yarn, and, in the case of the *Franklin* herself, a ton of elephants' tusks. These commodities, taken aboard at Batavia, were exchanged for copper, camphor and various articles of Japanese manufacture. On the ocean voyage the American ships flew their own flag, but upon approaching the Japanese coast, their instructions called upon them to hoist that of Holland and thereafter observe scrupulously the procedures prescribed by the Japanese authorities for the vessels of the Dutch East India Company. They were to fire a fixed number of salutes on passing certain points in the harbor, send ashore their arms and ammunition as soon as they had anchored, and carefully seal up all books and papers, especially any religious books. In preparation for being boarded by the Japanese officials, they were further ordered to make ready on the quarter-deck "a table covered with a piece of cloth & five cushions for the Officers to sit upon."

The harbor of what the Americans called "Nangasacca" presented a striking view to the curious sailors aboard these ships. Against its background of picturesque, wooded hills, the city had a very fine appearance. Its buildings were for the most part two-story wooden houses, the streets narrow and paved with cobblestones, and everything about the port seemed to be unusually well ordered. The island of Deshima, where the Dutch had for so long lived in the most strict confinement, was apparently even smaller than the American visitors had been led to expect. And while it was connected with the mainland by a little bridge, this sole entry and exit was closely guarded and the island was otherwise surrounded by a high wooden fence.

The American seamen were allowed to explore Nagasaki with possibly more freedom—though always accompanied by Japanese guards or official spies—than was permitted the Dutch. They were also permitted, as was generally the custom aboard merchant ships, to engage in a limited private trade on their own account.

They bought from the Japanese silks and porcelains, lacquerware, inlaid tables, writing desks, knife boxes, fans and, as recorded in the *Franklin*'s log, "boxes of birds . . . and cuspidors." These purchases, brought back to the homes of seafaring families in Boston and Salem, were the first Japanese imports into the United States and helped to inspire a lively interest in the artistic manufactures of the island kingdom.

Among the Americans visiting Nagasaki in these years were two young brothers, William and George Cleveland, of one of the most noted of Salem merchant families, and their journals provide the first eyewitness descriptions of Japan and the Japanese written by Americans. William Cleveland sailed aboard the ship *Massachusetts*, Captain W. V. Hutchings, in 1800, and George Cleveland took passage the next year aboard the *Margaret*, Captain Samuel Derby.

Both young men liked the Japanese with whom they came in contact and singled out, as would succeeding American visitors down through the years, the unusual courtesy and kindliness that appeared to govern all Japanese social relationships, quite as much among the poor as among the rich. This politeness, and the highly civilized character of the Japanese in general, greatly surprised the Americans. Jealous of their monopoly and seeking to discourage any interest in Japan on the part of other Westerners the Dutch had painted the Japanese in a most unflattering light. "We were taught to look upon the Japanders as a cruel people before coming in," William Cleveland wrote. "Many stories we now think exaggerated and some entirely unfounded."

Even though this young visitor reported of the Japanese that "their manners are very respectful and engaging," adding that everyone aboard the *Massachusetts* was "much pleased with them," he still realized that they had "great vices as well as great virtues." He was shocked by the number of brothels in Nagasaki, the callous practice whereby the daughters of the poor were so often sold into prostitution, and the generally inferior status of Japanese women. Observing this aspect of Japanese society, he compared it with the purer customs of New England and confided to his diary that he could not help thinking back "with affection of our own Country and of the fond sisters of America who are so necessary to our happiness." In time his enjoyment of his stay at Nagasaki palled. He was soon to write that he was "heartily sick of the island of Deshima," and with the passage of another month confessed that he was "thinking and sighing for home."

George Cleveland, a twenty-year-old ship's clerk, has left a somewhat fuller account of Japan than his brother. He was ill upon first arriving at Nagasaki aboard the *Margaret,* and it was only after some time under the care of a Dutch physician on Deshima that he was able to visit the mainland. He then noted approvingly the general order that prevailed throughout the city, the obedience to authority displayed by the people, and the cleanliness and neatness of the interiors of the houses however mean their outside appearance. He spoke of the floors being covered with mats, and that it was considered "a piece of ill breeding, to tread on them, without first taking off the shoes." He was if possible even more impressed by the courtesy of the Japanese than his brother. "As long as we were in Japan," George Cleveland wrote, "I do not recollect of seeing one person that appeared to be angry with another, but the most perfect harmony prevailed among them."

He was fascinated by the samurai, with their shaven heads and topknots, their two swords and their exotic costumes. Struggling to describe their clothes, he wrote of them wearing "a caloy, or loose gown . . . over this a kind of petticoat . . . [and] a shawl, which is generally made of black crape, and round the waist they have a band of either Silk or Cotton; thro' this band the Officers of Government put their swords."

In carrying on his private trade, for George Cleveland was one of those who brought home a collection of curios, he found the procedure impossibly tedious. Everything the Americans presented for sale had to be gone over with meticulous care, and in his case the Japanese merchants examined minutely every one of a set of wine glasses and tumblers he offered them. No one could have any idea, he complained, of the "trouble we had in delivering this little Invoice, which would not have been an hour's work in Salem." When their own purchases—the usual porcelain, lacquerware and various curious—were finally made ready, the young sailor had a further revealing comment. Everything was packed, he reported admiringly, "in boxes so neat that in any other country they would be considered cabinet work."

George Cleveland also caught at least a glimpse of another side of Japanese life when a fast, as he described it, was held in remembrance of the dead while the *Margaret* was in port. The graves on the side of Nagasaki's steep hills were all lighted with paper lamps making "a most brilliant appearance," and then on the fourth night of the ceremonies these lamps—or lanterns— were all "brought down to the water, and put into small straw barks, with paper sails, made for the occasion, and after putting in rice, fruit, etc., they are set afloat. This exhibition was very fine."

On one trip ashore a number of the Americans, including Captain Derby, were cordially entertained by "an eminent Stuff merchant" who took them to his home, to a temple, to what Cleveland describes as "a glass house," and finally to a teahouse where they were entertained with music, dancing and acrobatics. At the merchant's establishment, they met "the lady of the House," and whether or not this was a quite accurate identification of the person in question, the American visitor was much impressed. "She appeared to be a modest Woman," he wrote, "which cannot be said of many of her countrywomen."

"Towards dark we returned to the Island," George Cleveland concluded this account of the experiences of one of America's pioneer sight-seers in Japan, "& so great was the crowd, in the streets, to see us pass, that it was with great difficulty we could get along."

During these years of American visits to Japan under Dutch auspices, a new effort was made to open a direct trade. It was undertaken by William Stewart, who had first visited Nagasaki as captain of the *Eliza* in 1797. Another enterprising Yankee who had much in common with John Kendrick, Stewart was daring, shrewd and again not overscrupulous. He too had had his troubles with the Chinese authorities at Canton, and turned to possible commerce with Japan as offering greater opportunities than the closely regulated Chinese market.

He returned to Nagasaki several times after his first visit, seeking to conclude some sort of an arrangement with the Dutch East

India Company for his private business. They would have none of it. Fearful of this threatening interloper, the Dutch finally placed him under arrest and deported him to Batavia. Stewart escaped, however, and after going to India reappeared in Nagasaki once again in the summer of 1803. His new vessel, which he tactfully named the *Nagasaki Maru*, had been outfitted in India, but she sailed under American colors.

Stewart now told the Japanese authorities, who by this time knew him well ("courageous and resourceful, but gentle-spoken, like a lady," their records describe him), that he was officially commissioned to open trade in the name of the United States. He said he had been authorized by President Jefferson, whom he described as holding the offices of "Daimyo of Virginia" and "Shogun of the United States," to seek permission to set up an American commercial depot at Nagasaki. Moreover, he came bearing gifts: a camel, an Indian buffalo and a donkey.

The Japanese were immediately suspicious of this vessel flying the unfamiliar Stars and Stripes. The Lord of Omura, whose territory adjoined Nagasaki, ordered his guard boats to surround the *Nagasaki Maru* and hurried additional troops to the port. In spite of Stewart's gentle-spoken persuasiveness and the attraction of his unusual gifts, the Japanese had no idea of letting down their barriers to foreign trade in his favor. They accepted the camel (a sketch of it remains in the Japanese archives), the buffalo and the donkey, but they ordered this rash Yankee to leave Nagasaki and never again try to return to Japan.

The last we hear of Stewart is through a note in the journal of that same Amasa Delano who had reported on Captain Kendrick's departure from Canton twelve years earlier. Delano wrote of Stewart's returning to China from his unlucky venture in Japan, and further commented that while he praised the Japanese in high terms, describing their country as rich, prosperous and exceptionally well governed, he had been unable to make any progress whatsoever toward opening an American commerce.

Four years later an even more unusual attempt to break down the Dutch monopoly was made by an American merchantman which visited Nagasaki flying Russian colors. This ship was the *Eclipse*, Captain Joseph O'Cain, of Boston. After several years' trading on the Northwest Coast, O'Cain entered into an agreement with the Russian-American Company, whose ships were also engaged in buying sea otter skins from the Northwest Indians, whereby he would take a cargo of furs to Japan. When the *Eclipse* drew into the harbor at Nagasaki with an American crew (and also the captain's wife) aboard her, the Japanese promptly surrounded her with guard boats and took her into custody as they had the *Nagasaki Maru.*

One member of the crew of the *Eclipse* was a Scottish-born sailor, Archibald Campbell, who would later relate his experiences in Japanese waters in *A Voyage Around the World*, published in 1816. As he described the *Eclipse's* venture, Captain O'Cain, forewarned that the Japanese were highly suspicious of Russia, sought to make the American character of his ship quite clear by hauling down his Russian colors on entering port and hiding his Russian supercargo. But the Japanese were again unwilling to enter into any trade. "They told us," Campbell wrote, "they had plenty of everything we had to offer."

The officials at Nagasaki were nevertheless very friendly, and while they continued to keep a strict guard over the ship, allowing none of the crew to go ashore, they supplied her with fresh water, fish, vegetables and four hogs. After three days the *Eclipse* was ordered to leave and a hundred open boats, officered by samurai "dressed in loose frocks, or gowns . . . a sabre hanging at each side," towed her out to sea.

This was to be the last visit of an American ship to Japan—so far as is known—for a quarter of a century. And in the meantime the Japanese rigidly tightened their exclusion laws. Primarily as a result of the fear of Russian encroachments on their northern islands, and suspicions aroused against Great Britain when the sailors of an English ship became involved in an affray with Japanese villagers, the government gave new instructions to all local officials to guard more carefully against the approach of foreign vessels. This new edict—"*ninen nahu*" or "no second thought" —decreed that all such ships were to be immediately fired upon, and should they still attempt to make a landing, their crew was to be either arrested or killed and the vessels themselves destroyed.

A Japan so zealously seeking to maintain her ancient policy of seclusion obviously revealed very little of herself to the handful of

Americans who happened to visit her shores at the turn of the nineteenth century. They remained almost wholly ignorant of her political institutions and social organization. Their surprise at finding the people industrious, obedient to authority and so highly civilized grew out of their common failure to realize that Japan had a long history of cultural growth and advancement. Nor could they know that the prosperity and general well-being they observed were the product of some two centuries of almost uninterrupted peace both at home and abroad.

The country's population at this time was some twenty-six million. The great masses of the people were bound to the soil, raising the basic Japanese crop of rice, and lived in small villages. Four or five cities, however, had become flourishing centers of trade and commerce, and also of a lively social and artistic life among the more wealthy. Society was organized on a feudalistic basis with a fixed hierarchical order that placed first the soldier-ruler class of samurai, followed by the farmers, and then by artisans and merchants. Governmental power was centered in the Shogunate, with its administrative arm known as the Bakufu, and a host of samurai officials enforced its decrees and orders.

The Shogun, an office hereditary in the Tokugawa family since the days of Iyeyasu, was officially the military deputy of the Emperor. But he ruled from his capital at Yedo with unquestioned authority, while the Emperor, legendary descendant of the gods, remained in impotent seclusion—a virtual prisoner—at the imperial court in Kyoto. As first of the feudal lords, the Shogun had vast territorial possessions and also exercised a paramount suzerainty over the other great lords of the realm, or daimio, who held their lands as fiefs. But while he was in theory an absolute autocrat, and did fully control the *fudai*, or dependent lords, whose ancestors had been Iyeyasu's vassals, his authority was never so complete over the *tozama*, or powerful outer lords, who had militantly opposed the Tokugawa assumption of power at the opening of the seventeenth century. Entrenched in their castle towns, surrounded by their fiercely loyal samurai retainers, these daimio were in effect masters within their own domains.

At the time of the first American visits, new forces were thrusting up from below to threaten the whole structure of this ancient order which the successive Tokugawa Shoguns had attempted to

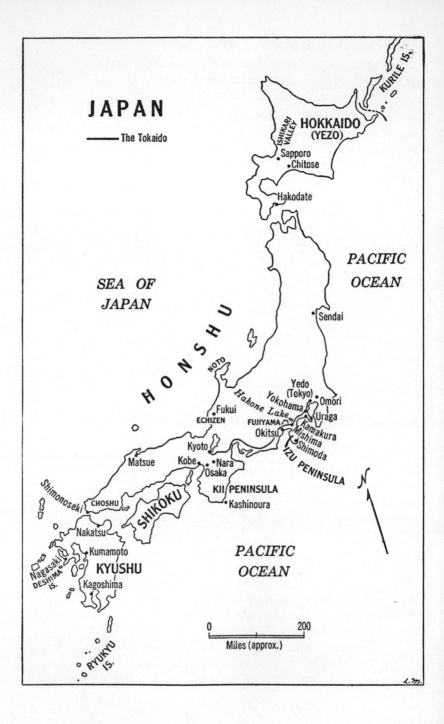

JAPAN
—— The Tokaido

KURILE IS.

ISHIKARI VALLEY HOKKAIDO (YEZO)
Sapporo
Chitose

Hakodate

PACIFIC OCEAN

SEA OF JAPAN

HONSHU

Sendai

NOTO

Hakone Lake

Yedo (Tokyo)
Yokohama
Omori
Uraga
Fukui
ECHIZEN
FUJIYAMA
Kamakura
Mishima
Okitsu
Shimoda
IZU PENINSULA

Kyoto
Matsue
Kobe
Nara
Osaka
KII PENINSULA
Kashinoura

N

Shimonoseki
CHOSHU
SHIKOKU

Nakatsu

Kumamoto
Nagasaki
DESHIMA IS.
KYUSHU
Kagoshima

PACIFIC OCEAN

0   200
Miles (approx.)

RYUKYU IS.

L. M.

freeze beyond possible change. The harsh conditions of country life, with increasing taxes being levied on the annual rice crop and other landlord exactions, had led to a series of bloody peasant revolts. The growth of trade and rise of cities were creating a new money economy which benefited the merchants and tradespeople but increasingly endangered the highly privileged position of the samurai. And the outer lords were becoming restive under the domination of the Shogunate, which sought to compel their loyalty by commanding their presence at Yedo during half the year and for its remainder holding their families as hostages. A transformation in the very bases of Japanese life, presaging the revolution which was to accompany the opening of the country in the mid-nineteenth century, was already under way. But all this was still beneath the surface. The Japan with which Americans first came into contact was still the old Japan whose feudal order had endured for centuries and whose manners and customs contrasted so sharply with everything about the West.

Apart from the governmental system, which most visitors never understood, making a false distinction in attributing temporal power to the Shogun and spiritual power to the Emperor, the status of the samurai afforded the greatest cause for foreign wonderment. They were soldiers, but a long period of peace had left them with few military duties while they still enjoyed the annual stipends granted them by their lords. The social rank exemplified by the right to wear two swords freed them from having to take part in any commercial or other income-producing activity—indeed prevented them from doing so—and until economic pressure forced the later drastic changes in Japanese society, the lower samurai lived lives of carefree irresponsibility. Their loyalty was to their feudal masters and they were bound by the warrior code of *Bushido* (nothing is more familiar about ancient Japan than "The Tale of the Forty-Seven Ronin"), but the times were beginning to undermine the discipline, the sense of duty and the Spartan frugality which had once been so characteristic of samurai conduct.

A few cities—especially Yedo, Kyoto and Osaka—where the rising merchant class was becoming very wealthy and correspondingly influential, reflected another aspect of contemporary Japanese life. Here there had developed what was called *ukiyo*—or the floating world—which was marked by urban frivolity and urban dissipation. As described by G. B. Sansom, the foremost Western historian of Japanese culture, it was a world of "fugitive pleasures, of theatres and restaurants, wrestling booths and houses of assignation, with their permanent population of actors, dancers, singers, story-tellers, jesters, courtesans, bath-girls and itinerant purveyors, among whom mingled the profligate sons of rich merchants, dissolute samurai and naughty apprentices." Its scenes and colorful characters are those depicted in the *ukiyo-e*—colored wood-block prints of the floating world—by such artists as Hokusai and Hiroshige, and they are also the stuff of modern Kabuki drama.

There were attempts at reform in dealing with the breakdown of old standards in this burgeoning town life. Sumptuary laws called for the arrest of prostitutes, outlawed betting, and even went to such lengths as to prescribe dress and forbid both barbershops and hairdressers. An army of spies reported on all infractions of the new codes. But the reforms came to little. As Sansom has written, they were "confounded in a great river of events and left hardly a trace."

Outside the cities, the life of Japan was still going on very much as it had throughout the whole long period of Tokugawa rule. The peasants planted and reaped their crops of rice, lived frugally and simply in small villages of thatched huts, and enjoyed the recurrent festivals centered about the Buddhist temples and Shinto shrines. The ancient virtues were upheld and, except for the occasional uprisings when crop failures broke down their stoic endurance, the people obediently accepted (as George Cleveland had noted) the rule of their lords and masters. And it could also be said that while they were governed firmly, they were on the whole governed justly.

Japan had a highly sophisticated civilization. Its spirit was expressed not only in the justice of government and the honor paid religion, but in the refinement of its artistic culture. The intrinsic value of its architecture, painting, sculpture, ceramics, theater and literature was hardly rivaled in the West. All that Japan lacked were the invention and technology that were the fruits of modern science.

Something of all this gradually became known in the United States. Descriptive accounts written by the Dutch living at

Deshima, especially the famous *History of Japan* by Engelbrecht Kaempfer, were translated into English and published in America. The fragmentary reports of the seamen who visited Nagasaki were spread abroad and appeared in newspapers or magazines. A growing popular interest in things Japanese was reflected, for example, in a review of one book about Japan, in this instance the record of a Russian naval commander held there in custody for several years, that appeared in the *North American Review* in 1818. It concluded:

> There is probably no part of the world which is so little known, and at the same time so worthy of exciting a national curiosity as the Empire of Japan. Its immense population, its great wealth and industry, its progress in the useful arts, and the peculiarity of its civil and religious government, and the manners of its people, give it a hold on our curiosity over almost any other part of the East.

Moreover, it was not only curiosity about Japan that was now being so greatly stimulated, but the idea that the United States might take the lead in trying to break down the walls of Japanese isolation and open up this secluded country to trade and commerce. The persuasive argument was advanced even in these early days that since America had not been involved in any of those episodes that had in the past aroused Japanese hostility toward Europe, and could not be properly charged with the imperialistic designs attributed to both Great Britain and Russia, she might be able to induce Japan to resume her ancient contacts with the outside world.

Probably the first American official to suggest definite action along these lines was Captain David Porter of the United States Navy. After voyaging in the Pacific in pursuit of British whalers during the War of 1812 (he captured a dozen or more), Porter addressed a letter to President Madison, on October 31, 1815, in which he discussed the potentialities of possible trade with the Japanese and urged that an attempt be made to inaugurate commercial relations. He was fully convinced, wrote this far-seeing naval officer, that the United States had a unique opportunity "to beat down their rooted prejudices, secure to ourselves a valuable trade, and make that people known to the world."

Another and more prominent exponent of such a project was John Quincy Adams, whose Massachusetts antecedents made him naturally interested in the promotion of the Far Eastern commerce in which New England merchants were so heavily engaged. His approach, however, emphasized not so much mercantile opportunity as the broader right and duty of Christian nations to bring Japan into the world community. No country, Adams maintained, was justified in withholding its private contribution to the welfare of the whole, and therefore Japan should somehow be persuaded, if possible by the United States, to tear down those isolationist barriers that she had for so long maintained.

Mounting pressures led the Jackson administration to consider a possible expedition to Japan, and Edmund Roberts, who had concluded the first American treaty with Siam, was actually commissioned to visit Yedo in 1832. He himself felt strongly that since it had not awakened the suspicions inspired by the Europeans, the United States could succeed where England and Russia had so repeatedly failed in persuading the Japanese to abandon their seclusion. "The Americans," he reported emphatically to the State Department, "are the only people who can probably effect it." However, a lack of funds and then his death in Macao prevented Roberts from carrying out his mission.

This was not the end, however, of these efforts in the days before Perry to open up Japan. In another five years a further venture, under private rather than government auspices, was launched to seek out trade. It was undertaken by Charles W. King, one of the partners of the American trading firm of D. W. C. Olyphant and Company, which had for many years been doing business at Canton. King had long been interested in Japan, and in the summer of 1837 he believed he had an unusual opportunity to ingratiate himself with the authorities and possibly win their consent to trade by returning to Japan seven Japanese seamen who had been the victim of shipwreck.

Four of these unfortunate castaways had drifted in a junk wrecked in Japanese waters to the shores of the Philippine Islands. After being rescued by friendly natives, they were finally brought to Macao and placed under the protection of American missionaries. The three others had had even more amazing and harrowing experiences. Four years earlier their junk, carrying a cargo of rice between two Japanese ports, had been swept by storm across the Pacific and wrecked on the Northwest Coast, near Queen Charlotte Island. After the Indians had held them captive for a year, the captain of a Hudson's Bay Company ship finally freed the helpless Japanese and took them to London. They remained there only briefly, kept aboard ship except for a single occasion when they were allowed to walk London's streets, and were then re-embarked on an American vessel, the *General Palmer*, which brought them on the long eastward voyage back to China by way of the Cape of Good Hope.

If King's primary motive in seeking to make "a favorable impression" on the Japanese authorities by returning these castaways was the promotion of trade, he also had another reason which reflected the historic pattern of so much American activity in eastern Asia. He hoped to break down the ramparts of Japanese seclusion in the interests of missionary enterprise and the further spread of Christianity. His firm had long been known for its sympathy for such endeavors, having afforded free passage for a number of missionaries coming to China, and its warehouses and offices at Canton were popularly known as "Zion's Corner." King himself was not only an enterprising merchant but also a man of personal piety and deep religious feeling.

To carry the message of Christianity to Japan, he consequently invited three missionaries to sail aboard the ship *Morrison*, which was being outfitted under the command of Captain David Ingersoll for the projected voyage. They were Karl Gutzlaff, a German who was at the time acting as interpreter for the Superintendent of British Trade in China; Dr. Peter Parker, a medical missionary, later secretary for the first American mission to China, and S. Wells Williams, editor and author, as well as missionary, who would return to Japan sixteen years afterward as interpreter for Commodore Perry. In this opportunity to initiate missionary enterprise in Japan, the three men happily envisaged, in Dr. Parker's words, "the glory of God in the salvation of thirty-five million souls."

It was with this unusual passenger list—Charles King (together with his wife), the Japanese castaways and three missionaries— that the *Morrison* sailed for Japan. In order to demonstrate the thoroughly peaceful character of the voyage and to avoid arousing any Japanese suspicions, she carried no armaments of any kind and no religious books or tracts. Her small cargo was made up of cotton goods and woolen cloth for possible trade, together with an assortment of presents for the Emperor ranging from a pair of globes to a portrait of George Washington. In two letters addressed to "His Imperial Majesty" from "the American merchant King," the expedition's leader stated that the *Morrison*'s primary purpose was to return the shipwrecked Japanese sailors, but also requested, after tactfully noting that Japan had once freely admitted foreign vessels to her harbors, that Americans might now be permitted "to carry on a friendly intercourse on the ancient footing."

After a voyage of some twenty-six days from Macao the *Morrison* anchored off Uraga, at the entrance to the Bay of Yedo, where Commodore Perry would draw up his naval squadron in 1853. A number of fishing boats quickly approached her, and in the hope of establishing a basis for friendly communications with the authorities, King allowed the crews of these boats to board the ship. There were some women among them. The Americans were rather taken aback by the odd and unattractive custom a number of them followed in painting their teeth black, but they showed themselves to be both curious and friendly. Dr. Parker was inspired by one "pretty lass" to conjecture over the possible effect on her life of a different environment. "What a change would there be in her future character," he wrote, ". . . could she be transferred from the society in which she lives to some Sabbath-school in England or America!"

The Americans aboard the *Morrison* did not, however, have much time for such reflections. Soon after their visitors had left them, one of the Japanese shore batteries ringing the harbor, without any sort of warning, opened fire on the unarmed and peaceful ship. Without knowing the strange vessel's mission or even her nationality, the local authorities, having hurried troops to Uraga, were prepared to drive her away.

The *Morrison* quickly shifted her position out of range of shellfire and again came to anchor. The next day she found herself subject to a heavier bombardment, one cannon ball furrowing the ship's deck and almost carrying away a mast. In the face of a reception somewhat less cordial than that which had been so confidently expected, the ship's sails were raised and she headed for the open sea.

King was nevertheless determined to make at least one further attempt to get in communication with the responsible authorities, and after clearing the Bay of Yedo the *Morrison* consequently put in to the port of Kagoshima, in the territory of the daimio of Satsuma in southern Kyushu. Once again many small boats approached the American ship in what appeared to be a most friendly spirit, and the local officials not only sent aboard a pilot and provided fresh water, but promised that a representative of the daimio would come aboard the *Morrison* next day. King sent his letter to the Emperor ashore and, very much encouraged, waited for an answer to his request that the castaways aboard his ship be permitted to land.

Whatever hopes he had that the authorities at Kagoshima would be more receptive than those at Uraga were soon dashed. It was observed that improvised forts—which actually amounted to no more than stretches of canvas masking a battery of guns—were being hastily erected along the shore, and the next day the unfortunate *Morrison* was once again subjected to heavy shelling—"a promiscuous fire of musketry and artillery." In attempting to escape she found herself becalmed, slowing drifting on shore, until a sudden squall which nearly laid her on her beam ends enabled her to get clearance. Even then it took the harassed ship nearly eighteen hours, under intermittent Japanese fire, to beat her way out of the harbor.

King decided that there was no alternative to complete abandonment of his project. With the fearful Japanese castaways, who had caught no more than distant glimpses of their native land, still aboard ship, the *Morrison* returned to Macao.

The expedition had been a complete failure. Its results, as Dr. Parker despondently noted, were "nil." Yet King remained convinced that by exerting official pressure, which had been of course beyond his capacity as a private citizen, the United States Government could easily persuade Japan to open her doors to trade. In a book published the year after the *Morrison's* unsuccessful venture (probably the first volume dealing directly with Japan under an American imprint), he urged the authorities at Washington to dispatch a small naval force to Yedo to protest against "the late treatment of the national flag" and insist on a friendly reception for all American vessels in Japanese waters. The United States had both the opportunity and the obligation, King insisted as had David Porter and John Quincy Adams, to take the lead in forcing Japan to change her arrogant policy.

"America is the hope of Asia beyond the Malayan Peninsula," he wrote in *The Claims of Japan and Malaya upon Christendom*. "*There* is the grand scene of human probation, the vast coliseum of the moral world; and there I summon the ablest companions of my country's benevolence to appear."

The situation exemplified by the experiences of the *Morrison* at Uraga and Kagoshima certainly could not continue indefinitely. It was bound to lead either to a changed policy on the part of Japan or an open clash with some one of the Western powers. The world was growing too small for any nation to maintain such strict isolation. Nevertheless there was to be no change at the time in Japan's traditional policy and no lowering of the barriers to trade.

"Since the ancestral law has been once fixed," the Great Councilors again declared, "posterity must obey."

2

⚛

Whalers, Shipwrecks and Iron Cages

THE ANCESTRAL LAW was strictly enforced for some sixteen years following the unsuccessful venture of the *Morrison*. In 1842 the Bakufu decreed that in special circumstances foreign ships entering Japanese waters might be supplied with food and water, but this was a minor concession. Further instructions to the local officials strongly emphasized that if the foreigners did not at once depart after being provisioned, "you will, of course, drive them away."

Throughout these years, Americans interested in the affairs of the Pacific and eastern Asia grew more than ever concerned with the need to break down this determined isolationism. The pressures being exerted by commercial and missionary enterprise gained increasing momentum, and there was soon added to them an entirely new influence in support of opening up Japan. This grew out of popular solicitude over American seamen cast upon Japan's shore as a consequence of shipwrecks among the whalers cruising in Japanese waters.

"If that double-bolted land, Japan, is ever to become hospitable," Herman Melville was to write in *Moby Dick*, "it is the whaleship alone to whom the credit will be due; for already she is on the threshold."

The whalers ranging the wide Pacific in search of their elusive prey had discovered the Japan grounds, lying eastward of Japan, as early as 1820 and then extended their voyages to the waters about the northern Japanese island of Hokkaido, or Yezo as it was then known. They provided excellent hunting. Scores of the sturdy little ships hailing from New Bedford and other whaling ports in New England and Long Island were spending the season in these waters by the early 1840's, no less than eighty-seven being reported in one contemporary Japanese account.

The appearance of these ships off their coast alarmed the suspicious Japanese, who could not disabuse themselves of the idea that the barbarians, even though in this instance they were Americans rather than Europeans, could only be engaged in spying out the land with some aggressive purpose in mind. Whenever any of the crews of these whalers fell into their hands, through shipwreck or other misadventure, they consequently placed them under arrest and, holding them in the strictest possible confinement, transported them to Nagasaki, where they were turned over to the Dutch authorities at Deshima for deportation.

Reports of the suffering and hardship endured by American seamen in these circumstances made their way back to the United States. They might first appear, as told directly by the survivors, in such journals or newspapers as the *Chinese Repository*, published in Canton, the *Polynesian* and *The Friend* in Honolulu, or the *Straits Times* in Singapore, and then be picked up and reprinted by newspapers and magazines in the United States. Stressing as they did the harshness and even cruelty of the Japanese officials in dealing with the helpless American castaways, these reports aroused considerable popular feeling against Japan. Especially in shipping and whaling circles the demand was now voiced that, over and beyond all considerations of trade, the United States should take such measures as were necessary to force the Japanese to provide aid and succor for its shipwrecked citizens.

From their point of view the Japanese authorities were acting justly and logically. However ungrounded their suspicions might actually be that the American whalers were surreptitiously surveying the coast, forerunners of possible attack or invasion, past experience appeared to warrant the sternest measures against all foreigners in order to uphold the seclusion policy. Even though American seamen coming ashore might claim (as had Captain Kendrick a half century earlier) that they had been forced to do so under "stress of wind and wave," their presence in Japan violated the law. Arrest and deportation followed as a matter of course.

In the subsequent negotiations over this issue after the arrival of Commodore Perry, the Japanese were to maintain that they had not acted inhumanely. The orders of the Bakufu had been to take all stranded seamen into custody and transport them under guard to Nagasaki, but to treat them in a kindly and considerate way. They declared that this had not always been easy. The crews of shipwrecked American whalers were often rough and unruly ("not of good character") and had sometimes tried to escape from custody.

However, what might seem wholly considerate treatment in the eyes of the Japanese, accustomed as they were to consider all foreigners as barbarians beyond the law, could well be interpreted quite differently by Americans, who had firm convictions about their rights abroad as well as at home. There could be no reconciliation in these circumstances of the inherent contradictions in the two cultures. To this conflict of laws and customs were also added the insuperable difficulties of communication between the American seamen and their Japanese guards. In more than one sense, they were speaking different languages.

A further factor added to the popular resentment in the United States over Japan's failure to give stranded seamen the friendly assistance to which it was believed they were entitled by the laws of humanity. They forced these castaways to step on tablets bearing a representation of the cross, or of the Virgin and Child, in renunciation of what the Japanese considered "the evil sect" of Christianity. This practice, known as *fumi-ye* and soon to become notorious throughout the Western world as "trampling on the cross," was an outgrowth of the abiding fear of Christianity's dangerous influence born of Japanese experience with the Jesuit missionaries of the sixteenth century. It was enforced against all the Shogun's subjects suspected of harboring Christian beliefs (especially those coming in contact with the Dutch) and automatically extended to the unwelcome foreign visitors.

Nothing could have more greatly shocked and outraged the American public than the reports of this sacrilegious indignity being forced upon their countrymen. The nineteenth century was a deeply religious age, and such an affront to the only true faith could never be condoned. The stories of the shipwrecked seamen erased from the American mind everything that former visitors in Japan—the crews aboard the ships chartered by the Dutch East India Company—had ever said about the Japanese being a friendly and hospitable people. Even though these tales, as William Cleveland had once said of those told by the Dutch, may have been "exaggerated and some entirely unfounded," many Americans became persuaded that the Japanese were a wholly barbarous people.

The first direct encounter between the Yankee whalers and Japanese samurai in these years, ironically enough, did not involve shipwrecked Americans but shipwrecked Japanese. It had none of the unfortunate consequences that grew out of the landing of bereft whalemen on Japan's inhospitable shores. The novel experience of Captain Mercator Cooper, of the whaleship *Manhattan* of Sag Harbor, Long Island, may perhaps be told before taking up those instances in which the Japanese imprisoned and reportedly maltreated the American trespassers in their own domain.

On March 15, 1845, the *Manhattan* was hunting whales off the Japanese coast, and on her approaching a barren little island known as St. Peter's, a boat's crew was sent ashore for wood and water. There the Americans discovered seven marooned Japanese and took them aboard ship. Three days later the *Manhattan* encountered a shipwrecked junk and rescued eleven more fishermen. Captain Cooper thereupon decided to take these castaways back to their native land. If his primary motive was one of humanitarianism, he also felt, as had Charles King eight years earlier, that here was a wonderful opportunity to combat Japanese prejudice. In his own words, he very much hoped "to make a strong and favorable impression on the government as to the civilization of the United States and its friendly disposition towards the emperor and people of Japan."

As the *Manhattan* drew near the Japanese coast, Captain Cooper decided to make for Uraga, but he first took the precaution of landing several of the castaways at another point along the shore in order that they might inform the Japanese officials of his intent to sail into the Bay of Yedo. These men were promptly arrested by coastal guards, but, as was later learned, they were well treated and their message relayed to the proper authorities. When the *Manhattan* arrived at Uraga she was not fired upon, as the *Morrison* had been, but was nonetheless promptly surrounded by what Captain Cooper estimated to be at least a thousand armed boats, ranged in three concentric rings, and for the five days she remained in the harbor these boats continued to maintain their close guard. At no time, however, did the Japanese make any hostile gestures or threaten the American ship.

The Americans were fascinated by the spectacle presented by the great number of small craft surrounding the *Manhattan*. They were gaily decorated, with pennants flapping in the breeze, and at dusk lighted lanterns were swung from every stern. A number of Japanese officials soon came aboard ship, including "several of the nobility" as Captain Cooper reported, and they were found to be "intelligent, polite and educated." Reflecting that further characteristic on which every American visitor throughout this early period commented, they were also "filled with an insatiable curiosity" which the Americans were hard put to satisfy. One of the officials however was found to speak some English. He was Moriyama Einosuke, a young samurai who had studied with the Dutch at Deshima and was to appear as an interpreter at every official meeting between Americans and Japanese for the next twenty years.

No member of the *Manhattan's* crew was permitted to go ashore, but the Japanese seamen rescued from St. Peter's Island and the shipwrecked junk were allowed to land, given some money and restored to their homes. Moreover, the authorities expressed their appreciation to Captain Cooper for having brought them back to Japan and sent aboard the *Manhattan* generous gifts—tea, rice, wheat flour, vegetables, fifty chickens, a basketful of flatfish, two octopuses, and also a set of lacquer bowls and ten painted dishes.

The friendly reception accorded the *Manhattan* had been

agreed upon, the Japanese sources state, only after long debate and largely upon the urging of the local officials at Uraga. They argued persuasively that it was hardly likely that the foreign ship could have any ulterior purposes in coming to Japan inasmuch as it had interrupted its whaling operations to effect the rescue of the Japanese seamen. Moreover, in a report made to the authorities as a result of his inquiries aboard the *Manhattan*, Moriyama confirmed the whaleship's peaceful character. He stated that she had sailed for the Pacific from New York ("situated on a small island in North America"), had caught some eight whales, and had aboard a small organ and a great number of books, several dealing with the American war against Great Britain. He described Captain Cooper as a man of about forty-three, tall, gentle and kindly, and added that while most of the twenty-eight members of the crew appeared to resemble Hollanders, eight had "faces and bodies as dark as charcoal."

After disembarking the Japanese waifs and taking aboard the supplies and gifts presented to him, Captain Cooper received a highly official-looking document. "The Emperor sends his compliments to me," he noted in his sea log, "and thanks me for picking up their men and sends me word that I must not come again." The substance if not the actual source of this message is again confirmed by the official Japanese records. In spite of their welcome to the *Manhattan*, the authorities did not want anything like it to happen in the future. They declared that should an American ship ever again have occasion to rescue any Japanese, it should "carry them to some Dutch port."

Captain Cooper had flown the American flag on a visit to Japan —the first friendly visit since those of the American merchantmen flying the Dutch flag in the early 1800's—and even though he had been ordered not to return, the Japanese guard boats pointedly escorting him out to sea in a mile-long file, he felt that his reception was encouraging. On his return to the popular whalers' rendezvous in the Hawaiian Islands, he reported to the Honolulu *Friend* that he was "highly gratified with the result of his adventure among this recluse but civilized people." But while Captain Cooper was hopeful that his reception opened up the possibilities of closer intercourse with Japan, events were soon to demonstrate that it did not foreshadow any real change in the ancient laws.

This was explicitly made clear within the year when Commodore James Biddle, in command of the ship-of-line *Columbus* and the sloop-of-war *Vincennes*, detached for this special mission from the Navy's East India Squadron, visited the Bay of Yedo on July 20, 1846. His mission was wholly exploratory. The first two American envoys sent to China about this same time had been commissioned to conclude if possible treaties with Japan, but for one reason or another they had been unable to undertake this further assignment. Commodore Biddle was instructed to try to find out whether the Japanese would consider treaty negotiations.

The answer was an unequivocal "no." Though no attempt was made to drive the American warships away, and the attitude of the local officials was generally friendly, the Bakufu stated its position in an "explanatory edict"—undated and unsigned—which was handed Commodore Biddle a week after his arrival off Uraga. As later translated, this note read:

> The object of this communication is to explain the reasons why we refuse to trade with foreigners who come to this country across the ocean for that purpose. This has been the habit of our nation from time immemorial. . . . We can make no distinction between different foreign nations—we treat them all alike; and you, as Americans, must receive the same answer with the rest. . . . We have to say that the emperor positively refuses the permission you desire: He earnestly advises you to depart immediately, and to consult your own safety by not appearing again upon our coast.

The visit of the *Columbus* and the *Vincennes* did not in any way advance the cause of Japanese-American relations or bring the people of the two countries any closer together. While hundreds of Japanese were allowed to come aboard the men-of-war, inquisitively examining everything about them, the American seamen were not permitted to go ashore. Two large junks came alongside the *Columbus* and the *Vincennes* with water, fresh vegetables and fruit (including, as one American sailor happily reported, "a quantity of small green apples, the first we have seen since leaving home"), but there were no other contacts between the Japanese and their visitors.

One incident occurred of which a good deal was to be made in later years. Commodore Biddle had agreed to go aboard a native junk to receive the reply to his request for treaty negotiations, but as he stepped on her deck a Japanese seaman struck or pushed him, and he stumbled back into his own boat. Biddle angrily insisted that the man be arrested and then returned to the *Columbus*. The Japanese apologized profusely, said the offending seaman would be severely punished, and expressed the hope that the Americans would not take the unfortunate incident too seriously.

Biddle was not prepared to make any more of it, accepting in good faith the officials' apologies and their promise to take disciplinary measures against the Japanese involved. In reporting the affair to his superiors, he explained that he had wished to maintain a friendly and conciliatory attitude which would help promote the utmost possible goodwill between America and Japan. He felt that the conduct of the seaman who had pushed him was inexplicable but should not be given too much importance, "especially as all the Japanese in and about the ship had evinced a great good nature in their intercourse with us."

The contretemps assumed its unexpected significance when successors of Commodore Biddle heard that reports were current among the Japanese that one of their common seamen had insulted an American naval officer with impunity. These later visitors were convinced that Americans henceforth would have to deal more authoritatively with the Japanese, stand more upon their dignity, in order to uphold the prestige of the United States. There is little question that the incident had a very real influence in causing Commodore Perry to maintain the stiff and unbending attitude that he exhibited in 1853 as a means of impressing upon the Japanese his high position as an official envoy of the United States.

About this same time there had occurred the first of that series of cases which found Americans in Japan suffering somewhat greater indignities than being rudely pushed about on the deck of a native junk.

In June, 1846, the whaleship *Lawrence*, Captain Baker, of Poughkeepsie, New York, was wrecked in the North Pacific. Seven survivors of the disaster somehow made their way to Etorofu, one of the Kurile Islands stretching northeastward from the main Japanese Archipelago. The local officials, in accordance with the prescribed laws, promptly imprisoned them, but confused and uncertain as to how they should deal with these unwelcome visitors, sent to Yedo for instructions. The Bakufu decided that, owing to the lateness of the season and the hazards of ocean travel, it would be necessary to keep the shipwrecked seamen in detention until the following spring and then convey them under guard to Nagasaki where they could be placed aboard the annual Dutch ship when it sailed for Batavia. This course was followed. One of their number died before the survivors of the *Lawrence* were finally released but the other six sailed for the Dutch colony in November, 1847.

The Japanese records of this whole affair emphasize the reasonable treatment accorded the shipwrecked Americans, and this is generally confirmed in the accounts to be found in the archives of the Dutch East India Company. But a quite different story of the survivors' experiences, as first told by the *Lawrence's* second mate, George Howe, to the Singapore *Straits Times*, was what reached the United States.

Howe related that during eleven long months of confinement on Etorofu the seamen were not once allowed out of their prison and, in the apparent belief that they were spies, were subjected to incessant questioning seeking to make them confess their real intention in landing on Japanese territory. Their only food was a most meager diet of rice and fish. On one occasion they were given "a sort of liquor called Sukee," but Howe was convinced that the only reason for this unusual treat was the officials' hope that the cheerful effects of imbibing what was obviously sake, the familiar Japanese rice wine, might lead them to admit they were seeking to spy out the land. It was "a miserable situation," the *Lawrence's* mate declared, and made all the worse by the "bad treatment from the guards who frequently struck us, and insulted us in every possible way."

On their trip to Nagasaki, Howe continued his narrative, the Americans were stowed away "in a dark, filthy place" on the junk transporting them along the Japanese coast and never permitted to go on deck. Occasionally on the infrequent stops at local ports they were taken ashore but invariably "put in a box, the lid of which was fastened down upon us." On finally reaching Nagasaki, they were first taken into a room where there was a print of the crucifixion on the floor, as Howe described it, and ordered on pain of death to step on it. They were then once again put in prison and, for the several months before the arrival of the Dutch ship through whose agency they were to be released, continued to suffer from "close and strict confinement, privation and ill-treatment."

Americans reading this vivid account of the unhappy experience of their countrymen (it was reprinted from the *Straits Times* in home newspapers) were naturally incensed by the treatment accorded them. It did not matter that past experience provided some justification for Japanese fears and suspicions of foreign activities. It was hardly taken into consideration that in imprisoning and then expelling the shipwrecked Americans the officials were no more than carrying out laws that Japan considered, however outrageous from a Western point of view, necessary for her own national security.

Moreover, Americans could not understand that what seemed such unfeeling harshness toward the seamen was often no more than accepted Japanese custom. The bitter complaints against a daily fare of fish and rice would have astonished the native officials. These were the normal staples of the Japanese diet. There is also the matter of the seamen being "put in a box." This was undoubtedly the Japanese norimon, an enclosed palanquin usually about four feet long and perhaps three and one-half feet high. It was in general use among the upper classes, and for a Japanese to travel by such a conveyance was a luxury rather than a hardship. The trouble was that for the much taller Americans the norimon was excruciatingly uncomfortable, as many later travelers, not prisoners, would repeatedly testify. The survivors of the *Lawrence* undoubtedly suffered grievously in being so cooped up, but this was not the malicious torture which the readers of Howe's story so easily imagined.

Still, nothing could extenuate the fact that, instead of giving a friendly reception to the hapless victims of shipwreck, the suspicious Japanese had kept them harshly imprisoned until they could be expelled.

Shortly after the release of the survivors of the *Lawrence*, John W. Davis, the American Commissioner in China, learned through the Dutch East India Company that the Japanese were holding fifteen other Americans as prisoners in Nagasaki. He so informed Commodore Geisinger of the East India Squadron, and, aroused by the accounts of the sufferings of the men from the *Lawrence*, Geisinger promptly ordered Commander Glynn, in command of the sixteen-gun sloop-of-war *Preble*, to proceed to Nagasaki and demand their release.

When the *Preble* entered the Japanese harbor on April 17, 1849, she was surrounded by guard boats, as the earlier American visitors had been, and additional troops were seen assembling on shore to man the batteries that ringed the harbor. Commander Glynn, however, was not to be deterred by any show of force and when his ship was boarded by Japanese officials, he peremptorily insisted on the immediate surrender of the American seamen. If he could not obtain full satisfaction at Nagasaki, he further stated, his orders called for him to proceed to Yedo itself and enforce his demands. This was something new. The local officials did not dare outrightly to refuse compliance, but they were fearful of taking the responsibility of handing the imprisoned Americans over without definite orders from the Bakufu. They tried to put off the importunate American naval officer with the excuses and evasions that would give them time to hear from the capital.

Glynn became more insistent. His knowledge of how Commodore Biddle's consideration had been interpreted as weakness in the earlier incident at Uraga led him, as he was later to write, to impart "a character of 'bruskness' to my intercourse which I have never regretted." A final exchange with the Japanese authorities, as reported in his dispatches to the Navy Department, thereupon brought matters to a head:

COMMANDER GLYNN—It is useless to talk to me in this manner. I
want no prevarication. I want a straight up and down answer. I have
waited five days—four days too long; and now I want something
more than "I think." You give a direct reply to my question, and
I will do the thinking. I will stay three days—certainly no longer—
but you must promise me now that in three days you will deliver the
men. Do you promise?

ANSWER—Yes, in three days you shall get possession of the men.

COMMANDER GLYNN—Very good (offering his hand to the chief who took it). I rely on your word—upon the solemn promise of a Japanese chief.

The men were handed over.

Here was a first instance, as noted by the modern Japanese historian Teijuhn Wada, "in which the stubborn policy of the Japanese government had yielded to the demands of foreigners." There was in the incident a foreshadowing of the shape of things to come.

The stories that these rescued seamen told of their imprisonment nevertheless at the time strengthened the popular prejudices against Japan becoming so prevalent throughout the United States. Getting its news from officers of the *Preble*, the New York *Herald* published a sensational account, widely reprinted in other papers, which graphically stressed the "ignominious and cruel imprisonment" to which the marooned American sailors had been subjected and the "inhuman barbarity" of their Japanese jailers.

If there were some extenuating circumstances from a Japanese point of view for the treatment of the survivors of the *Lawrence*, there were even more in the case of the men brought home in the *Preble*. They were not victims of shipwreck, as Commander Glynn originally thought and as they were represented to be in the newspaper stories. They were mutineers. They had deserted the whaleship *Lagoda*, Captain John Finch, and made their way by small boat to the Japanese shore near Matsumae (now Fukuyama) on the southern tip of Hokkaido. They were beyond question an unruly lot of men and even by their own account made such trouble for the Japanese that it is hardly surprising that the officials felt they had no alternative to confining them even more strictly than they had the crew of the *Lawrence*.

Through their frequent attempts to break away, the *Lagoda* mutineers further convinced the Japanese that they were indeed spies. And even after they had been brought to Nagasaki, once again for prospective release to the Dutch, they continued to make further and nearly successful efforts to escape from custody. The local authorities consequently tightened their restrictions, and the conditions under which these restive prisoners were held were certainly very onerous. They had no opportunity for recreation or exercise, had few clothes and no bedding, and the usual fish and rice diet was only occasionally supplemented by the addition of sweet potatoes and seaweed. Two of the men died, one from some mysterious disease and another apparently strangled in one of the mutineers' incessant and violent quarrels. After still another try at getting away, three of the prisoners were then placed in solitary confinement in what they themselves described as "grated cribs or cages" which did not even allow them to stand up.

When the Japanese surrendered these men to Commander Glynn, they warned that there would undoubtedly be complaints of ill-treatment but insisted that the prisoners' efforts to escape and their quarrelsomeness had necessitated the severity of their imprisonment. These seamen, the Japanese stated, were "truly vulgar and rude, giving the officials no end of trouble." In the publicity their own stories obtained in the United States, however, all this was glossed over and it was never understood that they were actually mutineers. Commander Glynn's official reports were to make their status clear, but the American public remained wholly ignorant of the possible provocation for what the *Lagoda's* men had so emphatically called the Japanese people's "inhuman barbarity."

To the great surprise of Commander Glynn, the Japanese also handed over at the same time they released the mutineers of the *Logoda* another American whose presence in Japan had not been known. He was neither a victim of shipwreck nor a mutineer. Ranald MacDonald, for such was the name of this unexpected guest taken aboard the *Preble*, had landed in Japan entirely of his own free will in a spirit of daring adventure. He had been arrested and held in custody as were the American seamen, but liking both Japan and the Japanese he had no complaints about his treatment.

MacDonald was born in the Oregon country while it was still under British rule, the son of a Hudson's Bay Company factor and a Chinook mother. Short, thickset, dark-complexioned, with straight hair, his appearance betrayed his Indian blood and puzzled the Japanese with their fixed image of "red-haired" barbarians. His early life hardly suggested adventure in Japan. He was working in a bank in St. Thomas, Ontario, when his imagination was fired by the story of the Japanese castaways whom the *Morrison* had attempted to repatriate. At once he made up his mind he would himself visit this far-off, secluded island kingdom. He left his bank and, after making a number of Pacific voyages as a common seaman on various American whalers, entered into an agreement with Captain Lawrence B. Edwards of the ship *Plymouth* to take passage on his next voyage to the Japan grounds and there be set ashore at one of the Japanese islands. "I thought it a good opportunity to crown my intentions," he wrote his father from Hawaii, and added that in spite of all warnings of the risks in trying to visit Japan, "I am going."

The next year, on June 27, 1848, he put the final stage of his plan into execution. Cast off in a small boat from the *Plymouth*, as he subsequently related his unusual experiences, MacDonald landed on the coast of Hokkaido and made his way to a small village. The native Ainus, friendly and very curious, took him to a nearby Japanese military post. The samurai officers in charge placed him under arrest and took him by junk to the port of Matsumae, where the sailors of the *Lagoda* had also been held before being removed to Nagasaki. He was confined in a small cabin for this two weeks' voyage along the Hokkaido coast— "cribbed and thought-weary in the solitude of my prison on the ever-rocking sea"—but he was well treated by his guards and "amply supplied with all the conveniences," including tea, tobacco and sweetmeats. After reaching Matsumae he was taken to another town in the usual closed norimon, boxed up without even a peephole, and there placed aboard a larger junk for the trip south to Nagasaki.

Here his experiences followed what had become a more or less set pattern—the close confinement, the rigid restrictions on his daily life, the repeated interrogations. MacDonald's attitude, however, remained quite different from that of the seamen of either the *Lawrence* or the *Lagoda*. He had wanted to come to Japan, and he so successfully adapted himself to Japanese ways that the official records made at Nagasaki describe him as "exceedingly well mannered and polite." MacDonald also made the most of circumstances (again unlike the "vulgar and rude" whalemen), and sought to learn everything he could about the strange country which had so insistently drawn him across the Pacific.

He became very friendly with the interpreter who conducted the inquiries about his purpose in coming to Japan. This was none other than Moriyama Einosuke, who had gone aboard the *Manhattan* four years earlier at Uraga. Soon the two men were meeting almost daily in the interchangeable roles of teacher and student, the one learning Japanese and the other trying to perfect his halting English, and their meetings later broadened to include others among the young samurai in Nagasaki. MacDonald found himself giving lessons in English to a group of some fourteen students, who proved to be "quick and receptive" in their eager study of this new foreign language.

In the course of their questioning, the Japanese officials made minute inquiries as to MacDonald's nationality, his parents, his religion and conditions in his own country. The religious issue came up again and again. His jailers induced MacDonald to place his foot upon a representation of the Virgin and Child, though he did so unknowingly, by his own account, in the mistaken belief that he was trampling on an image of "the devil" of Japan, but at the same time they somewhat paradoxically allowed him to retain the Bible which he had managed to keep with him through all his travels. On one point he was firm: he refused to kowtow to the Governor before whom he was summoned, but standing on his own feet "looked him fearlessly but respectfully, full in the face." Moriyama later told him that the Governor recognized his brave independence of spirit and in addressing him had said, "You must have a big heart."

At some time word reached MacDonald that a number of other Americans were being held prisoner at Nagasaki—the mutineers of the *Lagoda*—but he was never permitted to see them. He was to write, however, that they were all "young, violent, habitually quarreled amongst themselves, and gave much trouble." He felt that their own fractious behavior was responsible for the severe treatment meted out to them by their Japanese guards.

MacDonald was himself kept throughout the seven months of his imprisonment at Nagasaki in what might again be described as a "cage"—a little barred room, seven by nine feet, in the courtyard of a temple. But as he later wrote, it was furnished with neat matting on the floor and a brazier to provide heat. He was comfortable, and his meals, including pork once a week, "were served with almost lordly state." He was even provided the appropriate table service of knife, fork and spoon instead of chopsticks. His daily relations with his guards, over and beyond his meetings with the students of English, were also on a most friendly basis, and he was to write that he "never had a cross word with any of them."

MacDonald had almost everything he needed or wanted— except his liberty. He was consequently overjoyed when he learned of the arrival of the *Preble* and was taken to Deshima, where he had his first Western-style meal since landing in Japan. He then, as his narrative concludes, "with a true 'Cheery men, Oh!' embarked on the good ship *Preble*, warmly welcomed; and with her noble Captain and right good crew, sailed for freer and more genial shores."

There was to be no return to Japan. MacDonald went to sea again and ultimately came back to British Columbia, where he resumed the more prosaic life he had followed before being so unaccountably drawn to his great adventure. His narrative was not to be published until nearly half a century later, and while a romantic sentiment may have softened his recalled memories, what he stressed throughout the book was the kindliness of the Japanese rather than the rigors of his captivity.

There were other Americans marooned in Japan during these years and kept imprisoned until finally released for deportation in Dutch ships. For example, three seamen of the *Trident*, a New Bedford whaleship, were so held for some fifteen months in 1849-50. The Japanese accounts go into great detail about their being arrested and transported to Nagasaki. They even list the personal possessions of the men, one record noting such items as "1 small knife, with a leather thong, 1 shaving brush, 1 pair of leather shoes."

Rumors persisted that these and additional seamen were being kept in even closer confinement than the *Lawrence*'s survivors and the *Lagoda* mutineers had been. A report in *DeBow's Review*, with no more authority than the claim it was "stated by writers," added to popular concern by saying that the Americans who had more recently fallen into Japanese hands were being "exhibited in iron cages in various parts of the Japanese territory."

Other and counteracting accounts of Japan and the Japanese were by this time available in the United States. Contemporary geography books provided reasonably accurate descriptions of the country, the form of its government, and economic and social conditions. One of them, Smith's *Geography*, flatly stated that Japan was "the most civilized and refined nation of Asia." Moreover, there was published in 1841 as a volume in the popular Harper's Family Library an excellent little book called *Manners and Customs in Japan*. Originally brought out in England, with extensive quotations from the Dutch authorities, it was advertised as a first attempt to present to both English and American readers a convenient compendium of all that was known about Japan. It very nearly did so, providing a full and generally sympathetic description of the country. Nevertheless the outraged accounts of the experiences of the shipwreck victims inspired a spate of popular magazine articles painting highly colored and far less favorable pictures of the island kingdom.

An essay in the *Democratic Review* stated that the Japanese people were so completely controlled by their despotic government as to be "little more than automata in every affair of life," and also affirmed that after having once been nearly Christianized they had been forced back by the cruelest persecution "into barbarism and idolatry." A contributor to the *Christian Remembrancer*, emphasizing what was so generally accepted as "the grossest paganism" in the life of the people, wrote that everything about Japan appeared to offer "a great exception to the family of mankind." And an even more rancorous critic in the *American Whig Review* placed the Japanese "about on a level with the Feejees of the South Seas, or the Esquimaux of the northern continent."

Whatever else might be said or written, the more imaginative accounts of "truculent islanders" who welcomed those cast upon their shores "to a dungeon or a cage," had at this time a pervasive influence in forming the general American image of Japan. "When I was a child," an early contributor to *Harper's New Monthly Magazine* wrote in mid-century, "I had an underdeveloped idea that the Japanese were a species of semi-cannibal race, who indulged in an annual practice of 'trampling on the cross.'"

3

✿

The Discovery of America

WHILE AMERICANS were hearing such conflicting and often irresponsible stories about Japan, the Japanese were gradually acquiring a good deal of information—and some misinformation —about America. When in July, 1853, Commodore Perry arrived in the Bay of Yedo on the first stage of his mission to open up the country, the officers of his squadron were amazed at how knowledgeable the Japanese officials boarding the ships actually were about the United States. "The first interviews," John Sewall, the captain's clerk aboard the sloop *Saratoga*, later wrote in his reminiscences, "were a surprise to us, we found our visitors so well informed."

They knew all about steamships, although those in Perry's squadron were the first that had ever visited their shores; they even knew the make of the guns with which the vessels were armed. When they asked their visitors where they came from and were somewhat superciliously answered the United States, they quickly made it clear that they meant what city: New York, Philadelphia, Washington? "There can be no doubt," the official report of the expedition compiled by Francis L. Hawks stated, "that however backward the Japanese themselves may be in practical science, the best educated among them are tolerably well informed of its progress among more civilized or rather cultivated nations."

This information had been obtained through various sources, including the interrogations of the shipwrecked American seamen, but primarily from the Dutch at Nagasaki. For many years a group of Japanese intellectuals, the so-called "Dutch scholars," had understood the importance of Western science and technology. In the face of the proscriptions imposed by the Bakufu upon all association with foreigners, they had been assiduously learning from the Dutch everything they could about the West— its geography, history, government, military organization, medicine, industry, way of life. Their interest was first of all in Europe, but it also came to embrace America.

Two of the foremost of these Dutch scholars were Watanabe Noboru and Takano Nagahide, young samurai who took up Western learning in the 1830's and formed what they called the "Old Man's Club" to study particularly history and foreign policy. They also translated or wrote a number of treatises on such diverse topics as medicine, coast defense, physics and chemistry, and, in the case of Takano, articles on pneumonia, ulcers and soap. Their interest in the West soon brought them under suspicion and the authorities charged them with treason.

Their position was made all the worse when they dared criticize the policy of the Bakufu at the time of the abortive visit of the *Morrison* in 1837, stating that it had been a mistake to drive this ship (which they did not even know was American) out of Japanese waters. Takano also wrote a somewhat naïve and yet prophetic pamphlet entitled *Yume Monogatari,* or *The Story of a Dream,* in which he suggested that regardless of matters of trade Japan should welcome such foreign vessels in order to learn all it could of the West, and he even forecast a day when the barriers of isolation would be wholly broken down. Both Watanabe and Takano were thereupon arrested for their temerity in criticizing the Bakufu. Feeling he had brought shame upon his feudal lord by his behavior, Watanabe commited hara-kiri in 1841, and eight years later, after having escaped from his prison and lived for a time in hiding, Takano also took his own life according to the samurai code. The influence of these two men nevertheless contributed substantially to a further growth of Japanese interest in both Europe and America, and in time they were to become national heroes, recognized as pioneers in urging the basic changes in Japanese policy that were to take place after 1853.

Watanabe and Takano were not alone in their absorption with Western civilization. Others among the Dutch scholars less conspicuously continued their work and were indeed encouraged to do so. A number of the outer lords went so far as to set up special schools for foreign studies, and in time even the Bakufu was to find it necessary to establish an "Institute for the Investigation of Barbarian Books."

It was not that Japan's rulers were becoming sympathetic toward the West, but rather that they realistically understood how important it was to learn the secrets of its technological advance. They were fully aware that in physics and chemistry, in medicine and, most ominously for Japan, in military and naval science, the once scorned barbarians had tapped new sources of knowledge. Moreover, there was always among the Japanese, in spite of their seclusion, a natural curiosity and thirst for knowledge. Apart from their interest in Europe, they were anxious to discover what they could of the new country which the Dutch told them had been established in the Western Hemisphere—those onetime English colonies that had become the United States.

The first more or less popular Japanese account of the American continent, according to the historian Shunzo Sakamaki, appeared in 1708 in a book entitled A *Study of the Commerce of Chinese and Barbarians*. When its author did not actually know the nature of the country he was attempting to describe or have any authentic information about its inhabitants, he peopled the scene with savages and wild animals much as the early Western geographers had depicted the countries of Asia. He described North America as "a country cold and large . . . with many lions, elephants, tigers, leopards, and brown and white bears . . . the natives are pugnacious and love to fight."

A number of more informed and sophisticated geographies were to be brought out in ensuing years, but one published a full century later still had New England lying between Virginia and Maryland with its capital at Boston, Maryland confronting New

Holland to the North and "the land of the Iroquois" to the west, and described Virginia as "a vast country, bordering on Florida on the south, on New Holland and the sea on the east, and on various wild lands on the west and north." "In various localities there," this account continued, "uncouth natives live in extremely mean dwellings."

Reports from the Dutch were, however, about this same time giving an account of the American Revolution, and they made a deep impression upon the officials at Yedo. One commentary, especially noting that "a chief called Washington proved himself a good and valiant general . . . who successfully defeated the English forces," created an interest in this revolutionary leader that was in time to make him widely and favorably known among all educated Japanese. When the members of Perry's squadron celebrated Washington's birthday at Uraga, on February 22, 1854, it was remarked that the "Japanese seemed perfectly acquainted with the name of the great father of our country." Because of their own mistrust of the British, Washington had become something of a hero to the Japanese, and a later American visitor was to write even more specifically of their familiarity with his exploits and those of other leaders of the Revolution. "The names of Washington, Franklin, Adams, and Jefferson," this contributor to the magazine *Galaxy* stated in 1868, "were as household words, being interwoven into stories for children, with illustrations more amusing than correct."

The early Dutch reports on the United States were not generally made public, but with the publication of a new *World Atlas* in 1847, this information was collated in a fascinating article. It described the settlement of North America, and then after recounting the colonies' growing discontent with British rule, gave this description of the Revolution itself:

The people found themselves in most desperate straits, and officials of the thirteen states assembled to ponder the situation. A military official named Washington, and a civil official named Franklin, promptly stood up and declared, "We must not lose this heaven-given opportunity. We must sever relations with the English forever." The assembly decided to adopt this proposal.

The English then realized they could not attain their ends, and that their words had been unreasonable, so they lifted the blockade and departed. In 1780, a certain official of this land reached an agreement with the English that this should forever be a free and independent nation. Since then, the nation's strength has steadily increased, and its territory has expanded enormously.

The article continued with the history of subsequent developments in the United States and a general description of the country, concluding with a short biography of Washington. Once again he is depicted as a noble, self-sacrificing leader, and no American writer could be more adulatory:

The people have not yet put up any monument to this great man, nor even a tombstone, with an inscription recording his achievements. His name, however, has an imperishable place in history, obviating the necessity for a tombstone. Nothing more could one ask!

A full-length history of the United States was also published on the eve of Commodore Perry's expedition—two years before any history of Japan was written by an American—under the title *Meriken Shinshi*, or in its English translation, *New Account of America*. In spite of many mistaken details and interpretations that may somewhat startle an American reader, the passages translated from this book by Shunzo Sakamaki appear to give a basically accurate picture of the United States and reflect a highly sympathetic attitude toward America and the Americans. Its treatment of contemporary customs in the United States is highly revealing of the quite different culture of Japan. It singles out, for example, the lack of distinction between ruler and subject in the United States; the similarity in homes, food, drink and clothing among all classes; the widespread use of carriages; and the strange and inexplicable customs of eating beef and drinking milk.

"They do not have monthly solar festivals or fete days," a further entry reads. "They merely go to some great man's house, or to their relatives', on every seventh day, and all clasp hands and worship. That is all."

Quite as interesting as the descriptions of American life seen through Japanese eyes are the illustrations. One that Shunzo Sakamaki has reproduced is a portrait of Washington, in a very strange foreign dress but with distinctly Japanese features. Another is a battle scene—supposedly Saratoga but also naming Yorktown—in which Washington, with drawn sword, has ordered his troops to fire on the fleeing Britishers, who are desperately scrambling over some cone-shaped Japanese mountains.

Other American studies were published in mid-century and generally stressed the point that the Japanese could no longer afford to ignore foreign countries. The barbarians, the author of *Amerika Soki,* or *General Account of America,* declared, were not as those of ancient times. They were educated and civilized. It had consequently become the responsibility of Japanese scholars fully to inform the public about such people as the Americans in order that preparations might be made to meet them "with respect but not fear."

Apart from what they learned from the Dutch, who were also to inform them in 1852 of a prospective American expedition with troops and arms under command of "a person named Perry," the Japanese could sometimes tap other sources of published information. Several translations of American books and documents which had originally been printed in China were currently available. They may even have reached a larger audience than such original Japanese histories or geographies as *Meriken Shinshi* and *Amerika Soki.* Seeking to discover how the Japanese visitors aboard Perry's ships could be so well informed, John Sewall was confident he had the full answer:

> This knowledge of America came straight from Dr. [Elijah Coleman] Bridgman's History of the United States, which had been published in China, and which had enjoyed what Dr. Bridgman had never dreamed of, a wide circulation in the Mikado's dominions. That book had already prepossessed them in our favor.

Among the shipwrecked Japanese fishermen or sailors rescued at sea and returned to their own country was one man, and only one according to available records throughout this whole period, who had direct and firsthand experience in the United States. There are reports of some Japanese being repatriated by the American ships sailing under Dutch colors in the early 1800's; other survivors of wrecks made their way back to Japan by Chinese junks after being brought by foreign ships to Macao, and there were most notably the sailors restored to their homeland by the *Manhattan* in 1845. All of these men were closely questioned by the Japanese authorities about what they might have learned of the foreigners, but none could give anything like the information provided by a young fisherman from a little village in the province of Tosa who actually lived for several years in the United States.

This Japanese was Nakahama Manjiro—known in his own day simply as Manjiro, or by his American name of John Mung—and his accounts of America following his return from the United States in 1851 apparently attained a very wide circulation. He was officially interviewed many times, and in addition to such official reports other contemporary accounts were compiled by people who came to listen to his fascinating tales. A great deal of this material is today available in *The Narratives of the Castaways*, an official record of his interrogations, and in the biography of Manjiro written by his son under the title *Nakahama Manjiro-den*. Within recent years much has been made of this early Japanese traveler—"the man who discovered America"—and several books about him have appeared both in Japan and in the United States.

Manjiro was shipwrecked at the age of fourteen while on a fishing trip in January, 1841. Together with four other survivors of the storm that had disabled their junk, he drifted ashore on a lonely Pacific island and for some six months eked out a precarious existence until dramatically rescued by a providential American whaleship, the *John Howland*, Captain William H. Whitfield, of Fairhaven, Massachusetts. After taking the five Japanese aboard, the *John Howland* continued her voyage to Honolulu and there set the castaways ashore.

During this time, however, Captain Whitfield had become captivated by the young Manjiro, a bright, intelligent and cheerful boy. He offered to take him back to the United States and send him to school at Fairhaven. Manjiro had the imagination and the courage to accept this unique invitation and, after completing the long eastward voyage about Cape Horn, found himself in Fairhaven in the spring of 1843. He lived there three years, learning English and going to school, and won the cordial respect and liking of the entire community in this little whaling port which for all its outward appearance may not have been so completely unlike his native fishing village. One untoward incident marked his early days at Fairhaven. Captain Whitfield, a deeply religious as well as friendly and generous man, took the young Japanese boy to his church. He was requested to sit in the pews reserved for

Negroes. The irate sea captain, incensed at this bigoted attitude on the part of the congregation, left the church and found another where Manjiro was more welcome.

After his several years of schooling and a period in which he was apprenticed to a cooper, the young Japanese felt the old lure of the sea and in 1846 signed on as a seaman aboard the whaleship *Franklin*, Captain Ira Davis, for a voyage to the Pacific. This life apparently did not satisfy him, however, and he longed somehow to get back to Japan. After returning to the United States he became excited by the stories of the discovery of gold in California, and with the idea of earning enough money to buy his transportation to Japan, he joined the gold rush in 1849 and the next year worked for five months in the mines. Having saved some $600, he took passage to Honolulu. There he met two of his former companions of shipwreck days and, as they too were anxious to return to Japan, agreed to include them in his plans.

With a supporting letter from the American consul in Honolulu ("John Manjiro has sustained a good character and has improved in knowledge"), he then succeeded in making arrangements, with his two companions, to sail aboard the merchantman *Sarah Boyd*, Captain Whitmore, and be set ashore on some island in the Ryukyus, the southern islands which were then under the control of the daimio of Satsuma. This project was successfully carried out. However, on their landing in the Ryukyus on February 2, 1851, the three Japanese were, as they had every reason to expect, promptly arrested. After being minutely questioned by the local officials, they were taken to Kagoshima for formal trial on the charge of having broken the law forbidding Japanese to live abroad. Here they were minutely questioned by Shimazu Nariakira, the daimio of Satsuma, during a series of hearings that lasted some forty-eight days. Finally a report was forwarded to Yedo stating that, in spite of their technical guilt in living abroad, Manjiro and his companions appeared to be "innocent of the evil foreign religion or other crimes."

Their lives were to be spared, but they had not yet finished with the ordeal of continued imprisonment and seemingly endless questioning. On orders from Yedo they were taken to Nagasaki and examined even more carefully, if that were possible, on everything they knew about the United States. Manjiro was the spokesman of the trio and, as the contemporary *Narratives of the Castaways* suggests, gave a picture of the American way of life that must have strangely intrigued his inquisitors.

Manjiro described the domestic political situation ("The present king is called Taylor") and gave a full accounting of the war with Mexico; discussed in detail such important technological phenomena as steamships, railroads and the telegraph; answered innumerable questions on manners and customs; and freely gave his opinion about the American people themselves.

"They are perfect in body with white skins," he is reported to have said. "They are naturally gentle and sympathetic and prize integrity. Above all, they are industrious and trade with countries in all directions." And another time: "The people of America are upright and generous, and do no evil. Among them are neither homicides nor robberies, as a rule. If such things occur, there are laws covering them, and the offenders are promptly seized."

The favorable impression Manjiro had received of the United States and his frank willingness to impart it to his antiforeign questioners at Kagoshima and Nagasaki proved to be very important. There is no question whatsoever that his report on the United States had a very real impact on high authorities at Yedo. It served somewhat to dispel, as Shunzo Sakamaki has emphasized, the unwarranted fears and suspicions of the intent of the Perry expedition in 1853.

In answers to further questions, as filtered through ancient Japanese reports and more recent translations, Manjiro painted a wonderful picture of American life as seen by a young Japanese exile well over a century ago. Again it is clear that what he was describing for his countrymen were those aspects of life in the United States that most differed from the customs of Japan, and we learn from him almost as much about Japan as about nineteenth-century America.

Manjiro was greatly interested that ordinary men wore watches, took off their hats when paying a visit, and had the strange custom of sitting on chairs. He was amazed to find stores "surrounded by glass in which they display things for sale" and very much shocked at markets selling "cows, sheep, pigs and many kinds of birds." He had a good deal to say about drinking. "Refined people do not drink intoxicants," he reported rather surprisingly, "and only a

small quantity if they do. Vulgar people drink like the Japanese."
It was his further opinion that the intoxicants in the United States
were worse in quality than those of Japan.

Living conditions were a strange revelation, with homes so clut-
tered with furniture in comparison with the simplicity of Japanese
houses, and he singled out two features that must greatly have
astounded the audience at his trial. "There are no baths in that
country like those of Japan, but they use a bath tub," Manjiro
reported, and then added: "Toilets are placed over holes in the
ground. It is customary to read books in them."

He found relations between man and wife "very loving and
families peaceful and affectionate," but a further statement that
"both American men and women make love openly and appear
wanton by nature" and his account of American marriages might
have startled Fairhaven: "For their wedding ceremony, the Americans merely make a proclamation to the gods, and become married, after which they usually go on a sightseeing trip to the
mountains. They are lewd by nature, but otherwise well-behaved."

It might be added that Manjiro also reported that George Washington, a great hero, could not tell a lie "even when it was discovered he had cut down a cherry tree"; that American women did
not use "rouge, powder, and the like"; and that the people enjoyed
singing "and often do this when walking along the roads." Finally,
there is the recurrent tribute in which he characterized Americans
as "very generous and honest and they do little wrong."

A full account of his various interviews was forwarded to the
Bakufu, with such of his personal possessions as might prove of
interest, including a life of Washington, Bowditch's *Navigator* and
the *Farmer's Almanac*, and at long last Manjiro (together with his
companions) was released. After a total absence of eleven years,
and a year and half after landing on the Ryukyus, he returned to
his native village and saw again the mother who had long since
given him up for lost.

He had not been home long before he was summoned to Yedo.
Forewarned of Commodore Perry's arrival, the authorities
wished to consult him further about the United States and also
have him advise them as to how to deal with the Americans. He
was given samurai rank, with two personal attendants assigned to
him, but fearful that he might try to make his own contacts with

the Americans ("a baby phoenix escaping by riding on the winds and clouds when a storm comes"), the ever-suspicious officials kept him in protective custody. It was later rumored that he was present at the American treaty negotiations, secreted in a room adjoining the council chambers, but Manjiro actually remained in Yedo throughout Commodore Perry's entire stay in Japan.

Six years later he again visited the United States. His experience and the knowledge of navigation he had acquired aboard American whalers led to his appointment as a special officer aboard the *Kanrin Maru*, a ship that was to accompany the Japanese embassy to the United States in 1860. Aboard her was also Captain John Mercer Brooke of the United States Navy, who had been detailed to assist the *Kanrin Maru's* crew in this first transpacific voyage undertaken by a Japanese vessel. Captain Brooke was greatly impressed by Manjiro. He described him as a broad-shouldered, compact, fine, intelligent fellow, and one of the most remarkable men he had ever seen.

As a result of their talks on the long Pacific voyage, Brooke became convinced that the information Manjiro had given the authorities at Yedo and his advice on things American had played a very important part in persuading the Japanese to accede to Commodore Perry's demands in 1853. "I am satisfied," Brooke wrote, "that he had more to do with the opening of Japan than any man living." While this may have been an extreme judgment, hardly warranted by the known facts, this first Japanese to know the United States at firsthand was certainly highly influential in persuading the officials of the Bakufu that the objectives of the Perry expedition were wholly peaceful.

On his return from his trip in 1860, which took him no further than San Francisco but enabled him to bring back with him a sewing machine, photographic apparatus and a copy of Webster's dictionary, Manjiro followed a varied career. He lacked the education to reach high position in Japan, but was influential in the development of a native whaling industry, served for a time as an instructor in English in one of the schools that was eventually to become a part of Tokyo Imperial University, and continued as an adviser to Japanese officials on foreign affairs. The government sent him abroad in 1870 to observe the Franco-Prussian War, and going to Europe by way of the United States, he took occasion to visit his old home and see his friends at Fairhaven. The New Bedford *Morning Mercury* described the visit of this onetime resident of the nearby whaling port, now a man of forty-five, and its friendly article noted with interest the position he had attained in Japan. Soon after this last trip abroad, Manjiro's health gave way and he remained a semi-invalid for the rest of his life, dying in 1898 at the age of seventy-two. He had lived to see the creation of a wholly new Japan, bound in close friendship with the United States, and where he had been a pioneer in first visiting America, hundreds of his countrymen were every year following his trail across the Pacific.

On July 4, 1918, the Japanese Ambassador in the United States, Viscount Ishii, presented in behalf of his government a samurai sword to the town of Fairhaven in appreciation of the welcome it had accorded Manjiro some seventy-five years earlier. And in 1933 President Franklin D. Roosevelt wrote a letter to Manjiro's son, Nakahama Toichiro, in which he recalled that one of his ancestors—Warren Delano—had been a part owner of the ship that had rescued Manjiro and brought him to America. "I well remember," Roosevelt said, "my grandfather telling me about the little Japanese boy who went to school in Fairhaven."

With the information gleaned from Manjiro added to that provided by the translations of the Dutch scholars and other books on America, educated Japanese may well have known in mid-century quite as much about the United States as educated Americans knew about Japan. However, most of the samurai and the common people—the peasants, fishermen and villagers—remained almost wholly ignorant of everything beyond their own shores. For them the long years of seclusion had encouraged strange legends about the Western barbarians who were forbidden to land in Japan, and ancient memories of the distant days when they had been welcomed were colored by the superstitions that had been especially built up about the impious influence of Christianity.

When the first news spread through the land of the arrival of the mysterious ships of Commodore Perry, two of them steamers belching an unlikely black smoke, all these old fears were revived. A contemporary ballad reflected this uneasy alarm:

Through a dark night of cloud and rain,
The Black Ship plies her way—
An alien thing of evil mien
Across the waters gray.

The officials of the Bakufu, even though forewarned by the Dutch of the Perry expedition and assured by Manjiro that the United States was a peaceful nation seeking no more than possible expansion of its trade, were themselves fearful of what this visit augured for the future. But the common people had no idea of what to expect as the dreaded barbarians anchored off their country's heretofore inviolate shores.

4

A Treaty Is Signed

IT WAS ON JULY 8, 1853, that the little four-ship squadron of Commodore Perry, under instructions from President Fillmore to undertake negotiation of a treaty with Japan, made its cautious approach into the Bay of Yedo and anchored off the shore near the village of Uraga. From the moment it was first sighted, according to a contemporary Japanese chronicler, excitement "seethed like a cauldron" and the Shinto priests were ordered to offer prayers at the great shrines of Ise for "the sweeping away of the barbarians." Beacon fires were lighted all along the coast and special guards in light armor with pikes and rusty flintlocks ("Some were holding aloft their rising-sun embossed war fans") manned hastily improvised forts. The people fled to the hills. In Yedo the commotion was reported to be even greater than in the countryside:

The whole city was in an uproar. In all directions were seen mothers flying with their children in their arms, and men with mothers on their backs. . . . The tramp of war-horses, the clatter of armed warriors, the noise of carts, the parade of firemen, the incessant tolling of bells, the shrieks of women, the cries of children, dinning all the streets of a city of more than a million souls, made confusion worse confounded.

53

At Uraga itself, where the nearby headlands were guarded by breastworks occupied by troops in scarlet uniforms, the Japanese sought to surround the American ships with their usual guard boats. Determined to prevent their coming too close, Perry ordered his sailors to cut the lines the Japanese tried to attach to his ships. He let it be known through his interpreters that he would open up communications only aboard the flagship *Susquehanna* and speak to no one himself except an officially designated imperial envoy. His immediate purpose was to deliver the letter he bore from President Fillmore to the Emperor; there was to be no temporizing in fulfilling his mission nor any submission to Japanese demands that might limit his full freedom of action. "The question of landing by force," the official report of the Japan Expedition states significantly, "was left to be decided by the development of succeeding events."[1]

Fortunately the Japanese had no idea of offering any resistance, and after some preliminary discussion between the Governor of Uraga and Commanders Buchanan and Adams, ranking officers in the squadron, arrangements were made for a formal meeting on shore between emissaries of the Emperor (they were actually officials of the Shogunate) and Commodore Perry. There were some difficulties, some delays, but this most significant meeting duly took place at nearby Kurihama on July 14.

After taking every precaution against possible treachery, with decks cleared for action and the guns of his ships trained on the meeting grounds, the American naval commander came ashore with pomp and ceremony, and the Japanese envoys, proceeding for their part with no less ceremonious display, received him in the Emperor's name. The occasion was very brief. After handing over the official documents with which he was charged, Commodore Perry stated that he would not remain in Japan for a reply. He intended to leave within a few days and would then return in the spring (with a larger naval force, he pointedly said) in the expec-

[1] This official report was compiled by the Rev. Francis L. Hawks, but Commodore Perry had first asked Nathaniel Hawthorne, whom he saw on his return voyage at Liverpool, where Hawthorne was serving as United States consul, to undertake the assignment. In declining to do so, Hawthorne nevertheless wrote, "The world can scarcely have a less hackneyed theme than Japan."

tation of entering into the negotiations suggested by "the reasonable and pacific overtures contained in the President's letter."

This was all that happened during the first stage of this historic undertaking to open up Japan to the Western world. Having had his officers make the most careful surveys of the Bay of Yedo and himself proceeded some twenty miles beyond the original anchorage off Uraga in the direction of the Japanese capital, Commodore Perry prepared to leave. There had been no opposition to his movements by the Japanese and no attempt on the part of American seamen to go ashore. Whenever the survey boats approached close to the land, crowds of Japanese gathered to watch them and gave every evidence of having overcome their first fears of the barbarians. The American officers and men returned from these surveying ventures, in the words of the official report, "in raptures with the kindly disposition of the Japanese and the beauty of their country." On July 17, after a short nine days in Japanese waters, the squadron set sail with Commodore Perry reiterating his promise to be back early the next year.

The varied influences that had finally led the United States to dispatch the Japan Expedition had been slowly building up ever since the unhappy venture of the *Morrison* sixteen years earlier. The insistent demand of the whaling industry that something had to be done to assure protection for sailors shipwrecked on the Japanese shores was only the culmination of mounting pressures on the government. Important commercial interests, represented most vigorously by Aaron H. Palmer, a New York commission merchant and director of the American and Foreign Agency, were heavily stressing the great advantages of opening up Japan to trade and commerce; the missions already operating in China were calling with renewed urgency for action that would enable them to extend their Far Eastern activities in the field of Christian endeavor. Influenced as well by the advice of Charles King and Commander Glynn, who were in turn reflecting the views first voiced by Captain David Porter in 1815, Congress had become persuaded that the United States should not lose its unique opportunity to promote trade and commerce in Asia and should take the lead in bringing Japan out of her ancient seclusion.

President Fillmore was clearly responding to such economic and political pressures. The need to secure some sort of pledge for more humane treatment of American castaways was given as the immediate reason—or pretext—for the expedition in his letter to the Emperor. "We are very much in earnest in this," he stated emphatically. But he also adroitly suggested in this personal message that the time had certainly come when Japan should consider changing her ancient laws banning all foreign commerce. But he made no threats. His objectives in sending Commodore Perry on his important mission were wholly peaceful, the President told the Emperor, and he summarized them as "friendship, commerce, a supply of coal and provisions, and protection for our shipwrecked people."

In a broader sense than Fillmore suggested, the Japan Expedition also represented a dramatic expression of the new sense of "Manifest Destiny" that had swept across America in the 1840's. The forces of continental expansion had reached the Pacific shore, but new worlds now beckoned—what Melville described as "unknown Archipelagoes and impenetrable Japans." It was not only the prospect of enlarged trade in a slowly awakening Asia, however important it might be, that caught the popular imagination. As would prove to be even more true a half century later, the opportunity to spread abroad the beneficent influence of American political and humanitarian ideals had a powerful influence in stimulating overseas adventure. It was a sense of mission, the fulfillment of the nation's historic destiny, that bulwarked the drive of the mid-century expansionists into the far reaches of the Pacific. The United States was believed to be obeying a moral imperative in seeking to bring Japan within the family of nations; that distant country's continued seclusion could no longer be reconciled with the interests of the modern world. "The time of God's working had come," in the phrase of the day, and He had laid upon America a great responsibility that she could not escape.

There were elements within the country a good deal less enthusiastic about the expedition than all this suggests. It was intimated in some quarters that it was designed for "the glorification of the Yankee nation" rather than the fulfillment of any broad humanitarian mission. Political critics petulantly attacked it as no more than a transparent trick to build up the prestige of a faltering administration. Yet the strength of the underlying forces making for American penetration in eastern Asia was undeniable. "The opening of commerce with Japan," the *Democratic Review* declared in April, 1852, "is demanded by reason, civilization, progress and religion."

To sustain the peaceful character of the expedition, President Fillmore explicitly ordered that there should be no use of force except in the last resort and for the safety of members of the squadron. In the person of Matthew Calbraith Perry, however, the expedition had a commander who never hesitated to make it very clear that he meant business and would brook no refusal of his demands.

An able and experienced naval officer, now in his sixtieth year, Perry was highly ambitious and deeply impressed both with himself and with the importance of his mission. A man of commanding appearance, broad-shouldered and sturdy, with thick unruly hair and beetling eyebrows, he stood always upon his dignity as a high naval officer and special envoy to Japan. He was never one to mix easily with his subordinates, was a strict martinet in maintaining discipline aboard ship, and would appear to have been singularly lacking in any light touch or sense of humor. Yet there was none to dispute his ability, his sense of duty or his fearlessness. "Old Matt," as the seamen called him, commanded great respect even though he did not inspire much affection.

In all his dealings with the Japanese, whom he considered "a weak and barbarous people," Perry acted with that haughty assumption of authority which he displayed on his first landing at Uraga. His instinctive arrogance and his conviction of the need to impress the Japanese led to his continued avoidance of any direct contact with them except in the case of officials of the highest rank. He made every public appearance a formal ceremony panoplied with all the trappings of his naval rank.[2] But while his officers and the civilians attached to the expedition were greatly irked by his authoritative and pompous manner, they also came to realize that it had a decisive effect on the Japanese. In the final analysis even the Commodore's most severe critics were willing to admit that the expedition's ultimate success was largely due to the

[2] To heighten his prestige Perry insisted throughout the negotiations on being called "Admiral."

"prudent and sagacious" way in which he had conducted himself. Bayard Taylor, the future poet and diplomat who at this time was a youthful journalist, had succeeded in attaching himself to the American squadron as a master's mate. In his subsequent account of the expedition he gave Perry all credit for "the firmness, dignity and fearlessness" which he exhibited throughout the entire venture.

There was something in the nature of this naval commander that foreshadowed the character of another American military figure who nearly a century later steamed into this same Bay of Yedo—or what was then the Bay of Tokyo—aboard the U.S.S. *Missouri* to make far more drastic demands upon Japan. For Commodore Perry had much the same personal arrogance and much the same sense of destiny that would stamp General MacArthur. Moreover, both men succeeded in greatly impressing the Japanese and, through their peaceful implementation of policies whose consequences Japan could not hope to escape, they have won memorable places in the history of that country as well as in the annals of their own.

The letter which Commodore Perry sent to the Emperor created a grave crisis for the government of Japan. The Bakufu was at a total loss as to how it should deal with this challenge to a foreign policy that had been followed for more than two centuries. And while the Americans hardly realized it, they were making their demands at a time when the challenge to the power of the Shogunate, arising from opposition of many of the daimio and new forces of domestic discontent, was approaching a climax. A movement was growing to overthrow the Shogun and restore the ancient authority of the Emperor; serious lines of cleavage were developing between Yedo and the imperial capital at Kyoto.

In these circumstances any step toward acceding to the American request for opening up the country might prove disastrous for the prestige and position of the Shogunate, and yet to refuse it risked possibly even greater dangers. The officials at Yedo well realized from their knowledge of the United States that Japan could not possibly hope to resist successfully the armed force that Commodore Perry had so strongly intimated might be brought to bear against her on his return to Japanese shores. After the American squadron left, the Bakufu consequently shattered all precedents—and nothing could more clearly have revealed its own weakness and indecision—by appealing to the daimio for advice on what course should be followed.

The replies of these lords of the realm showed at one and the same time the strong, unrelenting hold of tradition, the continued suspicion of the West, and the fierce, patriotic pride that animated the Japanese people. The daimio were convinced that opening the door to trade would invite the immediate danger of foreign conquest. Once the Western barbarians were admitted to the country, the Lord of Tosa warned in a typical statement, they would then seek "to subdue and round up our innocent people by giving the impression of brotherhood and good will."

There was hardly one among the daimio who favored freely letting down the barriers of isolation. Some of them realized that times had changed since the exclusion decrees had been first issued ("This we should explain to the spirits of our ancestors"), but even these more modern-minded leaders did not dream that Japan should now turn about and welcome foreigners to her shores. The replies sent to the Bakufu differed only on the point of whether Japan could run the risk of peremptorily rejecting Commodore Perry's demands or might better pretend to give in to them until she could build up the strength to offer more effective resistance to Western aggression.

The moderates counciled delay and equivocation, but nonetheless insisted that it should be clearly understood that "whatever we do, will be but a stratagem to last until the Bakufu can complete its military arrangements." The extremists were ready to defy Perry and demonstrate "our martial vigor to the whole world by completely destroying his ships." Reflecting very much the same chauvinistic spirit that would mark Japan's leaders in 1941, these super-patriots were ready to go down fighting whatever the odds against them rather than meekly surrender. To sustain Japan's honor and prestige, they called upon the Bakufu to forbid at once "all foolish talk of peace."

As the confused officials at Yedo pondered the replies to their questionnaire, they found no easy escape from their hard dilemma. They could not reason with the powerful forces insisting upon outright resistance to any foreign encroachments whatsoever, and they realized there was no hope of turning aside the importunate demands of the Americans. There seemed to be no solution to the crisis which threatened both the position of the Shogunate and the entire structure of Japanese society.

The Americans, however, were at the gates. As the time approached for Commodore Perry's promised return early in 1854, something had to be done. The Bakufu, though still wavering and uncertain where such a step might lead, reluctantly instructed the commissioners sent to greet the expedition's commander to enter into treaty negotiations. But while they were at all costs to avoid any break that might lead to war, they were to make no concessions that could possibly be avoided. What the Bakufu really hoped was that somehow the Americans might be persuaded simply to sail away. Yet its officials very well knew that this was an impossible dream.

"This day, if it be not hereafter remembered by our own, will at least be kept long in mind by the people of this country."

So wrote, on March 8, 1854, a young midshipman aboard one of the ships of the Japan Expedition now once again lying at anchor in the Bay of Yedo. Commodore Perry had returned, this time with a squadron of nine vessels, including three steam frigates, and the Japanese commissioners had announced they were ready to begin the negotiations to which the Bakufu had finally agreed. The consequences that were to flow from this encounter have certainly led to the day on which it was held being remembered in Japan, and it also deserves a conspicuous place in American history.

The meeting between Commodore Perry and the Japanese commissioners was held in a gaudy, flag-bedecked pavilion which had been erected for this special occasion on the shore near what was then the obscure fishing hamlet of Yokohama. About it the Japanese had stationed bands of musicians and flag-bearers; soldiers armed with matchlocks and wearing brightly colored costumes and glistening lacquered caps; pikemen carrying burnished spears with crimson streamers. Their commissioners, landing on the beach from a great, gaily painted barge also decorated with flags and tassels, preceded the Americans to the "treaty house" where they awaited Commodore Perry's arrival. "They were intelligent-looking men," wrote one of the American naval officers, "richly dressed in gay silk petticoat pantaloons, and upper garments resembling in shape ladies' short gowns."

The expedition's commander came ashore with even greater pomp than on his first landing the previous year. It was not felt necessary to take such stringent military precautions as had then been thought advisable, but Perry was determined to make as impressive an appearance as possible. Some five hundred marines and sailors, bayonets fixed, were drawn up on shore, and, with two six-foot Negroes bearing the broad pennant of the expedition's flagship, the *Powhatan*, they formed a guard of honor with "the bluff, burly commodore marching up between the bristling ranks." The guns aboard the American naval vessels fired a series of crashing salutes, the marines presented arms, and three bands struck up "The Star-Spangled Banner." Against the background of Japanese guards, companies of archers and spearmen, and hordes of curious villagers pressing in on all sides, the landing of the Americans, reads the official report of the expedition, made "quite a martial and effective show."

An exchange of courtesies, the Japanese serving their guests tea, cakes and confectionery, opened the ceremony. Moriyama Einosuke, whose associations with Americans now included Captain Cooper of the *Manhattan*, Ranald MacDonald and Commander Glynn (about whom he asked), served as interpreter. In the presence of the august commissioners Moriyama remained on his knees, somewhat to the disgust of the Americans ("What respect can a man have for himself in such a position?" one of them expostulated), but scuttling back and forth, he helped to keep the conversation going on a friendly basis.

After the formal exchange of greetings the principals withdrew to a smaller room and the chief Japanese commissioner handed Commodore Perry a long scroll which proved to be an answer to President Fillmore's letter. While emphasizing the importance of "the laws of our imperial ancestors," this note acknowledged that times had changed and the consequent willingness of the Shogunate to consider the proposals that the President had advanced for the opening of friendly relations. "We are governed now," the

Japanese reply stated, "by imperative necessity." Perry expressed his gratification at this decision and asked that negotiations over the actual terms of the projected treaty be commenced as soon as possible. After some further discussion as to just how and when this should be done, the Commodore rose to leave. His guard presented arms, the drums rolled, the bands once again "sounded their martial strains," and Perry returned to his flagship. The meeting had been successful. As one American observer commented: "Everything passed off pleasantly in every respect."

In accepting the consequences of imperative necessity, the Japanese were not only acting on the broad assumption that they could no longer hope to resist the mounting pressures of the West. In the preliminary talks which led up to the formal treaty negotiations, Commodore Perry had again clearly revealed that behind the friendly words of President Fillmore was a determination to achieve the expedition's objectives by whatever means might prove necessary. If the Japanese commissioners had any lingering doubts on this score when they first came to Yokohama, they had been quickly disabused of them and also of any fleeting hope that through procrastination or evasion the Americans could be persuaded to just go away.

The chief commissioner was Hayashi Daigaku-no-Kami, the Lord Rector of the University of Yedo, who had been raised to the princely rank indicated in his title ("Daigaku-no-Kami") solely for the purpose of negotiating with Commodore Perry. A man of about fifty-five, rather handsome but gloomy-looking, he had on the evidence of every American diarist "exceedingly courtly manners." They were often strained. The record Hayashi kept of the the negotiations, translated in 1930 as *Diary of an Official of the Bakufu,* repeatedly emphasizes the unrelenting pressure under which the Japanese labored throughout the negotiations and their helplessness in resisting the American demands. On the eve of the first official meeting at the treaty house, Hayashi wrote that Commodore Perry had declared that if his proposals were rejected, he "was prepared to make war at once . . . [and] if he sent word he could summon a command of one hundred warships within twenty days." And the Japanese official later quotes the American Commodore as further stating at the meeting itself that "we are fully prepared to engage in a struggle for victory."

These powerful threats are confirmed by S. Wells Williams, the onetime missionary interpreter of the *Morrison* who was now serving in a similar capacity with Perry's squadron. In commenting on the American position at the beginning of the negotiations, he wrote in his journal of the expedition that the Commodore "threatens them in no obscure terms with a 'larger force and more stringent terms and instructions'" if they did not promptly comply with his demands. While Williams was later to agree with other members of the expedition in giving Perry high praise for his skillful diplomacy, he was at this point sympathetic with the Japanese and very critical of such an intemperate threat of force.

He had talked with Moriyama, the Japanese interpreter, and been impressed by the views of that experienced official. "You must give us more time," Moriyama had said. "It is all very plain to you, but we are like people coming out of a dark room into the glare of sunshine, and we do not yet see the bearing of things clearly." Williams felt that Commodore Perry wholly ignored such reasonable considerations. He was "making ambition the test of all his conduct toward the Japanese" and seeking to "advance his own aggrandizement and fame."

Yet in spite of what might be considered Perry's overbearing attitude, he nonetheless revealed an unexpected tact in adjusting himself to Japanese ways once the negotiations for the treaty really got started. From then on, a surprising measure of goodwill marked the meetings between the Bakufu officials and the American naval officers. There was a lively dispute when Perry insisted that the Japanese treatment of shipwrecked sailors had been inhumane and cruel. Hayashi denied the charge, upholding the right of the authorities to imprison these seamen because of their unlawful behavior. He declared that they were "not of good character . . . violate our laws and do as they please." But he finally agreed that in the future such castaways should be left free as they would be in other countries and not subjected to either arrest or confinement. With this issue resolved, the negotiations proceeded smoothly, and in little more than three weeks, on March 31, a treaty was duly signed.

"Eureka! It is finished! The great agony is over!" Lieutenant

George Henry Preble, a deck officer aboard the sloop-of-war *Macedonian*, wrote that evening in his diary. "In vulgar parlance the egg has hatched its chicken today. The Treaty of Amity and Friendship between the United States and Japan was signed today to the satisfaction of everybody. Even Old Bruin (i.e., the Commodore) would smile if he only knew how to smile."

The scope of the treaty, which has become known as the Treaty of Kanagawa, was very limited. In addition to their pledge not to imprison the crews of shipwrecked vessels, the Japanese opened the two ports of Shimoda and Hakodate (the one on the southern tip of the Izu Peninsula, about one hundred miles from Yedo; the other in the northern island of Hokkaido), where American ships could obtain wood, water and other supplies, and also agreed to the residence in these two ports of American consular officials. The treaty did not, however, contain any specific provisions for future trade. As subsequently described, it was "a wood-and-water treaty" rather than a commercial treaty, and another four years were to pass before the United States attained this underlying objective of its Far Eastern policy.

Two further aspects of the treaty may also be noted. It included a "most-favored nation" clause, that is, a provision that any future privileges granted to any other nation would also be extended to the United States, but unlike the treaty recently signed with China, it did not include any cession of extraterritorial rights. Furthermore Hayashi reported (though this was not in the treaty itself) that Commodore Perry pledged American aid should Japan become involved in controversy with any European power. Here was a demonstration of sympathy for Japan and also a clear expression of an intention to safeguard American rights.

In arriving at its difficult decision to negotiate with Commodore Perry, the Bakufu had by no means resolved the dilemma which his demands had created for the Shogunate. A historical sketch of these negotiations included a century later in the official Japanese tourist guide states that the Japanese eagerly welcomed the American expedition: "It was as if the whole nation heard the loud clanging of bells announcing the dawn of a new era." This is of course arrant nonsense. The forces of tradition remained far too strong to permit any such sudden change in popular feeling; the ancient fears of the barbarians were not so easily stilled. Neither the authorities at Yedo nor those at Kyoto nor the powerful outer lords were as yet prepared to accept the new treaty other than as a temporary concession which might hold the barbarians in restraint until Japan became strong enough to defend her interests more effectively.

The Americans were almost wholly ignorant of the real state of affairs in Japan. Failing to understand the role of the Emperor and the Shogun in the Japanese Government, believing as they did that the one was a spiritual emperor ("worshiped as a god") and the other a temporal emperor ("a matter of fact person"), they could no more realize the significance of what was to become the widening rift between the rival political camps in Yedo and Kyoto than they could properly appreciate how stubbornly antiforeign the daimio still remained. They took the treaty at its face value. They accepted it as not only marking a fundamental change in Japanese policy, but one which commanded positive support. They were consequently to be bitterly disillusioned when in succeeding years the Japanese sought by every possible stratagem to avoid living up to the treaty's terms and, as long as they possibly could, withheld any further concessions affecting trade and commerce.

Nevertheless, when Commander Adams, the officer who had been designated to exchange ratifications of the treaty after its approval at Washington and in Yedo, returned the next year to Shimoda, he found both the officials and the people very cordial. The former inquired solicitously about their friends aboard the American squadron and told Adams that the name of Commodore Perry "would live forever in the history of Japan."

It has most certainly done so. Had he not sailed with his black ships into the Bay of Yedo in the summer of 1853, some other naval officer, whether American, English or Russian, would very soon have knocked even more clamorously on Japan's tightly closed door. The pressures being built up in the West in favor of opening up Japan were gathering an irresistible momentum. But the fact remains that it was Commodore Perry, with a skillful combination of tact and firmness, who successfully forced the issue.

The consequences were all-important for Japan, highly significant for America, and they helped to shape the entire course of subsequent Far Eastern history. Although the United States may not fully deserve all the credit that it has sometimes arrogated to itself for opening up Japan, the conclusion of the Treaty of Kanagawa was nonetheless a spectacular achievement.

5

"Nippon and America, All the Same Heart"

WHOLLY APART from either its immediate or future political consequences, the second visit of Commodore Perry's squadron provided the initial occasion for any really significant contacts between Americans and Japanese. The samurai officials of the Bakufu visited aboard the American ships; Yankee sailors went ashore to explore this strange new land of Japan. At first rigid restrictions were enforced. To their constant annoyance the Americans found themselves followed by guards or spies wherever they went. S. Wells Williams was to complain that the easy intercourse for which he had hoped was prevented by "the thraldom of Tokugawa tyranny." But the restrictions were gradually relaxed. When the American ships put into the newly opened ports of Shimoda and Hakodate after signature of the treaty, both officers and men had an opportunity to see something of Japanese life and to mix rather freely with the village people.

There were difficulties. The Japanese remained for a time very suspicious of these outlandish barbarians; the Americans often tended to look down upon the Japanese as an inferior, semicivilized, heathen people. Incidents arose where the vast disparity between the cultures of the two races led to misunderstanding and friction. Yet the over-all record as shown in contemporary American and Japanese accounts emphasizes a surprising measure of goodwill. Naval officers and samurai had rousing parties both aboard ship and ashore. As for the sailors landing at Shimoda and Hakodate, they found themselves after the initial distrust had worn off being greeted most cordially. For all their mutual doubts on coming together under such unusual circumstances, Americans and Japanese discovered in 1854 a basis for enduring friendship.

Again it was not altogether unlike the situation that was somewhat ironically to prevail nearly a century later when victorious American military forces landed to occupy a Japan defeated in war. In the 1940's there were on either side grave apprehensions. The Americans were prepared for a hostile reception; the Japanese were fearful of the conquering troops. But contrary to all expectations this latter-day American invasion, as when Commodore Perry's seamen went ashore, led not to sullen hostility but to an amazingly cordial *rapprochement.*

"They are without exception," Edward Yorke McCauley, an officer aboard the *Powhatan,* wrote of the Japanese in striking reaffirmation of the very first American visitors' impressions, "the most polite people on the face of the earth." If the keen intelligence and unexpected knowledge of the United States displayed by the samurai first coming aboard the American ships had astounded the expedition's officers, their unfailing courtesy was a further demonstration that they represented an advanced and highly sophisticated civilization. Bayard Taylor, no more than echoing the views of William and George Cleveland a half century earlier, was to characterize the two-sworded, petticoated samurai as "perfect gentlemen."

The obverse side of this engaging quality, many of the Americans nevertheless soon became convinced, was an hypocrisy which courtesy could only partially conceal. The exasperation of Commodore Perry with the Japanese commissioners' polite evasions, what he came to consider their flagrant falsehoods, is repeatedly reflected in the official report of the expedition. Williams, who liked the Japanese, considering them very much "superior" to the Chinese, reported that some of the naval officers came to judge them as no more than "savages, liars, a pack of fools." Taylor also commented on their artful dissimulation, becoming convinced that cunning was somehow second nature to these otherwise perfect gentlemen.

This is no place to attempt to analyze Japanese character. What is interesting is that the impressions formed by the members of Perry's squadron helped to set a pattern of American thinking about the Japanese that has persisted for a century: courtesy and hypocrisy. If there is indeed something in the nature of Japanese society that emphasizes such qualities as national characteristics, the situation the Bakufu officials faced in 1854 would have sharply accentuated them. These officials were walking on very thin ice. They had to meet the demands of the foreigners as politely as they could without making commitments that their superiors would not only disavow but for which they would hold them responsible. The samurai meeting the Americans at Yokohama were less concerned with Western concepts of truth and honesty than in avoiding mistakes that might well cost them their lives.

The insatiable curiosity of the Japanese again struck their visitors. Those coming aboard the American vessels examined everything about them with the utmost care and asked countless questions. They were intrigued by the woolen jackets and trousers of the seamen no less than by the swords and epaulets of the officers; they were as fascinated by the engines and machinery in the hold as by the guns and equipment above deck. "When visiting the ships," Francis Hawks wrote in the official report, "the mandarins and their attendants were never at rest; but went about peering into every nook and corner."

They took copious notes of everything they saw, convincing one American that the Japanese were "a nation of reporters . . . a nation of readers." Many of them were forever sketching. They drew the war vessels, the officers, the Commodore himself; they drew every piece of armament and equipment aboard ship. Many of these sketches have survived, an occasional one still turning up in a Tokyo secondhand bookstore, and they provide graphic evidence of the Japanese people's consuming interest in everything foreign. The portraits done in color of Perry and his officers generally have two things in common: great, long noses and red hair.

The traditional Japanese image of the Western barbarians was confirmed by these eager artists scrambling about the decks of the American ships.

A most fascinating reproduction of such sketches is found in *The Black Ship Scroll,* published only in 1963, which brings together several contemporary portraits of Americans, drawings of the *Powhatan* and, even more interesting, various pictures of American sailors enjoying shore leave. Here in vivid color are the Japanese artists' renditions of common sailors, a Negro member of a ship's crew, the instrumentalists of a ship's band, members of a surveying party, and one wonderful scene of sailors "dancing under the influence of strong drink." Still another very revealing sketch shows three seamen arranging to take a photograph of an elaborately dressed geisha. It bears the Japanese inscription:

> This picture shows how at Daian-ji, a temple in Shimoda, they took great pains to record the appearance of a courtesan to show the American king.

On going ashore the Americans soon discovered that the peasants and villagers (once they realized the visitors were not bloodthirsty ogres) were no less curious than the samurai officials. Dr. James Morrow, the expedition's agricultural expert, was interested in both distributing seeds and collecting them (he was to take home seventeen full packing cases), and this project led him to make more forays into the countryside, generally accompanied by Wells Williams as interpreter, than any other American. The people would not leave him alone. His towering height (six feet, two inches), fair skin and blue eyes contributed to making him an object of very special interest, and the villagers pressed closely about him, inquisitively fingering his clothes, wherever he went. They also asked, as Dr. Morrow recorded in his journal, innumerable questions "about geography, natural history, and the news of the world."

The Americans for their part showed no less curiosity than the Japanese, noting in their diaries and journals whatever they found strange or unusual. They described at length the countryside, with carefully tended rice fields climbing up the steep mountains, and the little villages with their neatly thatched houses. They especially singled out, as had their predecessors, the colorful two-sworded gentry, the submissive married women so exotically garbed in "nightgowns" and the grave, dignified, shaven-headed priests.

Sometimes actuality did not live up to expectations. "It is astonishing," wrote Lieutenant Preble, "how travellers have been carried away by their imaginations. . . . The Golden pillars and walls of palaces and temples, which have excited the admiration and wonder of travellers, are but wood and plaster—gilded." He also tells in one journal entry of how he heard an "old salt" growl out that "for his part he could any day lick a hundred of such fellows in petticoats, who hid themselves behind canvas forts and used paper pocket handkerchiefs." But making due allowance for all exaggerations, Preble was not himself disappointed in either Japan or the Japanese. He liked both the country and its people.

Another diarist who has left a youthfully naïve account of his experiences was John R. C. Lewis, a twenty-year-old Virginian of good family (he was a grandnephew of George Washington) who had, like Bayard Taylor, signed on for the voyage to Japan as a master's mate.

Lewis described the Japanese as a very quiet, inoffensive race ("though they do wear a large sword"); emphasized their cleanly habits; spoke of the children happily greeting the Americans with "*o-hio*" (then as today the common greeting for good morning); and wonderingly noted that the women always walked several paces behind their menfolk. He was interested in food and the ever-present "*sackee*," but, in common with most members of the Perry squadron, took a very dim view of Japanese refreshments in general. "A variety of heterogeneous native dishes," reads a description of one banquet, "many of them indescribable and partaken of only as a matter of etiquettey, deriving their charm probably from the dishes which were of the most magnificent description and pattern."

Many later visitors would probably agree with Master Mate Lewis in this description, and also with the appreciation he expressed on another occasion for Japanese confectionery, "especially a very superior quality of sponge cake." Interestingly enough, another American was in a quite different context to list this delicious sponge cake as one of the half dozen contributions (the others were gunpowder, firearms, tobacco, venereal disease and a few foreign words) which the Portuguese had contributed to

Japanese culture in the seventeenth century.

On first arriving Lewis had looked upon Japan with all the excitement and eager anticipation of adventurous youth. "Here then was the far-famed land of Japan," he wrote in his diary as his ship sailed into the Bay of Yedo. "Often in my childhood had my imagination wandered to this unknown region of the world hoping that by some enchantment I might be wafted there." But two months later, reminding one of William Cleveland, his tone had somewhat changed. "I certainly leave . . . without a single regret as I have never spent a more tiresome time in my life. . . . So farewell Japan and I hope I may never see you again."

Lewis did not concern himself with moral questions. Other members of the expedition, however, found many things to shock them: the frank and open system of prostitution, the acknowledged sale of young girls to the brothel keepers, and the ready availability of obscene pictures and pornographic books. Even though many of the American visitors believed that the Japanese were morally superior to other Orientals, they still asserted that they were "a lewd people." Every diarist (as well as the official report) notes what was felt to be this most serious blemish on the native character. "The remarkable sensuality of the Japanese," wrote Lieutenant Preble, "is everywhere evidenced by their habits, conduct and actions." And Francis Hawks declared that "there was enough in their popular literature, with its obscene pictorial illustrations, to prove a licentiousness of taste and practice among a certain class of people that was not only disgustingly intrusive, but disgracefully indicative of foul corruption."

One custom that convinced the Americans beyond any shadow of doubt of such moral depravity was that of men and women bathing together, openly and casually, in the public baths. "While passing through the village of Shimoda," wrote Dr. Morrow, "we saw more of the licentiousness and degradation of these cultivated heathen than ever before. It is common to see men, women and children,—old and young, married and single,—bathing in the same large open bath house." "A scene at the public baths, where the sexes mingle indiscriminately, unconscious of their nudity," the official report stated, "was not calculated to impress the Americans with a very favorable opinion of the morals of the inhabitants." "Their religion might encourage cleanliness," J. W.

Spalding, a ship's clerk, was to write, but in a "repulsive and indecent manner."

Such shocked reactions to public bathing were altogether to be expected of mid-century Americans. The age was one in which Victorian prudery had attained new and amazing dimensions, and nothing could possibly have presented more convincing evidence of moral degradation than this public display of the unadorned human form. After all, good Americans in these years, as the English visitor Captain Marryatt duly recorded, draped the nude statues in their museums and on occasion even put little trousers on the legs of their pianos.

It need hardly be pointed out that just as Americans could never reconcile themselves to what they judged to be the licentiousness of public bathing in Japan, so the Japanese, when they had greater opportunity to observe certain foreign customs, were in turn equally shocked by what they considered immorality. The reaction of Nakahama Manjiro, in reporting after his visit to the United States that the American people were "lewd by nature" because "men and women would actually kiss in public," is a case in point. In later years Lafcadio Hearn was to write that to the Japanese "the people of the West with their novels and poems about love seem a race of very lascivious people." There was no greater difference in the cultural patterns of Yankees and samurai than in their concepts of morality as applied to almost every aspect of sex.

These and other differences may have caused Americans and Japanese to look askance at certain of each other's customs, but what remains still more striking is how well they got along together. The naval officers and samurai officials happily exchanged cards and autographs (for which the Japanese, then as today, seemed to have had a veritable passion), talked freely through the medium of such interpreters as Moriyama Einosuke, and, what appears to have been even more memorable, drank together in happy conviviality. Accounts of these first Japanese-American parties sometimes give the impression that the door of Japan swung open on a wave of champagne.

When the local officials first came aboard his ship, Lieutenant McCauley, who was a rather brash young man, took them below decks and, after showing them the engines and machinery in the hold, offered them a drink. He was amazed at how enthusiastically they responded: ". . . bless my wig, they swallowed poteen, Brandy, Gin and sake alternately, a mixture that would swamp the devil himself." Dr. Morrow also noted (without disapproval) this cheerful proclivity of the Japanese. "They are free drinkers," he wrote after one shipboard party, "and many of them became very merry." Nor does the official report gloss this over. Describing one party aboard the *Powhatan* where the Japanese unabashedly showed their deep appreciation for the champagne, Madeira and punch, Hawks wrote that they "became quite uproarious . . . kept shouting at the tops of their voices, and were heard far above the music of the bands that enlivened the entertainment by a succession of brisk and cheerful tunes."

The most spirited occasion bringing Americans and Japanese together under very happy circumstances centered about the exchange of the gifts that Commodore Perry had brought to the Emperor and those which the Japanese presented in the Emperor's name to the Americans. This exchange was interesting also in that it revealed so sharply certain of the contrasting values in Western and Eastern civilization: the American presents were practical and utilitarian, those of the Japanese decorative and artistic. Moreover, while most of the former were in great, rough boxes or wrapped in brown packing paper, the latter were arranged on trays covered with woven mats "making a pretty show."

Among the American gifts were a quarter-size model locomotive, with tender and car; a telegraph set, a telescope, photographic apparatus, firearms and various types of agricultural machinery; also a collection of state documents, histories and technological books including Audubon's *Birds of America*, and a considerable quantity of whisky, champagne and cherry cordial. For the Empress, with a casual disregard of Japanese custom, there were a silk dress, a toilet dressing box and perfume.

The Japanese presents included gold lacquerware boxes, writing tables and bookcases; rich brocades and silks, and a set of porcelain cups of "wonderful lightness and transparency" to be given to the President; several samurai swords and a collection of coins for Commodore Perry; and for the officers of the expedition, lacquer tables, trays and "chow-chow" boxes; pipe cases, fans and umbrellas, and pieces of pongee and flowered crepe. In accordance with ancient custom, the Japanese also made a symbolic presentation of token quantities of dried fish, charcoal and rice, together with four small dogs.

There was no question that in this mutual exchange the model locomotive was the outstanding triumph. The Americans first brought their gifts ashore, and then a few days later the Japanese presented theirs. In the meantime seamen from the squadron (with the help of some Japanese, who proved themselves to be surprisingly expert at such an unfamiliar task) set up a circular railway track on the beach. On the ceremonial occasion all was ready. The little train was soon "scudding round and round the circus like a Shetland pony," with the fascinated samurai taking their turns for a ride, precariously perched on either the locomotive or its tender. "You can imagine," John Sewall, the captain's clerk aboard the sloop *Saratoga*, wrote in describing the experience of one official, "with what a death grip he clung to the eves of the car, and how his teeth chattered and his robes fluttered as he flashed around the circle."

In return for the entertainment provided by rides on the model train, the Japanese staged for their guests a "curious, barbaric spectacle.' This was a series of *sumo* matches, the traditional Japanese wrestling, in which two enormously fat athletes ("the stoutest men I ever saw," McCauley wrote) struggled by every means possible to force each other either out of the ring or to the ground. This unique form of combat has always been immensely popular among the Japanese (today it is an outstanding television attraction), but the members of the Perry expedition saw no more than a confused "shoving, yelling, tagging, howling, twisting, and curvetting about." Forgetting the savagery of the bare-knuckle prize fights of their own country (although one diarist was certain that the current national hero, "Yankee" Sullivan, could knock any Japanese out of any ring), and the bloodthirsty butting, biting, gouging free-for-alls of a frontier frolic, they condemned *sumo* as but another expression of Asiatic brutality and violence.

The scene on the beaches of Yokohama on that distant day— March 23, 1854—wrote one of the Americans, presented "a curious melange . . . a juncture of the east and west." Here were two-sworded samurai and their attendants with "shaven pates and nightgowns" jostling the soberly uniformed sailors of the visiting squadron; the model locomotive scudding about its little circuit; the massive *sumo* wrestlers pushing and grunting in the ring; the maneuvering of the marines in close order drill—"All these things, and many other things," this observer wrote, "exhibiting the difference between our civilization and usages and those of this secluded, pagan people."

A few days later Commodore Perry gave a great formal banquet aboard the *Powhatan*, the Japanese commissioners dining with the expedition's officers in the cabin while the lesser officials were entertained on the quarter-deck. It was a tremendous meal, which for all its strangeness the Japanese would seem to have enjoyed immensely. At its close, according to their custom, they gathered together everything that had not been eaten, carefully wrapping up "morsels of turkey, asparagus, pie, ginger, sweetmeats and the like" and stuffing these delicacies away in the long sleeves of their kimono.

Throughout the dinner and on into the afternoon, the sherry and the port, the whisky and the gin, the claret and champagne, flowed with a freedom that must almost have exhausted even the ample supplies of the flagship's storeroom, and the resources of the interpreters were surely taxed in the exchange of toasts on the quarter-deck. After honoring the President of the United States and the Emperor of Japan, pledging peace and friendship between the two peoples, this toasting came to something of a climax when one happy naval officer exuberantly proposed, "The ladies of Japan. May we become better acquainted."

At this point Commodore Perry appeared on deck with the Japanese commissioners to announce, "Gentlemen, we will now adjourn to hear the minstrels," and one of the samurai let out a startling whistle. ("The Commodore looks grave," Midshipman Sproston of the *Macedonian* recorded in his diary. "No one appreciates a joke less than he does.") It was occasioned, this unexpected whistle, by the appearance of a band of seamen from the *Powhatan's* crew elaborately made up in blackface.[1]

As these "sable gentlemen" broke into the familiar patter of

---

[1] A broadside of this affair which had appeared in the *Japan Expedition Press* is attached to the manuscript diary of Lieutenant Preble. It announces an "Ethiopian Concert" followed by a burlesque of Bulwer-Lytton's *The Lady of Lyons*.

"Mistah Tambo" and "Mistah Bones," went through a gay, rollicking "walk-around," sang and danced, the Japanese apparently gave way to almost uncontrollable mirth. The minstrels were a huge and unqualified success. While Sproston was further to write that he thought "the Commissioners would have died with suppressed laughter (for they never laugh out loud as we do)," other reports state that they all let go completely. "Even the saturnine Hayashi," Hawks said, "was not proof against the grotesque exhibit, and even he joined with the rest in the general hilarity."

With the gaiety reaching such unexampled heights, the *Powhatan* presented a scene that must be unique in the annals of the American navy. Then, as the liquor began to run low, one of the flagship's officers substituted a mixture of catsup and vinegar for the whisky. The Japanese hardly knew the difference by all accounts, and with the band music blaring forth, the ship's deck became an impromptu dance hall for the samurai and their hosts. "Some of our greyest and gravest officers danced with them," Lieutenant Preble wrote. "A funny sight to behold—these bald-pated bundles of clothes—and Doctors, Pursers, Lieuts. and Capts. all jumping up and down to the music."

A long afternoon finally came to an end. As the Japanese made ready to leave (their report of the affair, incidentally, merely stated that the commissioners came aboard the *Powhatan* "where they dined"), the censor attached to the Japanese commissioners, who was described on one occasion as having "a long drawn-out meager body, a very yellow bilious face," provided a fitting climax for the festivities:

The jovial Matsusaki threw his arms about the Commodore's neck, crushing, in his tipsy embrace, a pair of new epaulettes, and repeating, in Japanese, with maudlin affection, these words, as interpreted into English, "Nippon and America, all the same heart!" He then went toddling into his boat. . . .

Upon conclusion of the treaty negotiations, ships of the American squadron visited both Shimoda and Hakodate, and in these ports, more than had been the case while off Yokohama, the seamen as well as officers went ashore. In spite of the original reluctance of the Japanese authorities to permit them to go about freely, on Commodore Perry's emphatic protest they promised to withdraw all guards and permit the Americans to explore the village and countryside. As could only be expected with sailors on shore leave, there was trouble over drinking and women. The official report tells of a number of unfortunate occasions when the sailors got drunk and became involved in scuffles with the natives, and the Japanese records are somewhat more frank about patronage of brothels. One of the pictures in *The Black Ship Scroll* depicts "an American in a Shimoda inn dallying fondly with harlots," and the accompanying text further describes this phase of the sailors' life ashore.

Nevertheless the diaries of the expedition members continue to praise the Japanese (apart from the comments on their "lewdness") and to extol their friendliness and hospitality. The local villagers, for Shimoda was only a small fishing hamlet, had all "the characteristic courtesy and reserved but pleasant manners" of their countrymen elsewhere. It was felt that they would have liked to open up trade, and that it was only an arbitrary government that sought to cling to the age-old restrictions on any commerce with foreigners.

All accounts describe Shimoda at length, with general agreement on its attractive appearance even though it seemed to have little business and was quite poverty-stricken; and they also stressed the picturesque and varied beauty of the surrounding countryside with snow-capped Fuji occasionally visible in the far distance. The Americans went sight-seeing. They walked the streets, visited the temples as well as the bathing houses, wandered in the nearby hills, and wonderingly observed "the customs and habits of this seemingly simple and good-natured people."

When several of the squadron's vessels next sailed northward to visit Hakodate, they found the people there still somewhat mistrustful of their visitors, and it was some time before the villagers were fully reassured as to the peaceful intentions of the Americans. One local official, a district headman and owner of a grocery store, recorded events at Hakodate, and this novel diary has recently been translated and published.

The authorities, on learning of the approach of the black ships, ordered the people to hide everything of value; put up the shutters on their windows, sealing all the cracks; build barricades to protect their storehouses; and, having learned that the barbarians "are said to notice women particularly," either conceal their wives and daughters in the storehouses or carry them off to the hills. They further warned, the Hakodate diarist reported, that the foreigners were short-tempered and angry, very fond of drinking and always ready for a brawl.

That these instructions were taken very much to heart is clearly evident from American sources describing the first landings at Hakodate. One account speaks of the "perfect panic" which prevailed among the general populace; another states that the villagers "seemed much alarmed . . . and many of them took to flight"; and a third complained about "the Japanese police who follow you about and keep all the women shut up and their houses closed."

It was apparently with both surprise and relief that the Hakodate villagers gradually realized that their visitors were not going to give way to an unrestrained orgy of theft, murder and rape. But while the local diarist was soon recording that the Americans were by no means as fierce and unprincipled as had been expected, he still found them a very strange breed of men. He described them as averaging at least six feet, five inches in height, continually smoking cigarettes, and wearing a most unusual costume of jackets and trousers, with a wool cap "like that worn by the god Daikoku." He found their way of eating without chopsticks "unpleasant to see" and their manners very bad, but generously excused such social lapses as resulting from "the custom of the country." More importantly, our diarist reported that instead of laying waste the town, the worst that could be said of these foreign visitors (wherein they set a precedent for generations of American tourists) was that they "asked for food, gazed at the women, petted the children, and stayed a long time in temples."

Lieutenant Preble gave a brief description in his journal of a Sunday shore excursion that admirably supplements the account of the Hakodate district official. "After visiting the temples," he wrote, "made a tour of the shops, and bought a few Japanese things." He then added that the people were "inquisitively civil, looked at our watches, admired the cloth of our coats, and particularly our boots and shoes." Preble saw no women, believing that the soldiers who usually accompanied the Americans' rambles had ordered them to stay indoors. "We often notice little holes torn in the oiled paper windows," he recorded, "and imagine the sharp eyes of the Japanese fair are peeping through them at the terrible rough bearded strangers."

At Shimoda if not at Hakodate there were further banquets comparable to those at Yokohama bringing together naval officers and samurai, and one final occasion on shore again found cordial toasts being freely exchanged. It was perhaps not so lively an affair as the festivities aboard the *Powhatan* some weeks earlier. Nevertheless the official report states that everything "passed pleasantly and convivially, mutual compliments being freely exchanged, and healths drunk in full, if Liliputian, cups of saki."

On the eve of the squadron's final departure, S. Wells Williams expressed his view that the proceedings of the expedition had been "peculiarly prospered by God." Not a shot had been fired, not a man wounded, and not a piece of property destroyed. He remained convinced of the friendliness of the Japanese and felt in turn that on the whole "the impression left on the people by the squadron has been favorable." Over and beyond the signature of the Treaty of Kanagawa, with all its importance as a first step in prying open the door of Japan, there had been a meeting between people and people which was to be no less significant in laying the foundations of American-Japanese friendship.

6

❦

Envoy Extraordinary

ABOARD THE *Macedonian* one day as the ships of the Japan Expedition lay at anchor in the harbor of Shimoda, Midshipman Sproston was somewhat carried away by the loveliness of the view. "As I gazed over the beautiful landscape spread before me this afternoon," he wrote in his diary, "I thought the hills crowned with trees, their sides sloping gracefully to the water's edge and covered with verdure, to be as pretty a sight as I had seen for a long time."

The scene today is somewhat changed. Indeed, when Commander Adams returned the next year aboard the *Powhatan* to exchange treaty ratifications, he found that a great earthquake and typhoon had overwhelmed central Japan, "leaving abundant evidence of its ruinous effects at Shimoda." Nevertheless this little village until very recent years presented much the same general appearance as when Perry's ships first anchored in its harbor.[1] And even now the rocky shoreline, dramatically accented by twisted, stunted pines, and the sharp-pointed, heavily wooded hills lying in the near distance are just as Midshipman Sproston saw them. Also there survives an old temple—Gyokusen-ji—where

---

[1] It was only in 1961 that a railroad was built linking Shimoda with Tokyo; since then the village has become a popular tourist resort.

there may still be seen the gravestones of several American seamen who died in Japan in 1853 or 1854.

In the front courtyard of this temple is a stone monument, and on it is inscribed an extract from the journal of quite as illustrious a visitor to Japan as Commodore Perry himself. For it was at Gyokusen-ji that Townsend Harris lived, the American envoy who was appointed to carry forward the task on which the better known naval officer had started. The journal entry, dated September 4, 1856, reads:

Slept very little from excitement and mosquitoes,—the latter enormous in size. At seven A.M. men came on shore to put up my flagstaff . . . and, at two and a half P.M. of this day, I *hoist* the "First Consular Flag" ever seen in this Empire. Grim reflections—ominous of change—undoubted beginning of the end. Query,—if for the real good of Japan?

To an even greater extent than the signature of a "wood-and-water treaty," the establishment of this American consulate marked the effective beginning of the new era of foreign intercourse upon which Japan was so hesitantly embarking. It was a first step toward the conclusion of a further Japanese-American treaty which provided, as Perry had not been able to provide, for trade and commerce, and also for Japanese acceptance of an American legation at Yedo. "The genius of Perry had unbarred the gate of the island empire and left it ajar," John W. Foster, diplomatic historian and onetime Secretary of State, wrote in 1903, "but it was the skill of Harris which threw it open to the commercial enterprise of the world."

Townsend Harris was a remarkable man. His great interest was in opening up Japan to foreign trade, but he was determined in doing so to safeguard Japanese interests as carefully as those of his own country. Ready to see every treaty Japan had signed torn up rather than "witness the horrors of war inflicted on this peaceful people and happy land," he wished to avoid even the threat of force in his negotiations and so to conduct himself as to win an honorable place in Japanese history. It was his profound hope, as he was to state on a later occasion, that Japan might prove to be "the one spot in the Eastern world [where] the advent of Christian civilization did not bring with it its usual attendants of rapine and bloodshed."

Largely ignored by his own country (a contemporary article in *Frank Leslie's Illustrated Newspaper* assailed the "criminal neglect" from which he suffered, "alike disgraceful to the Government and to the American people"), the services of Townsend Harris were appreciated and honored by the Japanese. They did not find him, as they had so often found Perry, haughty and overbearing, but on the contrary warm and sympathetic; they came to have more confidence in him than in any other foreigner in Japan. On his final departure the Shogun gave him a valuable samurai sword (which Harris later presented to General Grant for having saved "my beloved country from the ruin that threatened her") as a mark of his personal esteem.

Harris arrived in Japan in 1856, an appointee of President Pierce, with varied experience both as a merchant and as a wide traveler. In the 1840's he had been a partner with his brother in an importing firm in New York and one of that city's eminent citizens. He was for a time president of the Board of Education and was almost single-handedly responsible for founding the "Free College or Academy" that ultimately became the College of the City of New York.[2] With his business and civic interests, and teaching Sunday school, his life was one (as a sympathetic biographer has written) "overflowing with riches and radiant with promise." However in 1847, following the death of his mother, with whom as a bachelor he had been living, Harris suffered some sort of nervous breakdown. He apparently felt lost without what may have been his mother's stabilizing influence and "fell into convivial habits." He resigned from the Board of Education, neglected his business affairs and soon gave up altogether, perhaps under pressure, his partnership with his brother. Without telling his friends, he soon afterward left New York on a mercantile venture to California, at the time of the gold rush, and then embarked on a further voyage to the Far East. This latter enterprise failed. He nevertheless stayed away and apparently traveled widely as a supercargo aboard various merchant vessels trading in Asia.

Little is known about this period of his life other than that he

[2] His name is preserved in the Townsend Harris High School.

spent successive Christmas Days, as later recorded in his journal, at Manila, Penang, Singapore, Hong Kong, Calcutta and Ceylon. There is clear evidence, however, that, far from giving way to further dissipation, he fully recovered the deep religious faith of his earlier New York days and once again became wholly exemplary in all his conduct. He gave up drinking. There is one reference in his journal to "my old Asiatic habit—tea and cold water," and another time he writes of refusing a Fourth of July party as he wished to "avoid all such affairs which are sure to run into excess of noise and drinking."

Moreover, Harris now wanted to do something more than wander rather idly through Asia and applied for a United States consular post. An appointment to Ningpo, in China, did not, however, interest him, and learning of the Perry expedition while on a visit in Shanghai in 1853, he tried to join it. When this proved impossible he conceived the idea of becoming the first consul general to Japan, and after a further trip to India, where he was reputedly engaged in "a secret and romantic mission" for the London *Times*, he returned to the United States to make a formal application for the post. Secretary of State Marcy was an old friend, Commodore Perry was approving, and several other prominent New Yorkers (attesting that Harris was a good Democrat) came to his support. President Pierce was persuaded to make him consul general and, in officially notifying Harris of his appointment, stated that it was based upon "your knowledge of Eastern character and your general intelligence and experience in business."

Townsend Harris was fifty-two at this time, a strikingly handsome man with a heavy mustache and sideburns. His manner was dignified and courtly, one later visitor at Shimoda speaking of the "almost over-powering politeness for which he is distinguished." Other acquaintances emphasized what they considered his serious, devout character. S. Wells Williams described him as a "truly Christian man" whose success in negotiating with the Japanese had come about largely in answer to prayer.

This rather somber picture of Harris is countered by the comments of other visitors at Shimoda and later Yokohama. They found him a friendly, generous host, highly interesting in his talk about Japan and the Japanese, and a man of many and varied interests. Lieutenant Johnston of the *Powhatan*, who was briefly at

The ship *Franklin*, Boston, which visited Nagasaki in 1799.
Courtesy Peabody Museum

William Cleveland—a portrait made after he had become captain of his own ship. Courtesy Peabody Museum

Captain James Devereux, of the ship *Franklin*, which visited Nagasaki
in 1799. Courtesy of the Peabody Museum

JOLKTOWN

"Washington greatly defeats the soldiers of England at Saratoga"—(not Yorktown).
From *Meriken Shinsi* (*New Account of America*), Yedo, 1853

Departure of the U.S.S. *Columbus* and *Vincennes* from Yedo Bay on July 29, 1846. Drawn by S. F. R. from sketches by John Eastley. Courtesy of Harry Shaw Newman, The Old Curiosity Print Shop, New York City

A daguerreotype of Manjiro. Courtesy of Miss Emily V. Warinner

一バッホー 港頭之畠

Fairhaven—New Bedford, Massachusetts. Drawn from a contemporary sketch by Manjiro. Courtesy of Miss Emily V. Warinner

"A Black Ship." From a contemporary Japanese newsletter, 1854

First Landing of Americans in Japan—July 14, 1853. Drawn by W. Heine.
Collections of the Library of Congress

米利幹便節 ペルリ 年五十二

Commodore Matthew Calbraith Perry. Contemporary
Japanese print. Collection of the Norfolk Museum

"True Portrait of Perry." From *The Black Ship Scroll*.
Courtesy of Japan Societies of San Francisco and New York

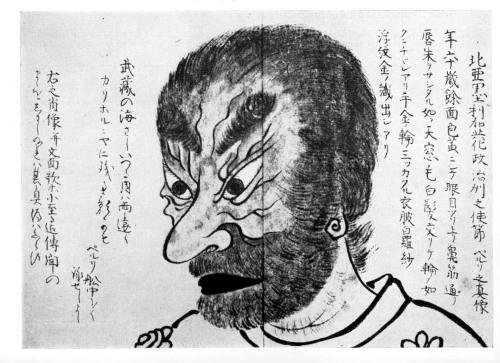

Matthew Calbraith Perry. From a daguerreotype by P. Haas

Commodore Perry and Color Bearer. Contemporary Japanese print. Collection of the Norfolk Museum

File of American Marines. Contemporary Japanese print. Collection of the Norfolk Museum

Commodore Perry and a Japanese Wrestler. Contemporary Japanese print. Courtesy DeWolf Perry

Public Baths at Shimoda. Drawn by W. Heine. From first edition *Narrative of the Expedition . . . to Japan* and subsequently suppressed

Commodore Perry Meeting the Japanese Commissioners at Yokohama. Drawn by W. T. Peters. From *Narrative of the Expedition . . . to Japan.*.

Dinner given the Japanese Commissioners aboard the U.S.S. *Powhatan*. Drawn by W. T. Peters. From *Narrative of the Expedition . . . to Japan*

Minstrel Show Aboard the U.S.S. *Powhatan*. A contemporary Japanese print. Collection of the Norfolk Museum

Sumo Wrestlers at Yokohama. Drawn by W. Heine. From *Narrative of the Expedition . . . to Japan*

An American Sailor Drinking with a Geisha. Contemporary Japanese print. Courtesy of Carl H. Boehringer

American Sailors Photographing a Courtesan. From *The Black Ship Scroll*. Courtesy Japan Societies of San Francisco and New York

Commodore Perry Paying Farewell Visit to Japanese Commissioners at Shimoda. Drawn by W. Heine. From *Narrative of the Expedition to Japan*

Townsend Harris. Portrait by James Bogle, 1855. Courtesy The City
College of New York

The Temple of Gyokusen-ji. Drawn by Henry Heusken. Courtesy Robert A. Wilson

Townsend Harris Meeting with Japanese Officials. Drawn by Henry Heusken. Courtesy of Robert A. Wilson

The First Japanese Treaty Commission, 1860. Photograph by Brady. From the National Archives

"Tommy"—the Favorite of the Ladies. From a photograph by Brady. From *Harper's Weekly*, June 23, 1860

"American Pleasure Riding in Yokohama." By Gountei Sadahide in *Yokohama Ukiyoe*. Courtesy Tsuneo Tamba

"Some Americans." By Yoshikazu. Courtesy Carl H. Boehringer

Floral Car Carrying the Japanese Treaty Box. From *Frank Leslie's Illustrated Newspaper*, June 30, 1860

"Foreigners Making Merry." By Ichimosai Yoshitora in *Yokohama Ukiyoe.* Courtesy Tsuneo Tamba

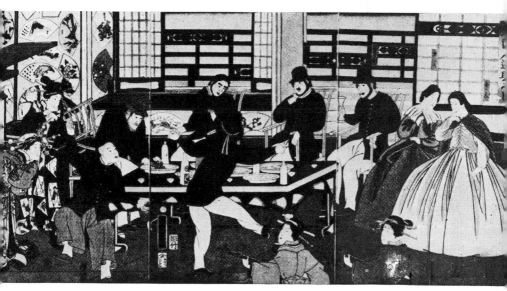

Ernest Fenollosa. From *Fenollosa: The Far East and American Culture*
by Lawrence W. Chisolm. Courtesy Yale University Press

Lafcadio Hearn. From *The Life and Letters of Lafcadio Hearn* by Elizabeth Bisland

Train and Waterfront at Yokohama. Collections of the Library of Congress

"Yokohama Dontaku"—The Famous Sunday Parade. By Gounter Sadahide in the *Yokohama Ukiyoe*. Courtesy Tsuneo Tamba

Shimoda in 1858, spoke of his enjoyment of the American coun-
sul's entertaining accounts of his life; three years later a missionary wife wrote of him as "very sprightly in conversation, and
easy and familiar in manner." His journal also reveals the more
human side of his character—flashes of humor and also occasional flare-ups of anger when the apparent duplicity of the Japanese officials overcame even his instinctive courtesy. There are a
few letters which further reveal a warm, affectionate nature beneath his sometimes frigidly polite exterior.

When Harris first arrived at Shimoda on August 21, 1856,
aboard the U.S.S. *San Jacinto*, under the command of Commodore James Armstrong, the local Japanese authorities made it
quite clear that they did not want to accept an American consul.
They asked him to go away; when he declined to do so, they asked
Commodore Armstrong if he did not have the authority to take
him away. The naval officer answered emphatically that his orders
were to bring Harris to Shimoda and "leave him there," and the
consul himself quite as stubbornly refused to entertain any idea of
foregoing his treaty right to remain. As recorded in the *Kinsei
Shiriaku*, a contemporary Japanese history, the Bakufu tried to
dissuade him from staying, but he "would not listen, and it had no
resource but to give way." Harris thereupon set up the consulate
at the temple of Gyokusen-ji, determined to persuade the Japanese
not only to accept rather more graciously his residence in
Shimoda, but to allow him to proceed to Yedo and negotiate the
commercial treaty that was his government's primary objective.
Harris stayed in Shimoda for some fourteen long and weary
months before he was permitted to set out for Yedo. He was alone
except for his Dutch-born secretary and interpreter, Henry
Heusken, an amiable young man—he was just twenty-four—who
had emigrated to America from Holland in 1853. Differences in
age and temperament sometimes placed a heavy strain on the
relations between the two men, but Harris was later to write that
they were "those of father and son, rather than *chef* and *em-
ploye*." Perhaps influenced by the older man, Heusken was also
fearful of what the impact of the West might mean for Japan.
"Oh country which has become so dear to me," he one time confided to his own journal, "is the progress really progress, this

civilization really civilization for you? . . . I fear, Oh, my God, that this scene of happiness is coming to an end and the Occidental people will bring here their fatal vices." Throughout their first year of exile Harris and Heusken were completely cut off from the outside world, the first ship to visit Shimoda arriving in September, 1857, and they were compelled to rely wholly on their own resources to while away the time. Even after Harris returned to Shimoda after his trip to Yedo, there was no break in the monotony of this isolated life. "The fatal sound of 'you are alone, you are alone,'" the consul general wrote during this latter period, "never ceases to strike upon my heart."

Harris was frequently ill and recorded rather dolefully his liver trouble, inability to eat, loss of weight and attacks of *cholera morbus*: "Ill, ill, ill, I am constantly wasting away in flesh." And another time, almost a year after his arrival when he was still waiting expectantly for the long-delayed return of the *San Jacinto* and almost despairing over what seemed to be the futility of his existence at Shimoda, he wrote: "My health is miserable, my appetite is gone, and I am so shrunk away that I look as though a 'Vice Consul had been cut out of me.' Where, oh, where is Commodore Armstrong?"

As the touch of humor in even this lament suggests, Harris never let himself become wholly downhearted. He busied himself with fixing up the temple more comfortably and made it into what one later visitor described as "a very commodious and romantic-looking residence." He built a pig pen and a poultry yard, started a garden where he planted Irish potatoes as well as cherry trees and camellias, and took long rambles (Heusken apparently did not accompany him) through the countryside gathering new plants and flowers. In one month, Harris recorded in his journal, he walked some 350 miles. In the temple grounds he had a fish pond with "*real live fishes in it*," as he wrote in an affectionate letter to the young daughter of one of his friends, and also described for her a collection of pets which included two dogs, five cages of birds, some tame pigeons and two "darling little hens." Such activities and a voluminous correspondence (even though he was going to have to wait a year for any answer to his letters) served to blunt the edge of his boredom.

What sustained Harris throughout this weary period was his stubborn faith that he would eventually succeed in his mission and break down Japanese resistance to his going to Yedo and having an audience with the Shogun. "Do not despair, my dear Kate," he wrote the same little girl to whom he had written of his pets, "for I shall go to Yedo one of these days and then I shall see what I can get for you." There were times when he became infuriated with the way the Japanese continued to put him off, and was quite as incensed as Commodore Perry over the evasions and duplicity of the officials in going back on their promises. The journal has many an outburst against "egregious lies" and "cool mendacity."

A further trial during the early days at Shimoda was the constant presence of the Bakufu's spies. They kept a watch on all the comings and goings of both Harris and Heusken and even attended their meetings with the local officials. Heusken relates how after repeatedly complaining of this maddening intrusion on his privacy, Harris finally came to realize that what his interpreter called his "gentle and courteous remonstrances" were of no avail and peremptorily demanded the immediate removal of guards "who treat like a prisoner the representative of the United States." He made his point; the guards and spies disappeared. "Now, when we walk about the streets," Heusken recorded on February 25, 1857, "police agents do not dare any more to follow us; I enter the houses freely; I speak with the common people without anybody daring to oppose it."

For all his difficulties and frustrations, Harris would appear to have maintained (except for this one outburst) a courteous and friendly attitude in all his dealings with the Japanese officials. Even though they might on occasion tell "egregious lies," he understood the difficult position in which they found themselves and tended to excuse them. He paid frequent tribute to their genial and affable manner, their hospitality and their innate kindliness. He also liked the common people—the villagers, fishermen and peasants—without qualification. The bonhomie that attended their politeness, Harris wrote, "convinces you of their sincerity."

His fondness for the Japanese was one time reported by English visitors to Shimoda. Great Britain (as well as Russia and Holland) had been quick to follow up the success won by the United

States by concluding their own treaties, and in 1858 the Earl of Elgin headed a special British mission to Japan for further negotiations. In his account of this venture Lawrence Oliphant, a member of Lord Elgin's staff, tells of the surprise of the Englishmen as their ships approached Shimoda and they saw "fluttering among the leaves of a Bo-tree, the well-known combination of red, white and blue which forms the national flag of our transatlantic cousins." The visitors were warmly welcomed, and after describing the temple of Gyokusen-ji, comfortably fitted up and with a well-stored library, Oliphant goes on to say that Harris' isolation did not appear in any way to have "disgusted" him with the people among whom he was banished. His experiences had seemingly only heightened his "high opinion of their amiable qualities and charming natural dispositions."

This cordial feeling for the Japanese, so important in the evolution of Japanese-American relations in this difficult period, was enhanced by Harris' belief that they were superior to any other Asiatic people. He especially admired the simplicity and frugality of their lives. Indeed, he noted somewhat wryly that it might be difficult to convince them that they really needed the goods and articles his countrymen were so anxious to sell them. He had himself been unable to persuade the Japanese, Harris said, that the sum of happiness is increased by the indulgence of artificial needs. But he wrote with little realization of what was actually going to happen a decade later when he went on to say that Japan was no country "for modistes, tailors, jewelers and the whole army that battens on the imaginary wants of the West."

He thought the Japanese (though his early observations were limited to what he saw in Shimoda and the surrounding countryside) generally well off and contented—"the best fed, clad and lodged, and the least overworked of any people on earth." Even after visiting Yedo he would repeat these comments and further stated that he had "never seen a case of squalid misery since I have been in Japan." His sympathetic acceptance of the Japanese way of life, so contrary to the views of those Americans who were convinced that only Christianity could save the country from its moral degradation, led him many times to reaffirm those misgivings that he had first voiced on raising the consular flag at Shimoda:

"God grant that the future generations may not have cause to regret the hour I arrived."

His journal has many descriptions of the people, their customs and their manners, and one perhaps may be singled out in which Harris undertakes to portray "a lady in full dress—i.e., made up for mischief":

Her face is thickly covered with rice flour, in which rouge—real rouge—is prettily placed, while her lips are brought to just that violet tinge that drives the Japanese lover even to making poetry; her robes are numerous and clumsy, and her girdle is so vast that its amplitude would make a robe for any ordinary woman; her head is bristling with metal ornaments that look like the grandfather of all tuning forks; her really pretty feet are protected by neat straw sandals; when she walks she minces her steps as though her legs were tied together at the knees.

His personal contacts with the Japanese grew primarily out of his continuing parleys with them over his living conditions—the procurement of supplies, problems with servants and other day-by-day matters. He was also entertained by the two governors of Shimoda, who were charged with the negotiations over his proposed trip to Yedo, and he occasionally saw other officials of the Bakufu. The interpreter at these meetings was once again Moriyama Einosuke, and he and Harris were soon on the best of terms. In this association, as in all his previous contacts with Americans, Moriyama's role was a good deal more than that of just interpreter. He was always a helpful adviser. Harris often speaks of his coming to the temple on "a mere visit of friendship."

In entertaining his Japanese friends, Harris would appear to have been well prepared, even though he was now himself a teetotaler, to indulge their fondness for Western drinks. The temple was fully stocked with champagne, cordials, brandy and whisky. On one of Moriyama's visits the consul tells of serving cakes and champagne which the interpreter enjoyed with unrestrained enthusiasm. There was another occasion when he reported that official callers voraciously consumed his brandy and whisky. But while Harris noted that the Japanese "drink more than enough," he was never really censorious of them. His tolerance reflected a far more

Christian spirit than that of the missionaries who later came prepared to be shocked at everything the Japanese did offending their own strict morality. Some aspects of their behavior might cause concern. Commenting on the public bathing, Harris said he could not account "for so indelicate a proceeding on the part of a people so generally correct," but he was not so completely scandalized as the members of the Perry expedition had been.

The Japanese attitude on matters of sex did involve Harris in one very curious episode which the records do not fully explain and which was to give rise to a beguiling and indestructible legend. This decorous, churchly American diplomat is romantically reputed to have enjoyed a liaison with a beautiful geisha whose name was Okichi-san.

The story begins, as recorded in the Harris journal, with a dinner at which the two governors of Shimoda, Inouye Shinano-no-Kami and Okada Bingo-no-Kami, lavishly entertained the American envoy. After it had come to a close with Shinano-no-Kami serving ceremonial tea with his own hand, the conversation took what Harris described as "the usual Japanese turn" in reverting to women. "Bingo-no-Kami informed me," the consul wrote, "that one of the Vice-Governors was specially charged with the duty of supplying me with female society, and said if I fancied any woman the Vice-Governor would procure her for me." Harris added nothing further in his journal—one is certainly left with the impression that he sternly rejected such an improper suggestion—but the Japanese accounts have something further to say on the subject.[3]

They state that a little later, during one of those periods when Harris was ill, he asked that a female nurse be sent to care for him at Gyokusen-ji. Not quite understanding the situation, the authorities instructed a local girl, Okichi-san, to go to the temple and put herself at the American consul's disposal. At this point what Japan's cautious modern historians state to be fact and the traditional legend abruptly part company. The historians declare that

---

[3] Heusken describes this same dinner and, while saying nothing of the offer made to Harris of female companionship, suggests his own interest in such matters in sadly noting that by Japanese custom no women were present. "This absence of man's angel of mercy," he wrote, "gives a sort of emptiness, a certain sadness to the Governors' dinner. Had some noble Japanese matron been hostess at the table, had we been able to dance a polka with the Governors' daughters, what a good time we would have had!"

Okichi-san was in fact "a washerwoman and a prostitute," and that the moment Harris discovered how the Japanese authorities had misunderstood him, he summarily dismissed the girl. Legend has not only made Okichi-san a beautiful and talented geisha, but has embroidered the story of her association with Harris with all the overtones of Kabuki drama.

The Shimoda authorities, according to the romantic version of the affair, instructed Okichi-san to serve Harris however he might wish and also to spy carefully on all his activities. Engaged to a young fisherman, she did not want to associate with the barbarian whom many of the people of Shimoda still looked down upon with considerable scorn, and was only persuaded to do so as a patriotic duty in whose performance she should be happy to sacrifice her fiancé and her reputation. On this basis she finally agreed to undertake the prescribed mission.

The diplomat and the geisha, so runs the story, thereupon and most properly fell in love, and for a time Okichi-san was "borne nightly to the Buddhist Gyokusen-ji Temple . . . in a palanquin." However, Harris eventually tired of his inamorata and with suitable gifts sent her away. Okichi-san then became deeply despondent. She took to drink, always using a sake cup given her by Harris, lost interest in everything, and finally (quoting one of the Japanese myth-makers) "plunged into a deep pool of the rivulet called Inubazawa, a mile from Shimoda, thus ending a life full of sorrow, sufferings and tribulation."

Harris makes no mention whatsoever of any one named Okichi-san in his journal (nor does Heusken), but the town records of Shimoda authenticate the existence of such a person and tell of her visiting Gyokusen-ji. But was she washerwoman, prostitute or an evanescent Madame Butterfly? In seeking to discredit the legend, a recent Japanese biographer of Harris, in the pro-American mood of the postwar years, does everything he can to erase what he emphatically declares to be an unjustified blot "upon the otherwise stainless escutcheon of the American diplomat." The authorities at Shimoda, however, still point to their century-old records as showing that there was some sort of romantic link between the lonely envoy and the young woman who was ordered to put herself at his disposal.

The supposed romance of Townsend Harris and Okichi-san, in

any event, has been the popular theme of so many plays, operas, moving pictures, radio and television skits that it has become a part of Japanese folklore. The trim little girl guides on the sight-seeing busses of Shimoda continue to point out the temple of Gyokusen-ji as the trysting place of diplomat and geisha a century and more ago.[4]

It was in late November, 1857, after his fourteen long months of isolation (with or without the solace of romance), that, having finally wrung permission from the reluctant Japanese, Harris was able to start on his journey to Yedo for a personal audience with the Shogun. He had in the meantime concluded a new convention that served to spell out some of the provisions of the Treaty of Kanagawa relating to such thorny problems as the residence of Americans in the treaty ports, the regulation of currency exchange and the rights and privileges of consular officials. But the grant of an official audience was a more signal victory. At the opening of the seventeenth century, the Shogun had received at his court the English merchant-trader Captain John Saris and on a few later occasions the head of the Dutch factory at Deshima. Still, there was no precedent for a formal meeting with the diplomatic envoy of a Western country. Harris was again dramatically pioneering in the breakdown of Japanese seclusion.

He started on what was then the long journey from Shimoda to Yedo—nearly two hundred miles as he traveled—with his company of attendant samurai, guards and porters making a very brave show. Three lads bearing bamboo wands and giving warning of the American envoy's approach by alternately crying out "Sit down, sit down," were at the head of the ambassadorial cortege. Then came a high military officer, with his attendants, and an official standard-bearer, carrying an American flag made of Japanese crepe, who was flanked by two guards in silk dresses with the arms of the United States embroidered over either breast. Townsend Harris on horseback was next in order, with his own two-sworded guards and followed by his norimon, or palanquin, with additional standard-bearers, shoe-bearers and fan-bearers. Heus-

---

[4] The legend was also the basis for an American movie, *The Barbarian and the Geisha,* directed by John Huston and produced without conspicuous success ("Beautiful but a bore," commented *Newsweek*) in 1958.

ken with his special guards and attendants followed his chief, and
in his train was a long line of porters carrying bedding, chairs,
food, trunks and packages containing the official presents for the
Shogun. Finally, the Japanese officials assigned to the mission,
including the Vice Governor of Shimoda, brought up the rear with
their special retinues. The entire party numbered some 350 persons.

Their way led northward through the pine-clad mountains of
the Izu Peninsula, and on the second day, bright and beautiful,
with the camellias in full bloom, Harris for the first time saw
Fujiyama, whose "perfect and glorious cone . . . glittered like
frosted silver." As recorded in his journal, Heusken was even
more rhapsodic in his enthusiasm over the lovely distant view.
"Ah! Why don't I have about twenty of the friends of my younger
days about me!" he wrote. "The surrounding hills would soon
repeat the echo of a thrice repeated hip, hip, hurrah in honor of
the sublime Fujiyama."

Coming the next day to the town of Mishima, the cortege
reached the famous Tokaido—the great trunk road linking Kyoto
and Yedo. After climbing to the mountain pass at Hakone, it descended gradually to the plain stretching out to the Shogun's capital and then traversed a lush countryside with many villages and
towns.

Along the Tokaido, a road some forty feet wide, bordered with
great cypress, pine and fir trees, there was usually a busy and
picturesque traffic: the daimio going to and from Yedo for their
six months' residence accompanied by great trains of attendant
samurai; numerous court officials and imperial messengers in their
swaying palanquins, borne by six to eight bare-legged coolies;
gowned Shinto priests and shaven-headed Buddhist nuns; companies of white-clad pilgrims; *kago* bearers, long lines of pack
horses and swarms of nondescript beggars. The color and life of
the highway, so faithfully depicted by Hiroshige in his "Fifty-three
Stages of the Tokaido," were traditional, but to Harris' amazement as he journeyed along it, it was deserted. "I have not as yet
seen a dozen travelers on the road," he wrote on November 27,
"nor met any of the great trains that attend the princes when they
travel."

Only later did he learn that the Japanese authorities had given strict instructions that the road should be cleared of all traffic, and even carefully swept, before the American envoy passed along it. However, there were crowds of people in holiday attire in the towns and villages, and as he went by they knelt on mats in the front of their houses and cast down or averted their eyes. Only those of a certain rank were allowed to salute him in any way and this they did, as Harris reported, by " 'knocking head' or bringing the forehead actually to the ground."

Harris spent his nights during the journey at the *honjin*, or rest houses, which were maintained at intervals along the Tokaido for the daimio and other persons of high rank. He generally found them very pleasant and comfortable, with their scrupulously clean rooms, unencumbered by any furniture, and he also enjoyed the little attached gardens with dwarfed trees, miniature lakes and diminutive mountains. The *honjin* at Hakone was "a perfect bijou of a rest house." Every evening on his arrival he was served the customary Japanese refreshments of tea and cakes, and noted one time that he was also offered live fish. He had, however, brought his own provisions with him and his own cook. This servant's instructions and training in preparing Western dishes, Harris wrote, "left his cookery . . . inferior to Delmonico's but much more to my taste than Japanese cuisine."

One night the cortege was held up and did not reach its overnight destination at Odawara until well after dark. Harris was far from sorry for the delay. They were lighted along the road with an immense number of flambeaux, he wrote his journal, and as the long train wound and turned in its descent down a steep mountainside, it made "a figure like the tail of an imaginary dragon."

On the eighth day, having rested on Sunday and held divine service according to his invariable custom, the American envoy approached Yedo with his retinue now stretching out in a line nearly half a mile long. The crowds were immense, packing the streets five deep on either side for the seven miles between the suburb of Shinagawa and the center of Yedo. Harris estimated the total at nearly 200,000 persons. Throughout this final stage of the journey guards in varicolored costumes and holding white staves stood in front of the spectators. They appeared wholly unnecessary; perfect order and complete quiet prevailed all along the line of march. "Among those thousands of faces, of men, women, boys and young girls," Heusken noted, "not one showed signs of antipathy, anger, or even indifference."

The American envoy, preceded by his country's flag, was now being carried in his norimon with a guard of ten samurai and followed by his umbrella-bearer, shoe-bearer and a stable boy leading his horse. After passing over the several bridges that linked the different quarters of Yedo, he was taken directly to the house set aside for him within the castle circle whose center was the residence of the Shogun.

To his astonishment Harris found this house furnished with a bedstead, some chairs and a table. Inouye Shinano-no-Kami, his old friend who had come ahead to welcome him to Yedo, "even pointed out a water-closet copied from mine at Shimoda." Everything possible had been done to make him comfortable and also to assure his protection. Shinano-no-Kami told him that the inner gates of the city had been closed to restrict the crowds, for otherwise the people would have rushed to Yedo "by millions (those are his numbers) to see me." Appointed to wait upon him as "Commissioners of the Voyage of the American Ambassador to Yedo" were eight distinguished princes of the realm, including two of the high officials who had attended the treaty negotiations with Commodore Perry.

The first move Harris made was officially to inform Hotta Bitchu-no-Kami Masayoshi, a liberal-minded councilor who had been appointed Minister for Foreign Affairs, of his arrival bearing a letter from President Pierce and credentials for the negotiation of a commercial treaty. This important Japanese, a man of about thirty-five with "a pleasant and intelligent countenance," was one of the few Bakufu officials who had come fully to accept the need for modifying if not wholly abandoning Japan's traditional policies. Harris was to conduct his preliminary negotiations with him, and while the American envoy was to be repeatedly put off with the evasions that were the accompaniment of all dealings with Japanese officialdom, he always found Lord Hotta polite and courteous.

Once the American envoy had formally announced his arrival, he found himself involved in a series of receptions and meetings while awaiting his formal audience with the Shogun. Everything about his stay in Yedo had been most carefully arranged in advance. Shinano-no-Kami, who acted as his host ("I do not know but keeper would be a more correct term," Harris wrote), complained that he lost considerable weight because of the anxious days and sleepless nights he had gone through in making certain that everything would go as it should.

Twenty years later Dr. David Murray, an American adviser in the Ministry of Education, obtained a copy of the minute and detailed instructions that had provided for every phase of Harris' stay in the capital: guarding the American envoy's lodgings and the routes he would follow whenever he went out, restricting sightseers and removing all beggars, establishing the order of precedence for every formal occasion, stipulating the costumes to be worn by the officials and setting up menus for all the banquets. One such menu included oysters, chestnuts, rice soup, mushrooms, turnips, eggplant, *bêche-de-mer*, rice, lobsters, omelet, lotus bulbs, horse-radish, bean sauce, mashed eggs, small tai, stuffed goose, clams, tea powder candy, bamboo sprouts, sugar, hot and cold sake. . . . These dishes were to be served in lacquered cups and porcelain dishes (painted red inside), and even the number of chopsticks and toothpicks was carefully prescribed.

On one occasion, when he was to receive a special ambassador bearing a present from the Shogun, Harris had to go through a careful rehearsal to be sure that everything was done according to protocol, standing at the door to his house with various officials on the appropriate lower steps while the courtyard was crowded with a multitude of kneeling samurai. "After the fatigues of this horrible reception," Heusken wrote of the ceremony itself, "Mr. Harris hastily opened the box which contained the gift from His Majesty. The box, my dears, contained a great quantity of bonbons. There was enough to fill the shop of a confectioner and make ill an infinite number of children."

Harris stood very carefully upon his rights in making certain that none of these regulations, especially the provisions for guarding him when he went abroad, restricted the freedom of action to which he was entitled as the American consul general. At the same time, he repeatedly demonstrated his willingness to adapt himself so far as possible to native customs and manners (including the use of chopsticks and the Japanese cuisine he so little enjoyed), and he made no demands upon his hosts that violated their traditions. Once again, as during the long, weary months at Shimoda, he demonstrated the patience and the friendliness that enabled him to win and maintain the confidence of his Japanese hosts.

The great day of the audience with the Shogun was December 7—just eighty-four years before Pearl Harbor. With an escort comparable to that which had accompanied him on the journey to Yedo, except for his luggage-bearers and personal servants, Harris proceeded in his norimon across the moats surrounding the Shogun's castle and through several quadrangles of buildings to the Audience Hall. He was dressed for the occasion in a very special costume: a gold-embroidered coat, blue pantaloons with a broad gold band, and a cocked hat with gold tassels. He carried a pearl-handled dress sword, and just before entering the Audience Hall ("The Japanese did not even ask me to go in my stocking feet"), he put on a brand-new pair of shoes! Taken in the first instance to a small room, with a screen of gilt paper, two chairs and a brazier with burning coals, he was served what he called "tea gruel" (undoubtedly the ceremonial green tea), and then moved to a larger room where he was joined by Inouye Shinano-no-Kami and Hotta Bitchu-no-Kami.

But let Townsend Harris himself take up the story:

At length, on a signal being made, the Prince of Shinano began to crawl along on his hands and knees; and when I half turned to the right and entered the audience chamber, a chamberlain called out in a loud voice, "Embassador Merrican!" I halted about six feet from the door and bowed, then proceeded nearly to the middle of the room, where I again halted and bowed; again proceeding, I stopped about ten feet from the end of the room exactly opposite the Prince of Bittsu on my right hand, where he and five other members of the Great Council were prostrate on their faces.

The Shogun—or, as Harris was to call him, the Tycoon—sat on a platform that stood some two feet off the ground. He was dressed rather simply in a silken gown with some gold woven into it ("I can say that my dress," Harris noted, "was far more costly than his") and wore a black lacquered cap on his head. Harris addressed him briefly, expressing the hope that his mission would unite Japan and the United States "more closely in the ties of enduring friendship."

The journal continues:

After a short silence the Tycoon began to jerk his head backward over his left shoulder, at the same time stamping with his right foot. This was repeated three or four times. After this, he spoke audibly and in a pleasant and firm voice, what was interpreted as follows:—

"Pleased with the letter sent with the Ambassador from a far distant country, and likewise pleased with his discourse. Intercourse shall be continued forever."

With some ceremony the American envoy then delivered the official letter from the President, and with a courteous bow the Shogun indicated that the audience was at an end.

I bowed, retreated backward, halted, bowed, again retreated, again halted, and bowed again and for the last time. So ended my audience, when I was conducted to my original room and served with more tea gruel.

The precedent-shattering ceremony had come off successfully: Townsend Harris had looked "the awful Tycoon" in the face without trembling or quaking, without the hesitancy of faltering voice that his Japanese friends had expected. Shinano-no-Kami afterward told him (with what Harris considered "some admixture of 'soft sawder'") that everyone present at the audience had been greatly surprised by his calm bearing in the presence of the mighty ruler of Japan and amazed at his "greatness of soul."

The principal concern of the American envoy, once the ceremony of the audience was over, was to get started on the negotiations for a new treaty. After a series of further meetings with Lord Hotta they finally began, Shinano-no-Kami and Iwase Higo-no-Kami having been appointed special commissioners, and Harris set forth the proposals he hoped he could persuade the Japanese to accept. They included freedom to trade, the opening of additional ports and the right of residence at Yedo for an American minister. In the course of his discussion, Harris undertook to instruct the Japanese commissioners in many aspects of diplomatic and commercial relations they did not fully understand, sought to make it abundantly clear that he was not requesting special or exclusive privileges for the United States, and insisted that his sole purpose was to establish the most friendly relations between the two countries.

"I may be said to be engaged in teaching the elements of political economy to the Japanese," Harris reported in one of his dispatches. "They said they were in the dark on all these points, and were like children; therefore I must have patience with them. They added that they placed the fullest confidence in all my statements. . . . I then gave them champagne, which they appeared to understand and to like."

Finally, the American envoy pointed out that Japan faced a very real danger from the possible forcible action of the other powers in seeking to break down her wall of isolation, and argued that a treaty with the United States, which had no ulterior designs whatsoever, would establish a peaceful precedent for bringing Japan into the family of nations and should serve to make her a prosperous, powerful and happy country.

Harris had an extremely difficult task, against the background of the uncertainties of Japanese foreign policy and the strong resistance which the Bakufu still faced in making any further concessions to the foreigners. He had to call upon all his reserves of self-control in countering the exasperating shifts and turns in the attitude of the Japanese commissioners and the continued evasions by which they tried to turn aside his arguments. "It requires an incalculable amount of patience," he noted in his journal on December 17, "to prevent my throwing the matter up in despair." But he kept doggedly at it and at long last, toward the close of February, nearly three months after his arrival at Yedo, a general agreement was reached on the proposed treaty.

It was not yet signed. The Japanese insisted that on such an important matter the approval of the Emperor, as well as that of the Shogun, had to be obtained. It would take several more months, they declared, to complete the necessary negotiations at Kyoto. There were several more meetings (Heusken described that of February 20 as "one of the most alarming, boring, tiring, erratic, ignorant, and childish conferences we have had so far"), but Harris could not budge the commissioners beyond winning their assurance that no matter what happened at Kyoto, the treaty would in due time be signed. He had no alternative other than to accept this still further delay in the final accomplishment of his mission.

The strain of the long negotiations had by this time greatly taxed Harris' health, and on February 27 the entry in Heusken's journal was brief and ominous: "Mr. Harris falls ill. He vomits and complains he has an awful headache and that all the bones in his body ache, his back, his legs, his arms, etc." A week later, having decided to return to Shimoda, the ambassador left Yedo in a heavy snowstorm and, embarking on the small steamer that was to take him back, was so weak and helpless that Heusken had to carry him from his norimon. On reaching the familiar temple of Gyokusen-ji, he then broke down completely with a fever of some sort that, as he later wrote, "left a perfect blank in my memory for about twenty days." Heusken was panic-stricken. "What am I to do?" he wrote in his journal on March 11. "I am alone entirely here. My God! This is a terrible thing." Learning of the emergency, the Shogun sent two Dutch-trained physicians from his court to Shimoda. "The doctors received peremptory orders to cure me," Harris later told a friend, "and that if I died, they would themselves be in peril."

He did not die; his health gradually improved. However, before he had fully recovered, the arrival of the *Powhatan* at Shimoda, with news of a new treaty which England and France had forced upon China, convinced him that he should return promptly to Yedo to safeguard his own treaty with Japan. When he arrived once again at the Shogun's capital his Japanese friends were shocked to see him still drawn and haggard, with his hair and whiskers turned completely white, but Harris was not going to let anything interfere with the completion of his negotiations.

The Bakufu was now finding itself in an even more difficult position than when it had first been confronted with the demands of Commodore Perry. The sharp differences of policy among the political factions at Yedo were exacerbated by a new quarrel over the succession to the Shogunate, and the breach between the Bakufu and the imperial party at Kyoto was also steadily widening. The great majority of the daimio still strongly opposed the treaty, especially any provision whatsoever for the residence and travel of foreigners within Japan, and were inflaming anti-Western sentiment. Only the realization of its own weakness, its complete lack of the military or financial resources to offer any resistance to the foreigners, was driving the Bakufu along the unpopular course it had adopted. Knowing he was combating tremendous odds, Lord Hotta had taken the unusual course (while Harris was in Shimoda) of going himself to Kyoto in an effort to persuade the Emperor that the treaty had to be approved.

Although Harris only vaguely understood the nature of the political crisis he had precipitated, he very well realized that things were going badly. "The matters at Miako [Kyoto] are more difficult than words can express," he noted in his journal on May 15, 1858. "A conspiracy exists . . . to murder Hotta, Bittsu-no-Kami; and placards threatening death have been posted on the walls." It soon became apparent that the Emperor was not going to give his consent to the treaty without the approval of the daimio, and as they remained stubbornly opposed to it (one of them intemperately advising that Harris should be decapitated), Hotta returned empty-handed from his journey to Kyoto.

Harris refused to give up. He insistently urged that the Bakufu sign the treaty, even without imperial approval, in order to provide a peaceful precedent for establishing commercial relations between Japan and the Western world. He made no threats; he had no naval forces at his command. He did argue strongly, however, that other powers might not be as forbearing as the United States, and he was able to drive this lesson home by reporting on the military intervention of the Anglo-French forces in China. This argument finally proved to be persuasive. By another turn of the political wheel there had come into power among the Grand Councilors at Yedo a statesman even more realistically convinced than Lord Hotta of the necessity of treaty relations with the West in order to avoid the possibility of a disastrous war. This was Ii Kamon-no-Kami Naosuke, and upon being appointed *tairo*, or regent, he was persuaded to make the fateful decision that the negotiations should be consummated no matter what the Emperor's attitude might be. Harris finally had the satisfaction of seeing his immense labors crowned with success when on July 29, 1858 the treaty was formally signed aboard the *Powhatan* in the Bay of Yedo.

The treaty provided for freedom of trade, for the opening of new ports including those that were to become Yokohama and Kobe, and for recognition of the right of Americans to reside in such ports as well as at Yedo. It also included, on Secretary Marcy's instructions—though Harris was to view these clauses as temporary and subject to revision—an agreed-upon schedule of Japanese tariff rates and extraterritorial rights for American citizens. Finally, there was formally incorporated in the new accord an undertaking that the President of the United States would act as a friendly mediator in the event that Japan called upon his services in a dispute with any European power.

The other nations—England, France, Russia, Holland—were almost immediately to conclude very similar treaties, but once again it was the United States that had pointed the way and its treaty was to be the basis of Japan's foreign relations for the next half century. By negotiating without any threat of military action, and so clearly seeking to safeguard Japan's interests as well as promote those of his own country, Harris had continued to retain the goodwill of the Japanese. He was also to be acclaimed by the envoys of the European powers. Even though he was later to have serious difficulties with the British, their minister, Sir Rutherford Alcock, characterized him at this time as "thorough-going and clearheaded" and praised highly his "strategic skill." Some among the foreigners declared that he had unjustifiedly played upon Japanese fears of an Anglo-French attack, but it was nevertheless a later British consul at Nagasaki, Joseph H. Longford, who in *The Story of Old Japan* paid Harris the most glowing of all tributes:

The story of how, unbacked by any display of force under his country's flag, he succeeded by his own personal efforts in overcoming the traditional hatred of centuries to even the smallest association with foreigners, is one of marvelous tact and patience, of steady determination and courage, of straightforward uprightness in every respect that is not exceeded by any in the entire history of the international relations of the world.

Upon ratification of the treaty, President Buchanan appointed Harris the American minister to Japan and he took up his residence at Yedo. Once again his lodgings were in a Buddhist temple, Zempuku-ji, which still stands in the Azabu district of modern Tokyo, near the busy, crowded shopping center of the Juban. It is today rather neglected and somewhat forlorn, but a granite shaft in the courtyard states that "On this spot Townsend Harris opened the first American legation in Japan, July 7, 1859." Here he stayed for nearly three more years, continuing to uphold with effective firmness but also unfailing tact and courtesy the interests of his country.

Antiforeign sentiment was to flare up dangerously during this period for the Japanese felt frustrated and betrayed by the concessions that the Bakufu had felt it necessary to make to Western demands. The two-sworded samurai, with their patriotic traditions, and especially the *ronin*, masterless samurai who had no allegiance to any daimio, were not only violently opposed to the new departures in foreign policy but implacably hostile to the foreigners themselves. Quick to take offense and all too ready with their swords, they were to stage a number of attacks on foreigners and foreign property. A wave of assassinations came to a tragic climax for the Americans when on January 15, 1861, a band of *ronin* struck down and killed Henry Heusken. He was returning late at night from the Prussian legation, accompanied by three mounted samurai and footmen bearing lanterns, when the assassins attacked. Putting his horse to a gallop he called out that he had been wounded, and then fell dying to the ground. The Japanese officials, as Harris reported to Washington, at once expressed their "horror at the tragic event and condoled with me on my great loss."

Even in the face of this shocking evidence of the mounting antiforeignism in Yedo, Harris remained staunchly faithful to his basic principles—friendship with the Japanese and confidence in their goodwill. He recognized, as the other foreign envoys were unwilling to do, the immense difficulties which the Bakufu officials faced in trying to handle an almost impossible situation. A month before the attack on Heusken he had written a friend warning him not to believe "any of the 'raw head and bloody bones' stories of our living here in constant dread of assassination," and in spite of the murder of one of his own official staff (Heusken had become secretary of the legation), he still refused to take alarm, stoutly reaffirming his confidence "in the good faith of the Japanese Government, and of their earnest desire to protect me."

When the other ministers withdrew from Yedo after Heusken's assassination on the ground that the Japanese officials were either unable or unwilling to safeguard foreign lives and property, the American minister, standing alone, refused to leave. His attitude incensed his British colleague, for it broke down an otherwise united Western front, but with "admirable indifference and courage" Harris continued to reside in the Shogun's capital.

The position he took on this occasion, and the many other instances in which he showed his sympathetic attitude toward the Japanese, undoubtedly had a far-reaching influence. Indeed, a Japanese historian of this period, whose writings have been translated by Akimoto Shunkichi, paid Harris the greatest possible tribute. He declared that the gradual stamping out from the minds of the people of their bellicose enmity toward Westerners had been chiefly brought about "by the patient efforts of this able American diplomat."

The burdens Harris was carrying were nevertheless once again physically wearing him down, and he grew increasingly anxious to be relieved of his ministerial post and get back to America. "I am very homesick and want to return," he had written as early as the close of 1859. He was soon to emphasize even more strongly that his many years of difficult, isolated living, deprived of the comforts of Western civilization, had greatly impaired his health.[5]

When President Lincoln came into office Harris formally submitted his resignation, but to his disappointment it was still another full year before Secretary of State Seward was willing to honor it. He finally left for home in May, 1862, having been in Asia, except for the one very brief trip to Washington when he received his consular commission, for nearly fourteen years, six of which had been spent in Japan.

On finally accepting his resignation, Seward generously acknowledged the distinguished ability with which Harris had conducted his negotiations, but on his return to the United States this first American minister to Japan suffered the unhappy neglect

---

[5] Rumors were current in the United States about this time that he had died.

against which *Frank Leslie's Illustrated Newspaper* so vigorously complained. The Civil War engaged both governmental and popular attention too deeply to make his services, or indeed anything about Japan, seem very important. Harris lived quietly in a New York boardinghouse, spending much of his time at the Union Club where he was known as "the old Tycoon," until he died almost forgotten in 1878.

7

"Hither from Niphon"

Two YEARS AFTER signature of the pact negotiated by Townsend Harris, the Shogunate took an equally unprecedented step. It sent an embassy to the United States for an exchange of treaty ratifications, and for some seven weeks this novel mission, made up of some seventy-seven Japanese—the major envoys, their samurai attendants, secretaries, physicians, clerks and servants—toured America amid great popular excitement. Immense crowds greeted the envoys' every appearance in the four major cities they visited, and when they finally reached New York, that city's *Illustrated News* enthusiastically declared that they had provided "the greatest spectacle we have ever beheld."

At the instigation of Harris, who had enthusiastically promoted the project ever since the Japanese themselves first suggested it, the United States Government made the steam frigate *Powhatan*, of Commodore Perry's old command, available for the embassy's transpacific voyage. Some of its members, however, crossed on the three-hundred-ton *Kanrin Maru*, a warship the Japanese had purchased from Holland and the first Japanese-owned vessel ever to make such a voyage. This in itself was an epochal event, and in the person of the little ship's captain, Katsu Rintaro, there was a further dramatic foreshadowing of the future. As Count Katsu, this pioneer Japanese seaman was to become known as the chief organizer of Japan's modern navy. It was also on this voyage of the *Kanrin Maru* that Nakahama Manjiro, the Japanese boy who "discovered America," made his second transpacific crossing as navigator and aid to Captain John Brooke, the American naval officer assigned to help a green and inexperienced Japanese crew.

The *Kanrin Maru* made a rough voyage, and as Captain Brooke reported in his journal, it was "certainly an experience for the Japanese." The crew hardly knew how to handle the steamship's auxiliary sails, understood little of the rigors of naval discipline and, including Captain Katsu, who took to his bed, were repeatedly seasick. But with the help of the handful of American seamen aboard her, the *Kanrin Maru* made San Francisco successfully after a two months' voyage, arriving on March 17, 1860, several days before the *Powhatan*, which had stopped at the Hawaiian Islands.

After a brief stay in San Francisco, the entire embassy boarded the *Powhatan* (the *Kanrin Maru* returning to Japan) and sailed for Panama. Here they took the railroad across the isthmus ("The train sped like an arrow," wrote one member of the mission in describing this novel experience. "The noise sounded like a thousand peals of thunder"), re-embarked on another American naval vessel, the frigate *Roanoke*, and after arriving at Hampton Roads on May 12, went immediately to Washington.

There were two principal ambassadors, Shimmi Buzen-no-Kami and Muragaki Awaji-no-Kami, and a high-ranking censor, Oguri Bungo-no-Kami. Together with their entire retinue they were guests of the nation. Congress appropriated $50,000 for their entertainment, and President Buchanan delegated an experienced naval officer, Captain Samuel F. DuPont ("our good Captain Du-Pont," as the envoys repeatedly characterized him), to serve as guide and comforter throughout their travels. The mission's first responsibility in Washington, the major objective of the whole undertaking, was the official exchange of treaty ratifications. The embassy then remained in the capital for some three weeks of sight-seeing and entertainment, briefly visited Baltimore, went on to Philadelphia, and then brought its tour to a close with the final celebrations in New York. On June 29 it embarked on another government vessel put at its disposal, the U.S.S. *Niagara*, and set out by way of the Cape of Good Hope on the long homeward voyage to Japan.

The scene was very much the same on each stage of the embassy's triumphal progress. The guns fired their rousing salutes, the bands played, the flags flew, and what the contemporary newspapers invariably called "the sovereigns of the nation" lined the streets to shout and cheer. At the receptions, banquets, assemblies and balls given the ambassadors in each city they visited, society crushed its guests in eager welcome. The members of the mission were importuned for autographs or pieces of paper with even a scrap of the unfamiliar Japanese writing. "Japonee, Japonee!" shouted the children, "give me a fan!" When the envoys appeared on the balcony of whatever hotel at which they were staying, quickly gathering crowds demanded souvenirs, and the Japanese sometimes threw down small iron coins for which the people below scrambled like small boys. There was a nationwide mania for things Japanese, and in every city the envoys aroused "the same wild, bewildering excitement."

The daily newspapers and such popular magazines as *Harper's Weekly* and *Frank Leslie's Illustrated Newspaper* gave great play to the embassy's visit—columns of description, full-page drawings, extravagantly embroidered human interest stories. They listed every guest at every reception and each item on the menus of the official banquets. They struggled to report accurately just how the Japanese looked and what they wore. It was easy to describe their shaved heads and topknots, and the richly mounted samurai swords, but how picture their strange and exotic costumes? The baffled reporters fell back on "spotless pajamas," "clean talmas," "skirt-trousers," "black crape ponchos," "kemmuno" and "incipient petticoats."

The reserve and dignity of the ambassadors themselves occasionally acted as a brake on journalistic enterprise, but the reporters followed the less important officials everywhere and made the most of their adventures and misadventures. One completely uninhibited Japanese, an interpreter, made more popular copy than all the other members of the mission put together. Tateishi Onojiro, who soon became known throughout the land as "Tommy," was a short, plump, seventeen-year-old boy whose zest in kissing the girls and other startlingly un-Japanese antics endeared him to the public, the ladies especially welcoming him effusively whenever he appeared as "darling fellow" and "sweet child." He was the embassy's comic relief, its popular clown. " 'Tommy' was as usual, in great request," the Baltimore *American* reported on one occasion, "and by his lively manner and facetious ways gave much amusement . . . decidedly a jolly fellow and loses no opportunity for fun." Upon the arrival of the embassy's special train in Philadelphia, the *Press* reported that "the inevitable Tommy was seen on the locomotive pulling the bell."

The newspapers were not above making fun of the country's visitors in reporting what was for Americans their strange appearance and outlandish clothes. The tone was generally good-natured but at the same time often revealed a sense of racial superiority marked by a note of rather lofty condescension. Admitting that the Japanese might be "civilized," many writers emphasized how astounded they must nevertheless be to discover the higher values of everything about the West as compared to their own culture. As time went on, however, the dignified bearing of the envoys amid all the popular hullabaloo of their welcome, and the contrast between their unfailing courtesy and the vulgar curiosity of the American crowds, brought about something of a change in the newspapers' supercilious attitude.

Some sort of combination of Red Indians and medieval knights had been expected on the embassy's arrival, wrote a contributor to *Frank Leslie's Illustrated Newspaper*, but it had become clear the Japanese were men of character and refinement to whom the New World could teach nothing in "propriety of demeanor." *Harper's Weekly*, significantly comparing the unruffled dignity of the Japanese with the rudeness of the Americans, wrote that "there are undoubtedly ladies and gentlemen in America, but what a pity that the Japanese will never know it. . . . The barbarian and savage behavior has been entirely upon our part."

There would appear to have been something almost hysterical in the popular furor stirred up by the Japanese tour. The crowds of a metropolis were in this period always eager for excitement; they turned out by the hundreds of thousands for every new or novel spectacle. But while the Japanese naturally aroused great curiosity, as the first of their race ever to visit the United States, there was perhaps something more to account for what one newspaper called "the perfect insanity" of the popular response to their visit.

The spring which found the embassy touring the United States also marked the hastening approach to that dread climax of events that in another year precipitated America's "irrepressible conflict." A few days after the Japanese arrived in Washington, the Republicans nominated Lincoln as their presidential candidate in direct challenge to the South. There was already talk of secession; the dark fears of possible civil war shadowed the land. An uneasy people may well have sought to find through their turbulent welcome of "the mystic, tawny, strangely dressed travelers" an emotional release from the harsh realities of the impending crisis.

The cheering crowds that so happily greeted the Japanese and the souvenir-hunters who scrambled for the iron coins tossed from hotel windows would have been surprised had they known how their guests reacted to all this popular furor. Outwardly the ambassadors remained calm and dignified, no matter what happened. "Not one of them by sign or word," a San Francisco paper commented in describing their arrival in America, "evinced either surprise or admiration." This reserve added to the fascination they had for the public, deepening the aura of Oriental mystery which surrounded them. What they felt, no matter how hidden at the time, nevertheless need not be wholly left to conjecture or vague surmise. The Japanese once again proved themselves to be "a nation of reporters." It would seem that almost every member of the embassy, from the Vice Ambassador to the lowest-ranking samurai attendant, kept a diary or a journal. There are also records compiled by the head of the stokers' gang aboard the *Kanrin Maru* and by one of the mission's cooks. Sailing with the returning envoys aboard the *Niagara*, an American naval officer wrote in his own journal that the Japanese were always at work on their diaries or "copying short books, words out of dictionaries and what not." Another time he noted: "The Japanese continue busy as bees at their studies."

As the entries in these diaries show, the members of the mission were generally amazed, and often amused, by all the excitement they stirred up. Their wonder and admiration for much of what they saw were also tempered by a healthy skepticism as to the ultimate value of some of the achievements of Western science and Western technology. They found from their own experience a good deal to be questioned in the social conventions and moral standards of this peculiar American civilization. ("In good sooth, I said to myself," reads one entry in the journal of Vice Ambassador Muragaki, "these foreigners did not earn their name of barbarians for nothing.") They were by no means so naïve as their general ignorance of the West might suggest, shrewdly recognizing the extent to which their unfamiliar clothes and customs simply piqued the curiosity of American crowds. They were on occasion extremely bored, finding the succession of parades, receptions, banquets and balls a weary ordeal. They looked back nostalgically to their own Japan ("I listened in vain," Muragaki wrote after one hectic day, "for the song of the cuckoo") and were extremely happy, apparently without exception, when their visit drew to an end.

The Muragaki diary is among the most interesting of those available (although he was sick a part of the time) and reflects the views of the most knowledgeable member of the embassy. On the first day of the visitors' stay in Washington, when they had been escorted by immense crowds to Willard's Hotel, he records how the high officials gathered in their room to talk things over. The crowds reminded them of those in Yedo on a festival day, according to Muragaki, but they were at a loss to understand how they could behave with such complete lack of restraint—so noisy and obstreperous. "Occasionally we could not help indulging in hearty laughter," the Vice Ambassador wrote, "so strange was almost everything that we had seen in the streets."

From the evidence of other journals as well, the Japanese were indeed more critical of the noisy and ill-mannered behavior of the crowds than of anything else. On their outings the minor officials entered into the spirit of the occasion, waving gaily at the spectators, throwing kisses, shaking hands with those who pressed about them. But nothing could have been further from their own customs. Reading the contemporary newspaper accounts of the people peering into the envoys' carriages and rudely fingering their clothes, one is reminded of the quite different reception accorded Townsend Harris when he passed through the streets of Yedo with the people in ordered lines and "not a shout or cry was heard." As for the insistent demands made upon the members of the mission for autographs and souvenirs, one diarist probably spoke for the entire delegation: "We dislike it."

The visitors were astonished by many aspects of the American scene: the seven- and eight-story buildings, with slate roofs and glass windows ("We cannot explain how beautiful they were"); the wide paved streets with their heavy traffic of carriages and omnibuses; the profusion at night of flaring gaslights (making it unnecessary to carry lanterns); and the elaborate shops and big department stores with little rope-pulled cages conveying goods from floor to floor.

It was perhaps the hotels, which they came to know so well, that struck them as most unusual. Their hundreds of rooms, requiring call bells to summon a servant rather than the quiet clap of one's hands, and such profuse furnishings (in addition to the unfamiliar beds, tables and chairs) as mirrors, clocks, fireplaces and statuary, could hardly have afforded a greater contrast to the quiet simplicity of Japanese inns. "Our eyes popped with amazement!" Yanagawa Masakiyo, one samurai diarist, wrote of his first experience with an American hotel.

The attendants and servants of the embassy found little use for the beds in these hotel rooms, generally sleeping on the floor, and the newspapers commented on how even the higher-ranking samurai were vainly struggling to adjust themselves to strange Western ways. "By degree they may become inured," said the New York *Tribune*, "to feather pillows and balmy blankets." There was some truth in such facetious remarks. Yanagawa wrote of an occasion when one of his companions could not find anything on going to bed to serve as the customary hard Japanese head rest until he finally discovered "a clean white jar under the bed." When told of the mistake made in appropriating this object as a pillow, Yanagawa reported, "We all laughed."

The bathrooms presented many novelties which the Japanese described in minute detail. The flow of water in the tin tubs, or in those baths which they spoke of as being covered with "white copper," and the provisions for flushing the unfamiliar toilets greatly intrigued them. But what seemed completely inexplicable in the light of Japanese custom was the practice whereby a person was supposed to take a bath all by himself, behind locked doors.

"Several of us bathed together," Yanagawa wrote. "The Americans were very much surprised to see this and went away. After this none of them came to this part of the hotel when the Japanese went to the bath."

Yanagawa illustrated his diary with careful sketches (always showing a very definite Japanese style no matter what he was drawing), which included many of the unusual objects found in hotels: chandeliers, tables, beds, bureaus, bathtubs, water closets. He admitted woefully, however, that there were far too many unfamiliar things in America for him to encompass them and that he lacked the skill either to describe them or to draw them with any sort of accuracy.

Although the newspaper accounts of the civic banquets often recorded that the Japanese "discussed the repast with apparent zest," their diaries suggest that American food and eating customs were a constant trial. They did come to like a few things very much, especially a delicious dessert which melted away in the mouth ("The name of this is ice cream"), and they were always highly appreciative of the wines and champagne. More generally, however, they did not like the hotel meals which were served them, usually in their own rooms.

"Our Japanese food alone is so unique and exceptional," Muragaki wrote, "that it is well beyond the power of my pen to describe what we, the Japanese, suffer in our journey in a foreign country."

There was too much meat, they disliked even the smell of milk, and they could not enjoy (no more can Japanese today) the way Americans cooked rice. They were hardly tempted by what one diarist described as "sliced bread like small pieces of wood." Yanagawa listed the dishes served on one occasion: soup, rice, baked chicken, corned beef and cabbage, boiled salmon and sponge cake, only to comment that this meal, supposed to be a banquet, was not at all savory because it was so greasy: "We did not enjoy it."

On a later "lecture tour" in Japan, the embassy's journalistic cook, Kato Somo, told his audiences of how he had examined the hotels' kitchens, tried to explain to Americans the way rice should be cooked, and watched the preparation of the strange and wonderful things that were served the envoys. He also recounted,

according to the record of his talks, the difficulties which the
Japanese experienced in trying to use knives and forks (the latter
described as silver spears which looked like little rakes), and their
trouble in learning what to do with finger bowls and "wiping
cloths." In pursuing their usual custom, which Commodore Perry's officers had so amusedly observed, of taking away whatever
might be left over from their meals, the Japanese were at a good
deal of a loss as to how to manage this politely. Kato reported,
however, that some of the members of the mission managed to
retrieve a good deal, putting eggs and oranges in the wide sleeves
of their kimono and even making away with sugar carefully
wrapped in tissue.

The after-dinner toasts and long formal speeches were wholly
mystifying to the visitors. "As the successive orators finished their
speeches," reads another of Muragaki's journal entries, "the noise
of clapping and the pistol-like reports made by the opening of
champagne bottles, simply deafened us, accustomed as we are to
the quiet manners observed at our banquets." It was the practice
of the first Ambassador, Shimmi Buzen-no-Kami, to answer these
speeches with what the New York *Tribune* characterized as "the
familiar and sententious reply: 'Thank you.' "

Among all the odd customs and strange mores of the American
people, the Japanese were most intrigued (to judge from their
reports on such matters) by the relationship between the sexes.
They were apparently attracted by American women. "How they
do ogle them!" a reporter for the New York *Illustrated News*
wrote on one occasion, and several of the diarists themselves
commented on "the beautiful young ladies." But the attendance of
women at receptions and banquets, and the precedence accorded
them, could not be reconciled with Japanese social usage. "It
seemed to us a most curious custom," Muragaki wrote after a
reception at the White House, "to permit the presence of ladies on
such a ceremonious occasion." And another samurai, Fukushima
Yoshikoto, noted wonderingly: "In this country, women are more
precious than men. For example, whenever there are not enough
chairs, men stand up and women take the seats. When a wife
wants a drink of water, she tells her husband to bring her a glass."

Kato Somo spoke of the good relationship that appeared to
prevail among married couples, saying that he had seen them

walking hand in hand on the street and even kissing in public. But he also noted in discussing family life that he had never observed a young person taking care of his old parents.

Women's clothes, not surprisingly, seemed very strange and in some aspects rather shocking. The huge immensity of the period's swirling hoop skirts contrasted sharply with the simple lines of the kimono, while low-cut evening gowns, displaying the wearers' necks and shoulders, deeply offended the Japanese sense of proper female modesty. One visitor admittedly found the women so arrayed very attractive, but with a curious reflection of how Americans oftened viewed Japanese women, he added that they nonetheless looked like so many wax dolls. Another reported after a reception that the ladies were indeed beautifully dressed but, influenced perhaps by the traditional Japanese image of Western barbarians, said that he found "their reddish hair uninteresting."

The Japanese were fascinated by American dancing. On first observing it at Willard's Hotel, Yanagawa Masakiyo wrote that "it looked to us just like exercise and did not seem a bit interesting." But he was young and adaptable. Within a month he was telling of a party in New York at which "we drank wine and danced with the Americans through the night until break of day." Such enthusiastic participation was hardly the practice of the ambassadors themselves; the more sober and sedate Muragaki always watched the dancing from the sidelines. On one occasion he wrote of "this extraordinary sight of men and bare-shouldered women hopping about the floor, arm in arm"; on another he said that the couples on the dance floor "went round and round as nimbly as so many white mice, on their monotonous walk, without making fluttering gestures with their hands even."

The members of the embassy did not discuss nearly so fully the country's political institutions or its burgeoning industry. It was probably all too baffling, and the almost insuperable barriers of language made it highly difficult for them to understand how the government actually operated or how the national economy was organized. Taken to a session of Congress, Muragaki made one acidulous comment that perhaps shows more perception than this suggests: "The scene, we whispered among ourselves, resembled somewhat that of our fish market at Nihonbashi." And on another occasion Yanagawa made a pithy observation on the national elections. "When the President of this country is to be elected," he wrote, "four or five of the leading men of the government choose a candidate who then stands for election in the presidential campaign. Anyone of good character except a negro may be elected president." There is no suggestion, however, that the Japanese appreciated the significance of the political campaign getting under way while they were in the United States.

All the diarists made broad generalizations about Americans. Vice Ambassador Muragaki spoke of them as a "wealthy, ingenious and industrious people" and also said they were "big-hearted and faithful." Nonomura Chujitsu, an attendant of the censor, characterized them as friendly and easygoing, "like the country folks in our country who have never seen the cities." Yanagawa Masakiyo had very much the same general impression, using the phrase "big-hearted, honest and faithful," and added (much as George Cleveland had said of the Japanese sixty years earlier) that "even on the streets we did not see any people quarreling." Fukushima Yoshikoto was greatly impressed by the general well-being and social equality that apparently prevailed among all classes. In further describing Americans he stated that "although we are unable to ascertain their real feelings, from the surface they look honest."

A number of journal entries refer to Negroes. Yanagawa was perhaps most explicit in trying to analyze their place in society, writing that because of "the gap between the white man and the negro," the latter had been made slaves and were not allowed to go into the hotels, auditoriums, teahouses or theaters of the whites. Although they were a very simple folk, he thought Negroes had "a bad disposition." The vagaries of race prejudice a century ago were further revealed in a curious incident that Yanagawa reported as occurring in the course of the embassy's procession to its Washington hotel: "A negro put his hand into the carriage, but none of us shook hands with him."

Several of the Japanese commented on Sabbath-keeping and the services at churches. "Today was called Sunday (*Dontaku*) and even merchants and workers take a day off," wrote one official. Another described the faithful observance of the Sabbath and what he felt to be the the sincerity of religious worship. The head of the stokers' gang, after attending a church service in San Francisco, wrote movingly of his experience. "In Japan," he confided to his journal, "we consider this sect to be an evil religion, but I find many proofs that it is not what we have thought."

The most unfavorable comments on life in the United States remained centered on what from the Japanese point of view were the Americans' lamentable want of manners. The contrast in social behavior inherent in the cultural patterns of America and Japan has always been very striking. It was probably even more pronounced at this time than ever before or since. Japan was still rigidly encased within the framework of the hierarchical ranking and ceremonial formality that distinguished her feudalistic society; America was in the midst of an egalitarian revolution, with the consequent eclipse of polite manners, that was a result of the rise of Jacksonian democracy. The gap could not be bridged.

Muragaki noted another aspect of the current scene that also deeply impressed European visitors in this same era. Americans were not only crude and impolite; they had a very superior opinion of themselves and of everything about their country. "The men usually essayed to impress us with a boastful account of themselves," Muragaki commented, echoing the opinion of other foreigners from Frances Trollope to Charles Dickens. And then he added: "This was indeed a custom unfamiliar in our country."

For all such criticism, Fukushima Yoshikoto probably expressed a general opinion among the embassy members when he concluded that they had discovered that many of the ideas they had had about Americans before coming to the United States were founded on ignorance and prejudice. "Almost all of us, seventy-seven members of the mission, have in the past hated Westerners," he wrote, "but now that we have come to understand their attitudes, we have changed our mind." For the Japanese to continue "to despise foreigners at all times as if they were dogs and horses," he continued, "would be discourteous and a great mistake."

The three weeks the mission spent in Washington were crowded with official ceremonies, formal calls on both President Buchanan and Secretary of State Cass, and by visits to almost every place of interest in the capital. The Japanese had been welcomed with elaborate ceremony. They were accompanied by mounted troops and military bands on their first progress to Willard's Hotel, and the crowds gathered to see them were immense, "The streets were like seas of human beings," wrote the second Ambassador. "I could not help smiling at the wonder in their eyes." Washington was full of sight-seers. They continued to mill about the hotel waiting for a further glimpse of the nation's guests, and the Japanese felt that they were under a continued siege of the curious.

The exchange of ratifications was carried through with a formal dignity that surprised the newspaper reporters. It had not turned out to be an absurd or amusing affair as so many people had anticipated, wrote a correspondent for *Frank Leslie's Illustrated Newspaper*; it was of "a solemn and serious character." The envoys themselves were immensely pleased when the real purpose of their mission was successfully accomplished. They saw no need for them to do anything else. Nevertheless they went graciously through their other public engagements and dutifully made official visits to the Smithsonian Institution (where they rather reluctantly submitted to being photographed), to the Patent Office, to the National Observatory, and to what appeared to interest them most, the Navy Yard.

A special feature of the Washington visit was the banquet President Buchanan tendered his distinguished guests at the White House. The newspapers gave it top billing and reported fulsomely on every detail: the company assembled to meet the Japanese envoys, the impressive formality of the occasion and the magnificence of the dinner itself. The impressions of the Japanese, however, were somewhat at variance with those of the newspaper correspondents.

They were not particularly impressed by the White House; it reminded one of them of the main hall of a deserted Buddhist temple. And Yanagawa reported wonderingly: "There is no policeman in the President's house and no fortress in his yard." While Buchanan struck them as being "genial and dignified," they could not understand how a man so simply dressed in black clothes, unaccompanied by special guards or costumed attendants, could actually be the head of a great state. They concluded that while Americans unquestionably thought a great deal of their country, they did not think half so much of their President.

Buchanan's niece and hostess made a much greater impression;

the Japanese envoys admired her beauty and hospitable courtesy. For all his general skepticism of the role of women in American society, Muragaki felt that her uncle might well have been taken for her prime minister, while Yanagawa commented that in acting as the President's secretary "the government was carried on at her command." Escorting her into dinner, the Vice Ambassador was somewhat embarrassed by her "delicate" questions about Japanese women, but he nonetheless greatly enjoyed her company.

The strain of official functions and the constant demands upon them by an insatiable public became increasingly wearisome for the envoys. They were never left alone. "We could not understand," Muragaki wrote after one occasion when they were called upon to make an unexpected appearance, "why we had to view a crowd of thousands from the balcony, during which time, no cups of tea were served nor any cigarettes offered, and why we were even restricted from leaving the place in search of the rest-room." But they obligingly went through their paces until finally the happy day arrived when they could leave the capital. After presenting their hosts with appropriate gifts—rich silks, porcelain vases, highly ornamented samurai swords—they went by special train to Baltimore.

On reaching that city they found themselves welcomed by even larger crowds than those which had turned out to greet them in Washington. Thousands of men, women and children lined the streets, which were gaily decorated with flags of the Rising Sun, as the usual procession of carriages, each drawn by four black horses, and the customary escort of bands and military troops conveyed them from the station to their hotel. And a tiring day was then followed by an even more onerous evening.

Baltimore had recently acquired several new fire engines, and the visit of the Japanese embassy was made the occasion of their first public display. As the city's guests stood on the balcony of their hotel, they were treated to an exhibition of the new engines' marvelous proficiency, eight fire companies taking part in the affair, and then watched a lavish fireworks display with rockets and fiery illuminations. This was something with which the Japanese were quite familiar; their own exhibitions of fire fighting had a centuries-old tradition behind them. But when the enthusiastic Baltimore firemen directed their hoses somewhat indiscriminately on the sputtering fireworks and the cheering crowd, one of the mission recorded that while it was a highly interesting sight, it had proved to be "rather wet for entertainment."

The next stage of their tour took the mission to Philadelphia. Their train hurried them over what one diarist surprisingly described as "a boundless plain, almost uncultivitated," and on their arrival at Philadelphia they discovered that a holiday had been declared in their honor. Artisans left their workshops, clerks deserted their counters, one Philadelphia newspaper reported, to gather at the station square where vendors' stands, shopping booths and itinerant barrooms had been set up to accommodate the throng. When the embassy arrived—this was the occasion when "Tommy" rode in the engine and pulled the bell—the populace crowded so closely about the envoys as they left the train that they could hardly make their way to their carriages.

The Japanese spent a busy five days in Philadelphia. A number of them visited the Mint, where they watched the weighing of coins and had the decimal system explained to them. The several physicians in the party went to a medical school and there had the unique experience of watching an operation at which the famed Dr. W. T. G. Morton, pioneer in the use of ether, administered the anesthetic. The ambassadors themselves were taken through Girard College and climbing to the roof of its main building were given an opportunity to look over the city spread below them. The Philadelphia *Inquirer* was inspired to conjecture over what they might have thought:

How must these dark eyes have gone back to Yedo, compared its vast expanse of cabins and humped-roof domiciles to the spires of shipping and temples which clove the sky beneath them. . . . Isolated civilization has sent its first subjects to confer with commercial enlightenment, and the sandals of the swarthy Mongols rested upon the palladium of our progressive school-house. Around and about them pressed the citizens of a city whose seamen have broken down the walls of their seclusion, and wooed them across the ocean.

There was also an evening at the Chestnut Street Theatre, the Japanese finding the play not unlike their own Kabuki drama ("with love scenes and fighting"), but they were greatly surprised that women performed the female roles rather than men as in

Japan. One memorable afternoon some of them watched a balloon ascension and were told that equipped with steam power it could make the long passage from America to Japan in six days. After a succession of such wonders, a great torchlight parade brought their stay in Philadelphia to a close.

The embassy's final visit was New York, and in its zeal to outdo all its metropolitan rivals, this proud city was determined to turn out more bands and troops, fly more flags, give more lavish entertainments than the Japanese had yet seen. Society staged a magnificent ball in the Metropolitan Hotel and adjacent Niblo's Gardens, with five bands playing incessantly, some six to ten thousand people crowding the rooms, and an equal number of bottles of champagne (according to the *Tribune*) helping to float the party through a gay evening. Men in formal evening clothes and women in ball gowns jostled and pushed, climbed on tables and chairs, to get a glimpse of the patient Japanese envoys seated on a platform above the crowd. The newspapers reported "a scene of festivity altogether unparalleled in the history of New York" and an occasion "whose memory will long shine like a rose-pink lantern."

Vice Ambassador Muragaki also made note of the ball in his diary: "We regret to say . . . that this sort of entertainment was very boring, and far from our taste."

The Japanese went sight-seeing and shopping—the Custom House and Barnum's Museum, Trinity Church, Brady's Gallery where they again sat for photographs, Stewart's Department Store, and Lord and Taylor's. They went to the theater, to minstrel shows and to the circus; they inspected factories and rolling mills. And nowhere had they been more mercilessly exploited as the directors of theaters and museums, the managers of shops and stores, advertised their appearance as a means of publicizing their own wares. Niblo's shamelessly announced that only in its gardens could the Japanese be "seen as they are"; the Academy of Music held a "Japanese matinee," and Christy's Minstrels staged a performance called *The Japanese Treaty*. Writing in the *Tribune*, an outraged Horace Greeley declared that every possible advantage was being taken of the Japanese envoys to gratify "the inordinate vanity, the inordinate greed, the inordinate folly of those with whom they come chiefly in contact."

The high point of the New York visit, however, was the welcoming parade, which had found tremendous crowds spontaneously hailing the city's unusual visitors. It eclipsed everything in the mission's entire tour, a climax of enthusiastic excitement bringing out an estimated half a million "exuberant Manhattanese" in the broiling sun of a mid-June day.

All traffic on Broadway was diverted for this great occasion (much to the disgust of the stage drivers), and not only were the sidewalks densely packed with eager spectators long before the appointed hour, but hundreds of boys had climbed the lamp posts or found some other precarious perch along the way. From the roofs, balconies and windows of the gaily decorated buildings on either side of the street, still more onlookers waited for the parade to come into view. Finally, there was a burst of distant band music and amid tremendous and tumultuous applause—"shouting, handclapping, waving of handerchiefs"—the vanguard of the marchers swung into view.

There was first a cordon of police, then troops of the Washington Grays and seasoned veterans of the Seventh Regiment, next a long line of open barouches with the official dignitaries and the city's honored guests, and after they had passed by, more bands, more marching troops, more files of police. The air was filled with the sound of "exquisite opera airs and stirring national melodies," but the cheering, huzzaing crowds repeatedly drowned out the music of the bands.

The Japanese ambassadors themselves, "very stately and reticent," sat unmoved as their carriages drove slowly up Broadway and past Trinity Church, proceeded by a somewhat circuitous route to Union Square where there was a halt for the review of the five thousand-odd accompanying troops, and then made their way to the Metropolitan Hotel. The minor officials and attendants showed somewhat less dignity and restraint than their betters during the long, slow ride. They lolled back in their carriages, smoking cigars and on occasion "gallantly flirting their fans" in answer to the plaudits of the crowd.

In that great milling throng along Broadway one rapt observer was a large, vigorous man, with iron-gray hair, full beard and mustache. This was Walt Whitman. He had earlier this same spring brought out a third edition of his *Leaves of Grass*, but in all subsequent editions there would appear a new poem which was first titled "The Errand Bearers" and then renamed "A Broadway Pageant:"

Over the Western sea hither from Niphon come,
Courteous, the swart-cheek'd two-sworded envoys,
Leaning back in their open barouches, bare-headed, impassive,
Ride to-day through Manhattan.

As the parades, receptions, balls came to an end, the weary Japanese envoys made their preparations to depart on the long voyage homeward. They shopped for gifts and souvenirs (for they were tourists as well as ambassadors), gave further generous presents to their hospitable if sometimes wearing hosts, and said their last goodbyes. On June 20 the entire party went aboard the *Niagara* for the final stage of their round-the-world journey. The usual crowds assembled to see them off; the boats in the harbor blew their whistles; the cannon fired a parting salute. Wishing them godspeed, the *Tribune* wrote:

And so farewell to the first Ambassadors that have ever been sent from the Empire of the Fragrant Islands to the shores of Christendom. Farewell, strange and swart Mongolians, with your rich, brocaded gowns, your swords of marvelous keenness, your dignity serener than the calm of your own Pacific.

In his cabin aboard the *Niagara*, Vice Ambassador Muragaki also took up his pen: "Looking back at the hills of the American shore joyous is our heart as we set out on our homeward voyage."

The embassy's visit had been a nine days' wonder. The American people enjoyed it immensely, however tired and bored their Japanese guests, and in spite of the occasional fun-poking and exploitation, its over-all effect was to create in the public mind a new and highly favorable impression of Japan. *Frank Leslie's Illustrated Newspaper* which had followed the progress of the mission, would state that it had become clearly evident that the Japanese had "a higher degree of culture and organization than prevails in any other of the Asiatic races." *Harper's Weekly* was to comment that "civilized as we boast of being, we can learn much of the Japanese." And a further assumption was indicated in the New York *Herald*'s final headline: "The Entente Cordiale of Japan and America a Fixed Fact."

Nevertheless the embassy had no more than sailed before it was almost wholly forgotten, and in the circumstances of the time it actually had little political significance. The administration of President Buchanan had far graver problems to consider in its brief, remaining days and no opportunity to follow up any leads in further cementing transpacific friendship. With the country once again totally absorbed in the mounting domestic crisis from which it had been only momentarily diverted, Japan receded far into the background. Nothing that might happen in Asia could excite any great popular interest in the light of Lincoln's election to the presidency and the secession of the Southern states.

Nor did the visit of these first Japanese to cross the Pacific on an official mission have any immediately significant consequences in their own country. The embassy had never had quite the importance that the American public attributed to it. Its dispatch did not by any means represent the adoption by Japan of a new, liberal policy toward the West. It was little more than a casual gesture. The ambassadors themselves were not men of real stature in their own country, having been given their simulated rank, as had the treaty commissioners first designated for the negotiations with Commodore Perry, only to impress the Americans.

The members of the mission, forever sketching and making notes, collected a good deal of heterogeneous information about the United States—though the New York *Tribune* suggested confused ideas rather than "precise notions"—and they purchased various interesting articles of American manufacture to take back to Japan. Something, certainly, they had gathered in the course of their tour that would help their countrymen better to understand the West. They did not, however, make any attempt to establish continuing contacts with the Americans. It was not until the days of the Iwakura mission, some twelve years later, that Japan began to enlist Americans as government advisers and importantly to encourage Japanese studies in the United States. The ambassadors sent by the Shogun carried out their specific task—the exchange of treaty ratifications—and that was all. When asked about trade and commerce, they answered haughtily, "We are not merchants." On their return to a Japan swept by a new tide of antiforeign agitation, they did not exercise any influence on policy. One further public appearance was their official attendance at the funeral in

Yedo of Townsend Harris' secretary, Henry Heusken, but they then sank back quietly into the relative obscurity from which they had been temporarily elevated.[1]

What does remain of importance, however, is that this first Japanese embassy to go abroad came to the United States rather than Europe. Even though it may have proved little at the time so far as any concrete results were concerned, it further emphasized the role that the United States was playing in seeking to lead Japan away from her traditional isolation. Its visit followed the pattern originally established by Commodore Perry and then strengthened by Townsend Harris. It made possible a first confrontation of Americans and Japanese within the United States. At least new ground had been broken, on either side of the Pacific, for the further development of friendly relations between the two peoples.

The way was not yet clear. The early 1860's were a time of turmoil and turbulence in both America and Japan. Each of the two nations was to experience civil war before circumstances permitted the evolution of the close accord of the Meiji era.

[1] Shimmi Buzen-no-Kami became for a time a privy councilor for the Shogunate but retired in 1866 from ill-health; Muragaki Awaji-no-Kami was sent on a minor mission to Hokkaido, and Oguri Bungo-no-Kami, after serving for a time as a local magistrate, was discharged and beheaded because he favored war against the foreigners.

8

***

A Time of Turbulence

THE WAVE of antiforeign agitation that was sweeping over Japan even as the members of the Shogun's embassy were being so royally entertained in the United States reached something of a peak within a few months of their return. At the opening of 1861 the rumor spread that six hundred *ronin* were on their way to attack the legations at Yedo and burn the little foreign settlement that had been established at Yokohama. The attack did not materialize. Nevertheless it was on January 14 of this year that Henry Heusken was assassinated and Townsend Harris stood alone in refusing to leave the Shogun's capital. It was a time of deep anxiety, almost panic, for the Westerners in Japan. Throughout the country the popular cry was everywhere raised of *"Sonno-Joi"*— "Revere the Emperor. Expel the barbarians."

The continuing political struggle which found the great daimio seeking to restore the power of the Emperor as a means of overthrowing that of the Tokugawa Shogunate provided the background for these turbulent days. The surrender of the Bakufu in opening up trade with the West was made a point of incessant attack. A year earlier the *tairo*, Ii Naosuke, who had been responsible for signature of the Harris treaty without imperial approval, had been assassinated. On a cold, snowy morning in March, 1860, a band of *ronin* attacked his cortege as it was approaching the gate of the Shogun's castle. They quickly felled his samurai guards, who were hampered by their raincoats and had wrapped their swords in cloths as protection against the snow. Then, thrusting their weapons through the palanquin in which Lord Ii was riding, they killed him instantly. As "the beautiful carpet of snow outside the Sakurada gate . . . turned crimson," the assassins made off with their victim's head. The murder was traced to Ii Naosuke's domestic political foes, but it grew out of the fierce, patriotic ardor that had been stirred up against the party favoring a friendly policy toward the West.

Even apart from the political intrigue and maneuver that fostered this antiforeign sentiment, popular resentment of the barbarians was a wholly natural phenomenon. The abandonment of the traditional policy of seclusion on the insistence of the United States and then of the European powers had been a frustrating and humiliating experience for a proud people. Moreover, the beginnings of foreign trade had brought about further deterioration in the country's distressed economic situation by draining away gold, raising prices and creating a nationwide feeling of social insecurity.

The samurai were especially affected. They could not but realize that expanded intercourse with the West posed an inescapable challenge to the whole structure of Japan's feudal society, immediately threatening their own power and social status. Their position was already being undermined by the rise of the new merchant class; the further growth of trade and commerce could be disastrous for them. Patriotism and self-interest were closely linked in building up an antiforeign attitude further supported by intense emotional prejudice.

"To hate a foreigner," the Japanese historian and publicist Nitobe Inazo would write of the samurai in these days, "became for them an act at once of utility, loyalty, and piety. I would fain draw a veil over a few years that succeeded the opening of the country."

The samurai were a proud, haughty class of men, going their own way with disdainful belligerency, quick to take offense and always ready to avenge any real or fancied insult with the bright flash of their swords. If they hated foreigners on principle, the latter often provided added cause for their anger. All too many of them were seeking to exploit the Japanese in this first phase of foreign intercourse, playing upon their ignorance in matters of trade, taking advantage of unfair currency regulations to speculate in gold, and conducting their business in general with scant regard for Japanese interests. Even apart from the more disreputable elements in the newly opened port of Yokohama, whom one foreign diplomat did not hesitate to characterize as "the scum of the earth," there were some money-seeking merchants who had only scorn for the Japanese, and indeed for all Asiatics. As a counterpart to the truculence of the samurai, the Frenchman De Fonblanque, in his contemporary *Niphon and Pe-che-li*, strongly emphasized "the insolent arrogance and swagger, the still more insolent familiarity, or the besotted violence, of many a European resident or visitor."

That a majority of neither the Japanese nor the foreign visitors were deserving of such harshly critical descriptions is obvious. Otherwise these early contacts between Japan and the West, between samurai and Yankees, would have ended in disaster. The Japanese people as a whole maintained the dignity, the friendliness and the politeness that Americans had from the first singled out as characteristic of the race; most of the foreigners were sympathetically seeking to develop a basis for cordial relations. On either side it was a minority that made for trouble. Nevertheless it was a minority numerous enough, as Townsend Harris wrote on one occasion, "to imperil the safety of the orderly and well-disposed, and seriously endanger the amicable relations that have been established with so much difficulty and labor."

Newspaper dispatches from Japan in these days, as in the case of one sent by a correspondent of the San Francisco *Bulletin* on June 28, 1860, repeatedly reported that "the white men here are in a state of constant alarm." The Bakufu provided special guards for the legations and consulates, Westerners rarely ventured very far abroad without armed escorts known as *betto* (the Americans called them "brown betties"), and every man kept his own gun or pistol ready at hand. "For four years," one American living in Yokohama stated, "I never wrote a note without having a revolver on the table, and never went to bed without a Spencer rifle and a bayonet at my hand." Others among the little foreign colony, including Robert H. Pruyn, who succeeded Townsend Harris as

American minister in October, 1861, were not quite so fearful. They felt free to ride abroad without guards, reporting that they encountered only friendliness on the part of the nearby villagers and peasants. Nevertheless the hostility was there so far as the samurai were concerned, and the recurrent assassinations made for an often tense atmosphere.

Among the attacks on foreigners, the most sensational was one which became known as the Richardson affair. A party of four Britishers, including one woman, was riding along the Tokaido on a mid-September day in 1862 when they met the train of the daimio of Satsuma, who remained one of the most antiforeign of the outer lords, and in flagrant defiance of law and custom recklessly tried to ride through it. The daimio's outraged retainers at once drew their swords and attacked the English party. The woman succeeded in escaping, two of her companions were injured, and the third, C. L. Richardson, a visitor at the British legation, was killed. The Englishmen maintained that they had been assaulted without having given the slightest provocation, but the fact that two Americans had earlier that same day met the Satsuma train and, by filing aside, passed by without let or hindrance, suggests if it does not prove that the arrogant attitude of the Britishers (for which Richardson was notorious) invited the attack. "The English insulted me," was the daimio's own succinct explanation of the incident, "and my escort inflicted punishment upon them."

This tragic incident had its importance in the forceful measures the British adopted in demanding redress for Richardson's murder. They had already taken stringent measures after an earlier attack on the British legation by sending ashore at Yokohama, in spite of the Bakufu's "ten thousand apologies," what the Japanese called the "Scarlet Regiment." They were now determined to step up their demands on the Shogunate. Whereas Townsend Harris, always conciliatory, had asked at the time of Heusken's assassination for no more than the arrest of the perpetrators of the outrage and a payment of $10,000 for Heusken's widowed mother, the British minister, Sir Rutherford Alcock, issued a stern ultimatum in the Richardson affair demanding hugely exorbitant indemnities from both the Shogunate and Satsuma.

The Bakufu capitulated under such strong pressure, agreeing

to pay Great Britain an indemnity of 100,000 pounds. However, when a British squadron proceeded to Kagoshima in August, 1863, to enforce the further demands being made upon Satsuma, the harbor forts there opened fire. The British bombarded the port in retaliation for this attack, sinking a number of Japanese vessels and destroying a great part of the city, but in the face of the continued fire of the forts then withdrew. The still defiant Satsuma people would have kept up the struggle, but their more realistic daimio accepted the futility of further resistance. Four months later he paid the British the 25,000-pound indemnity on which they had insisted.

The lesson taught by this naked display of the superior force at the command of the Westerners was not lost upon the Japanese. The Kagoshima affair revealed as had nothing else the hopelessness of continued resistance to foreign demands, convinced the other antiforeign daimio that they must build up their own military and naval defenses (Satsuma, somewhat ironically, was soon to conclude an agreement for the purchase of British-built warships), and still further weakened the position of the Shogunate.

The United States had not been involved in the hostilities against Satsuma. It continued its far more temperate policy and consistently sought to maintain friendly relations with the Japanese authorities. But it was soon to take part in an even more significant display of Western military power.

The daimio of Choshu, as rabidly antiforeign as the daimio of Satsuma, closed the Straits of Shimonoseki this same summer of 1863 to foreign vessels in complete defiance of all treaty obligations, and among the ships which his shore batteries shelled in enforcing this policy was the American steamship *Pembroke*. The United States countered by ordering the U.S.S. *Wyoming* to take punitive action, and entering the Shimonoseki Straits it sank two Choshu ships. But further attacks were made on other foreign ships. Aroused by the inability of the Shogun to control the situation, the United States consequently agreed to cooperate with the European powers in a joint expedition against Choshu. The next year a combined fleet of some seventeen vessels attacked the daimio's forts. It was a brief but bloody encounter ("Cannon balls flew about everywhere . . . the smoke of the guns covered the surface of the sea"), and Choshu was forced to surrender. Although only one small American ship participated in this action, the United States stood with the other powers in principle and in practice. It had swung away, for the time being, from the more moderate and independent position that it had formerly maintained. In this instance it was ready to act in military concert with the allies in forcing Japan to fulfill her treaty obligations.

This policy may or may not have been justified. Among the Americans in Japan it was both upheld as necessary to protect legitimate foreign interests and vigorously condemned (especially by the missionaries) as a willful exercise of aggressive power and needless shedding of blood. However, it brought further submission to Western demands. Not only did the daimio of Choshu have to surrender, apologizing for his act of defiance, but the Shogunate was compelled to pay an indemnity of $3,000,000 for the expenses of the allied punitive expedition. The United States was subsequently to return its share of this huge indemnity, winning new favor in Japan, but this was not until some twenty years later.

During this period of almost chronic crisis, highlighted by the attacks on Kagoshima and Shimonoseki, the hard-pressed Bakufu continued to find itself inescapably caught between the insistence of its domestic foes on measures to drive out the foreigners and the demands of the foreigners for further trade concessions. At one point the imperial party in Kyoto prevailed upon the Emperor to issue an official decree calling for expulsion of all Westerners within a prescribed time limit. The Bakufu was too weak to ignore this order and not strong enough to enforce it. The harrassed officials at Yedo formally acknowledged the decree, but in informing the foreign envoys that they had been ordered to close the ports, quietly let it be known that nothing would actually be done. They could not possibly have embarked on what would have been a suicidal course. The Bakufu's ambiguously dual role once again demonstrated the impossibility of reconciling the demands of the antiforeign forces with the stark necessity of acquiescence in the West's insistence on continued intercourse.

"The Shogunate as the governing force," one of the most eminent of Japanese educators, Fukuzawa Yukichi, was later to write in recalling these days in his *Autobiography*, "had lost all its prestige. There were almost daily assassinations. The country had become a fearful place to live in." The author of the *Kinsei Shiriaku* was even more decided in his viewpoint, quoting a contemporary as stating that the empire was "on the point of becoming hell."

It was against this inextricably confused background of conflicting domestic forces and mounting antiforeign agitation ("Everything is so enveloped in mystery here!" Minister Pruyn exclaimed helplessly in one of his dispatches) that direct associations between Americans and Japanese first developed on a scale beyond the fleeting experiences growing out of naval expeditions and foreign embassies. And in spite of the threatening aspect of the samurai and the occasional outbreaks of violence, the visitors from the United States, following in the tradition of Commodore Perry and Townsend Harris, were to exercise a pervasive influence on Japan as the foremost transmitters of Western culture.

The first Americans to attempt to establish themselves in Japan, for all the risks and hazards of living in that troubled country, were the traders and missionaries. Waiting expectantly in the wings as diplomacy opened the door for their entry, they had lost little time in making their way to the new treaty ports. They were soon followed by other Americans—their numbers were never very great—among whom were advisers to the Japanese Government, technical experts of all kinds, teachers and educators, and, after the turbulence of the 1860's subsided, more casual travelers who were the forerunners of the tourists of a still later day.

The pioneer merchant vessel to seek out the trade that Commodore Perry had hoped to initiate sailed from San Francisco immediately word had been received of the conclusion of the Treaty of Kanagawa. This was the clipper *Lady Pierce*, which arrived at Shimoda with her owner, Silas E. Burrows, aboard ship in June, 1854. The villagers were hospitable enough, but since the treaty had not actually provided for any commerce, the Japanese authorities gave the *Lady Pierce* a very frosty welcome. They would not allow Burrows either to sell his cargo or purchase any Japanese goods. It had been his desire to be the first American to visit Japan under the new dispensation, and that was just about all he achieved.

Nor were the next visitors much more successful. Two prospective merchants, W. C. Reed and T. T. Dougherty, arrived in Shimoda a year later, with their families, aboard the *Caroline E. Foote*, under the command of Captain A. J. Worth. It was their intention to go to Hakodate and there establish a trading station where American whaleships might stop for supplies. The Japanese authorities were not interested in this seemingly reasonable project. They refused to allow the Americans to land at Hakodate, and while they let them dispose of their cargo at Shimoda, they would not consider their staying anywhere in Japan. "We do not want any women," it was sternly stated, "to come and reside at Shimoda." In exchanging their own goods for silks and lacquerware, Reed and Dougherty nevertheless brought to San Francisco the first cargo of Japanese products directly imported into the United States.

In spite of other visits in Japanese waters (including that of the schooner *Wilmington*, Captain Brown, of New London, on August 17, 1855), it was not until Townsend Harris concluded the treaty of 1858 and Yokohama was opened up for trade that any extended commerce became possible. The Japanese authorities then made the port ready for foreigners in accordance with the agreements reached with the United States and the European powers (Great Britain, France, Russia and Holland). They built Western-style residences for the consuls and merchants, a customs house, a number of warehouses and two "imposing and beautifully constructed landing places." The American consulate was opened on July 4, 1859, to the strains of the "Star-Spangled Banner," and soon afterward an American commercial house, Walsh, Hall and Company, established its offices. A Japanese chronicler would now report that the "foreign merchants had been daily arriving in greater numbers at Yokohama, which so increased in wealth and importance as to form a new city of itself."

American expectations of a great burst of commercial activity were not, however, at once realized. The consular reports for the year 1864-65, even though this was a period "unprecedently free from excitement and baneful rumors," showed that the United States was lagging far behind Great Britain in the Yokohama trade. The imports of American merchants amounted to no more than $690,000 out of the port's total of $6,200,000, and their exports were valued at only $1,328,000 in comparison with an aggregate of $13,000,000. Soon, however, anywhere from twenty to forty Yankee ships (most of them engaged in the China trade) were calling annually at Yokohama, and by the time the civil wars raging in both the United States and Japan came to an end, this commerce began to take on significant proportions. The American ships were bringing to Yokohama such diverse products as petroleum, leatherware and shoes, tobacco, watches and clocks; they were carrying back to the United States sulphur, camphor, tea, manufactured silks, lacquerware, porcelain and fans.

Before the close of the century, United States imports from Japan had risen to $8,700,000 and exports totaled $16,000,000. In succeeding years this trade was destined to develop on an even more important complementary basis—the exchange of raw silk and raw cotton—to the immense benefit of both countries.

Americans, even though they were outnumbered by the British, played a leading role in the development of Yokohama. Almost immediately upon the port being opened up to trade, some forty-four foreigners took up their residence there; two years later the number had grown to 250. Among them were some sixty-four Americans; and in the municipal council set up in accordance with the foreigners' extraterritorial rights, there were eleven British, five Americans and four French members out of a total of twenty-six. The first chairman of the council appears to have been an American, a Baltimorean named Ralph Shoyer, who in 1862 established a pioneer English-language newspaper, the *Japan Express*. When he died shortly afterward from apoplexy, reputedly "overcome by excitement" at a council meeting, he was succeeded by still another American, one A. O. Joy.

The foreign community soon developed an active social life, though for a time it was largely made up of men, a first report stating there were "only two English women and three or four female American missionaries." Communal activities at first centered about a church, a theater and a club, but they quickly broadened to include race meetings, shooting matches and boat regattas, as well as bowling and billiards at the Hotel Anglo-Saxon, carefully restricted to "officers and gentlemen."

The latter note indicates that others than officers and gentlemen might visit Yokohama, and it soon acquired a floating population of varied persons who catered to the needs and wants of sailors from the visiting foreign ships. There were in 1865, only a half dozen years after the port had been opened, five hotels, twenty-five grog shops and an unrecorded number of brothels in the foreign settlement. Yokohama, that is, soon exhibited the contrasting aspects of sobriety and vice, of wealth and squalor, that so generally characterized the treaty ports of all Asia.

The foreign settlement was along the bund, or embanked quay, of Yokohama's harbor. It was lined with hongs and godowns, business establishments and warehouses that were replicas of those the foreigners had established in the treaty ports of China, and soon a paved main street led past an imposing row of banks, stores, hotels and restaurants. The residential quarter was on "the Bluff" overlooking the harbor. Here were the foreign consulates, the trim bungalows of the merchants, the public gardens and the race course. It might still be necessary for the foreigners to maintain guards against the threat of attack by antiforeign samurai and on occasion to carry arms themselves, but the Japanese with whom they associated in Yokohama bore them no ill-will. Whatever might be happening elsewhere in Japan, here was a little oasis relatively free from violence and providing a showplace of Western civilization.

The most vivid picture of the port in these early days is that provided by the various collections of contemporary *ukiyo-e,* which graphically reveal, as had the drawings in *The Black Ship Scroll,* what the Japanese themselves thought of their barbarian guests. They portray the great foreign ships, three- and five-masted side-wheelers with flags and pennants flying from stem to stern; the sampans unloading the foreign goods at the wharves along the waterfront; the interior of shops with counters piled high with porcelains and cloisonné ware; horse-drawn carriages on a street crowded with Japanese merchants, country folk in large straw hats, nearly naked porters and kimono-clad women. One *ukiyo-e* depicts the Yokohama *Dontaku*—or Sunday parade—with the foreign men in white trousers, black coats and top hats, and their women in ballooning hoop skirts and gaily colored shawls. One man carries an American flag on a tall standard, another a British flag. A second print shows foreigners "making merry" at a teahouse in the gay quarter. They are for the most part seated on the floor, drinking, but several of them are engaged in a sailors'

Highland fling. Costumed geisha in formal kimono and high head-
dresses are serving them their drinks or playing on their three-
stringed samisen.

The other treaty ports also had their foreign communities. A
new settlement at Nagasaki recorded some fifteen American land
renters as early as 1860-61, and their number was to grow steadily. The opening of Hyogo, which was to become the modern
Kobe, was postponed due to the antiforeign agitation and the
port's proximity to the imperial capital at Kyoto. It was not until
1870 that it had any considerable number of Western residents. In
that year, however, they totaled nearly four hundred and Kobe
was being described as a "model settlement." Nevertheless
Yokohama constituted the most important foreign bridge-
head in Japan. It was the center for most of the American residents
and the principal base for their broadening influence, commercial,
educational and missionary.

Among such Americans were a number who made strange and
unexpected contributions to the culture of Japan. They ranged
from the dedicated horticulturist who introduced geraniums in the
gardens on the Bluff to a pioneer importer of Singer sewing machines; from the crew which delivered for the Japanese navy a first
modern warship, the American-made *Fujiyama*, to the sports en-
thusiast who initiated the Japanese craze for baseball. There were
other even more unlikely transplantations of Americana. One
name that occurs frequently in the early records of Yokohama is
that of a "Professor" Risely. He successively established an ice
plant, a circus and a dairy (importing milk cows from America)
before he finally disappeared from the local scene as the manager
of a troupe of Japanese acrobats bound for the United States.

A special niche in this chapter of American-Japanese relations
is occupied by Jonathan Goble, a former marine in Perry's squadron, who came back to Japan in 1860. The official expedition
report refers to him as "a religious man," and his experiences
ashore in Japan apparently convinced him that he had a mission
to convert the Japanese to Christianity. Some time after returning
to his home in Hamilton, New York, he succeeded in persuading
the American Baptist Free Mission Society to send him to the
foreign field. Arriving in Yokohama he took up his self-appointed
task, contemporary records describing him as "half cobbler, half

missionary," and he became a very familiar figure in the little foreign community. As he himself later wrote, it was a hard life— "deep in poverty, much in debt, mending shoes to get a little food."

None of this accounts, however, for Goble's claim to fame. His place in history is due to the fact that when in 1867 his wife fell ill, he constructed for her convenience a unique type of man-pulled vehicle adopted from the illustration of a baby carriage that had appeared on the cover of *Godey's Lady's Book*. This is almost surely the origin of the jinrikisha—or man-power-vehicle, as the Japanese may be literally translated—which was to spread so rapidly not only throughout Japan, but to the treaty ports of all Asia. It was three years after Goble's experiment that a Japanese named Akika Baisuke is recorded as having applied for a government permit to manufacture jinrikishas in response to the growing demand for them, and before the close of the century there were forty thousand in Tokyo alone. For half a century or more no vehicle could compete with what became popularly known as the ricksha in the major cities of Asia; today where it has not entirely disappeared in an age of streetcars, busses and taxis, it has been replaced by the pedicab. In Japan, only the geisha still use the novel vehicle invented by that obscure "half cobbler, half missionary" who over a century ago was one of Commodore Perry's marines.

A quite different American visitor in this same early period was the well-known geologist and explorer, Raphael Pumpelly, who came to Japan in 1862, accompanied by a fellow scientist, William P. Blake, to explore the natural resources of Hokkaido. After the restoration of the Emperor many such scientists and technological experts visited Japan, but Pumpelly had the unusual distinction of being invited by the Shogun at a time when antiforeign feeling was still widely prevalent. After arriving in Yokohama aboard the clipper ship *Carrington*, he spent something like a year in Japan before going on to further travels in China and Central Asia. He later wrote of these unusual experiences in *Across America and Asia*, a pioneer record of American travel in the Japanese interior.

Pumpelly was a picturesque figure, "a great blue-eyed giant, with a long-flowing beard," who immensely impressed the Japanese, a man who combined a tremendous zest for exploration and adventure with a natural liking for people of whatever race or kind. While he was in Japan, unlike Townsend Harris and most of his fellow countrymen, he easily adapted himself to Japanese ways. He felt no need to carry foreign provisions with him when he traveled. He wrote cheerfully of sleeping on Japanese beds (the thin *futon* laid on the floor), using chopsticks at his meals and eating raw fish. His only complaint was about the hard, wooden block (for which the Japanese member of the mission to the United States in 1860 had found such an unlikely substitute) that was given him for a pillow. He singled out, as had his predecessors, the politeness, hospitality and curiosity of the Japanese, and also like them was critical of the official spying on his activities, the mixed public bathing and "the social evil" of the teahouses. "The ruling vice of Japan," he wrote somewhat surprisingly, "is undoubtedly drunkenness."

The Shogunate had employed Pumpelly at what he describes as "a viceroy's salary" to explore Hokkaido, but upon his arrival neither the officials at Yedo nor Pumpelly himself seem to have had a very clear idea of just what he was actually supposed to do. There was even the question, as one of the first of foreign experts, where he should be placed in the official hierarchy. It was only after Townsend Harris, still awaiting his replacement from Washington, advised that he would himself receive Pumpelly just as he would receive Commodore Perry that the problem was resolved. After this the visiting scientist was treated royally, but continuing uncertainties as to his mission and the general confusion at Yedo resulted in his being kept waiting at Yokohama some two months with nothing whatever to do. He spent his days as a sight-seer, wandering the countryside about Yokohama and visiting among other places Kamakura, where the famous Daibutsu, the great bronze statue of Buddha, still attracts all American tourists.

The Bakufu finally gave him permission to proceed to Hokkaido, and Pumpelly (together with Blake) then traveled on horseback all over that northern island. The authorities at first received him with conspicuous honors, the streets of the villages being spread with white sand and the local officials kneeling obsequiously as he passed by. He saw a great deal of the country and made what would prove to be highly valuable surveys of Hokkaido's resources, including its gold, silver and copper. He investigated the lead mines the Japanese were already working, gave instructions in modern mining methods, and introduced to Japan the Western technique of blasting with powder to extract the ore.

However, Pumpelly soon ran into increasing difficulties in carrying on his work, and the latent opposition of Hokkaido's antiforeign daimio led to his being refused permission to visit the coal mines in the island's interior. He decided that he had done about all he could. Having submitted an extensive geological report to the Shogunate, he left Japan and went on to his further explorations on the Asiatic mainland.

In some ways more important than any of the other early Americans in Japan were the missionaries. A first group of six men crossed the Pacific in 1859 to embark hopefully on the immense task, so joyfully anticipated in mission circles, of converting the Japanese to Christianity. There had been such large-scale conversions in those distant seventeenth-century days when the Portuguese Jesuits had preached the gospel that these eager pioneers confidently believed that Japan would soon enter the Christian fold.

In concluding his commercial treaty Harris had very much hoped that he could be "the humble means of once more opening Japan to the blessed rule of Christianity," but he had been unable to obtain permission from the Shogunate for any missionary activity. The Japanese were prepared to abandon the old custom of *fumi-ye*, compelling Christians to trample on the cross, to allow Americans free exercise of their own religion, and pledged themselves not to do anything that might excite religious animosity. Further than that they would not go. Their old fears of Christianity's subversive influence were not easily stilled. As late as 1868 an official decree reiterated that "the evil sect . . . is strictly prohibited."

In spite of this proscription of their faith, the missionaries were nonetheless confident that the old bans would sooner or later have to be lifted. They would prepare the way. While still forbidden to teach the gospel, they would engage in educational and medical work and at least indirectly, through their personal associations, lay the groundwork for more open proselytizing.

Their early activities are well illustrated in the careers of two of that little band which first came to Japan in 1859, James Hepburn and Guido Verbeck. Throughout the 1860's the respective roles of these two men were that of the physician and the educator, and while they later preached the gospel, it was for these secular activities that they are best remembered.

A graduate of Princeton and of the Pennsylvania Medical School, Hepburn had served in the missionary field before coming to Japan. He had gone out to Singapore, and then Amoy, as a young man, but then returned to the United States, where for thirteen years he practiced medicine in New York. He was forty-four years old, a man of strict Calvinistic principles but warm, humanitarian instincts, when he accepted an appointment from the Presbyterian Board of Foreign Missions to renew his missionary activities.

Upon arriving in Yokohama, Hepburn promptly set up a dispensary and medical school, winning the confidence of the Japanese by his dedication to their care as well as by his skill as a practitioner. Soon he was treating from thirty to fifty patients a day at his dispensary and visiting as many more in their homes. In later years the Japanese statesman Count Hayashi was to recall that Hepburn never flinched from any demands made upon him and, in spite of the risks and dangers that foreigners faced, was ready at all times to go wherever he was called.

His further interest in making possible the teaching of Christianity soon led him to embark upon an ambitious undertaking: the preparation of an English-Japanese dictionary that might help to break down the almost insuperable language barrier that stood between the missionary and his prospective converts. He devised a system for the romanization of Japanese, that is, its transliteration into Latin letters, that became the basis for his dictionary and the foundation for what the Japanese call *romaji*. Significant as his work in Yokohama may have been as physician and missionary (a visitor in 1870 described him as "the ablest and best missionary here"), Hepburn made his greatest contribution to the new life of Japan through his dictionary.

The most glowing tribute to his work comes from an Englishman. Living in Yokohama during this period, John R. Black often expressed in his book *Young Japan*, published in 1880, the critical attitude of the British toward Americans born of their political differences. But he had this to say of James Hepburn:

> If America would claim credit for anything she has done in connection with Japan, let it not be for what *Perry*, or for what *Harris*, accomplished in making their respective treaties. I have shown that these were only obtained by working on the fears of the Japanese rulers; and this fact takes all the gloss off them. But let her glory—if needs must—lie in the fact, that, *Hepburn*, one of her sons, has done more than any other, towards opening the door of knowledge to the people of Japan, and facilitating the acquisition of Japanese to those who come hither from afar.

Equally important, though in a quite different way, were the services of Guido Verbeck. Born in the Netherlands in 1830 and educated as an engineer, he had emigrated to the United States at the age of twenty-three and for a time practiced his profession in Arkansas. Deciding that what he really wanted was to become a missionary, he studied at the Theological Seminary in Auburn, New York, and when in 1859 the Dutch Reformed Church in the United States decided to send a missionary to Japan, he eagerly applied for the post. His Dutch background made him a logical candidate and he was assigned to Nagasaki. After some time spent studying Japanese, he opened a school for teaching English, which was largely attended by prospective interpreters. Unable to preach Christianity openly, he used the New Testament (and also the United States Constitution) as a text in these classes, and then somewhat surreptitiously began to hold a Bible class (it started with two members) in his own home.

Verbeck was a plain, simple man, dedicated to his work, courageous, at once tactful and firm in his convictions, who sought with unwearying perseverance to inculcate Christian ideals among a people he believed were almost wholly lacking in moral principle. His early letters home reveal how shocked he was by many aspects of Japanese life and particularly by "the flowery world" —the world of teahouses, geisha and the licensed quarter. "Christian countries are not quite free from similar immoralities," Verbeck wrote, "but it is in darkness, a world of darkness and shame. Here vice stalks about at noonday. . . . But thanks be to

God that the gospel will surely restore this people to holiness."
His concern over such moral issues, however, did not so preoc-
cupy him that he neglected the secular educational activities that
marked his stay at Nagasaki.

He developed his interpreters' school so successfully that in
1863 the Bakufu, recognizing the importance of this training in
language, gave it official recognition and governmental status. His
students, now totaling some hundred, were all samurai, and contemporary photographs show these earnest young men wearing
kimono and the two swords that marked their position in society.
A number of them were later to be encouraged by Verbeck to
study in the United States and became prominent in the new government established after the restoration of the Emperor.

After nine years at Nagasaki, Verbeck accepted an official invitation to come to the new capital at Tokyo. There he headed for a
time a school that was to become associated with Tokyo University and also served the government in various advisory capacities
relating to the development of education. The Emperor acknowledged the importance of his services ("pleased with your efforts as
headmaster") and his continuing role in helping Japan to meet the
problems of a new age. Throughout these years of government
service, however, Verbeck never lost sight of his primary interest
and kept up his religious teaching. In 1879 he resigned his advisory posts at Tokyo and, after a brief trip back to the United
States, returned to Japan to devote his entire time to the missionary activities that by this time the government had agreed to
tolerate.

There were other interesting figures in the little band of missionary pioneers who during the 1860's braved both the bans
upon Christianity and the general antiforeignism of the times in
seeking to spread their faith. Like Hepburn and Verbeck, they had
first to spend several years learning Japanese and teaching English
before they could hope to reach the people at all. Even then the
strict surveillance of the officials made it extremely difficult to
combat effectively what one missionary's wife typically characterized as "heathenism with all its revolting practices." They tried to
distribute tracts and hymns ("There Is a Happy Land" and "Jesus
Loves Me" were early translated into the vernacular); they pri-

vately held Bible classes and prayer meetings in their homes. But the missionaries were running grave risks, for themselves and even more for any possible Japanese converts, in the days of official proscription of Christianity. While the authorities encouraged secular teaching, especially in English, and were ready to seek out the advice of such men as Hepburn and Verbeck, it was not until the toleration edict of 1873, fourteen years after their first arrival, that American missionaries were permitted to embark openly upon the program whose glowing promise had led them to Japan.

During the years which witnessed this slow growth in the number of Americans in Japan, assiduously seeking to develop trade or to lay the foundations for missionary work, the internal strife between the Bakufu and its domestic foes in no way abated. Whether from conviction or expediency, the daimio favoring the restoration of imperial power continued to whip up antiforeign sentiment as a means of further undermining the position of the Shogunate. They had themselves learned the lesson of Kagoshima and Shimonoseki. They knew that resistance to the West was wholly futile, and a number of them were directly dealing with the foreigners if for no other reason than to learn the sources of their military and naval strength. But this did not stop them from accusing the Shogun of having betrayed the nation by failing to carry out the Emperor's original expulsion orders. The popular feeling on which they played so successfully was reflected in the bitter sarcasm of a contemporary verse:

> You, whose ancestors in the mighty days
> Roared at the skies and swept across the earth,
> Stand now helpless to drive off wrangling foreigners—
> How empty your title, "Queller of Barbarians."

The Western powers were unrelenting in the pressure they exerted on the Shogunate to carry out Japan's treaty obligations, safeguard the foreigners in the exercise of their rights and open new ports to trade. In making their sometimes arbitrary demands, however, they failed to realize that they were weakening the authority of the one political element in the country that was at this time willing to develop more extended intercourse. Baffled and confused by the vacillating attitude of the Japanese, they were still unable to understand the conflicting undercurrents of domestic politics.

And well they might have been confused. The rivalry between the contending factions at Yedo and Kyoto, plot and counterplot on the part of the jealous daimio, intrigue centering around possible successors to the Emperor and the Shogun who both died within a month in 1866, the angry clashes between the forces of the Bakufu and those of such recalcitrant clans as Satsuma and Choshu—all this makes up an incredibly complex story whose interwoven strands can even today hardly be unraveled. That fascinating contemporary history, the *Kinsei Shiriaku*, is one long, involved tale of revolutionary cabals, treacherous assassinations and quick, bloody battles.

American policy in these circumstances often lacked direction and continuity. In the hands of such ministers as Robert H. Pruyn and then R. B. Van Valkenburgh, neither of whom had the diplomatic ability or sympathetic understanding that had so distinguished Townsend Harris, it became largely subordinate to the more aggressive, demanding leadership of the British. The United States had participated in the punitive expedition against Choshu; it supported another naval demonstration off Osaka that finally forced the Emperor to ratify the foreign treaties. Sacrificing independence of action to cooperation with the European powers, America lost for a time the special position she had attained in Japanese eyes as their country's most generous foreign friend.

It was at best a difficult situation. Absorption in the Civil War pushed affairs in Japan ever farther into a distant background, and Secretary Seward felt driven to approve a cooperative policy with Great Britain and France. His one desire was to remain on the most friendly terms with them in order to prevent their possible recognition of the Confederacy. And finally the inability of the United States during these years to maintain any sort of naval force in Japanese waters made its voice exceedingly weak in allied councils.

Such slight influence as America did exert on Japanese affairs favored the Shogunate, whose at least relatively pro-Western policies appeared to be so much more in the foreign interest than the seemingly implacable hostility of the imperial party. Even the best-

informed Europeans and Americans in Japan failed to understand
the extent to which the latter's antiforeign agitation was primarily
a club with which to belabor the hard-pressed Shogun. When
domestic strife finally came to an end with victory for the imperialists, Minister Van Valkenburgh continued to misread the situation. He informed Washington after the restoration of the
Emperor that "there is not the remotest prospect of the people
being benefited." In his later years Seward was to write that he
had used every means at his disposal to prevent the revolution in
Japan because he thought it was a wholly retrograde movement.
"I little dreamed," he wrote, "that the restored Mikado would
excel the dethroned Tycoon in emulating western civilization."

In any event, the long internal struggle within Japan was now
approaching a final crisis. The impact of the West had been an
important contributing factor in the steady erosion of the Shogunate's power, but its weakness was rooted in the more basic
changes affecting Japanese society. It had by mid-century exhausted its popular mandate. The powerful daimio who had so
long been uneasy under the rule of the Tokugawa were now able
to command overwhelming popular support for their revolutionary cause. Accepting these harsh realities, with his hold over the
people shattered and his treasury empty, the new Shogun, last of
the rulers in the long line established by Iyeyasu more than two
and a half centuries earlier, was ready to surrender to the inevitable. Publicly declaring that the breakdown in government was "the
effect of my want of virtue and I cannot sufficiently deplore it," he
agreed in the fall of 1867 to relinquish his authority to the Emperor.

The last stage of the revolution was marked by a despairing
gesture of resistance on the part of the Shogun's loyal followers
who could not accept his decision to abdicate. They held out
briefly in some areas, especially in northern Honshu and Hokkaido, and fought one pitched battle in Yedo. This brief but
bloody engagement took place on July 4, 1868, in that part of the
city where Ueno Park now attracts its swarming holiday crowds,
but it could not stay the course of history. All Japan was ready to
accept the imperial rule.

What then happened, as the Emperor reassumed his ancient
authority, was an immediate and startling *volte-face* in the attitude

of the imperial party and its daimio adherents on the whole foreign issue. Once in power and no longer needing to drum up antiforeign sentiment as a weapon in overthrowing the Shogunate, the imperialists abandoned all idea of further resistance to the West. They were prepared, as the Emperor soon announced, to continue the foreign intercourse initiated by Commodore Perry and Townsend Harris and to accept in good faith the treaties concluded by the Bakufu.

Their new policy was no less nationalistic than it had been when their cry was "Expel the barbarians," but it was based upon the realities of the modern world rather than upon the romantic idea that Japan could hope to maintain her historic isolation. The new government was ready to learn everything possible from the foreigners, to welcome them to Japan and encourage Japanese to go abroad, in order to build up the strength, economic, industrial and military, that would then enable Japan to meet the West on equal terms. It would accept the inescapable challenge of foreign intercourse, but try to direct and develop these new relationships so as to safeguard the country's independence and security.

Never has a nation gone through a more dramatic transformation than that which Japan experienced in the years following the Emperor's restoration. The daimio surrendered their fiefs and the samurai their special rights and privileges. A centralized modern state was created. The bases were laid for commercial and industrial advances whereby Japan spectacularly forged ahead to an increasingly important role in world affairs. The past was not repudiated, even though for a time the intoxication with everything new gave such an impression. No greater mistake could be made than to believe that in its rapid modernization Japan wholly cast aside the traditions or the mores of her own ancient culture. But while clinging to much of the old, the country accepted the new with amazing enthusiasm.

The Emperor, installing himself in the Shogun's capital at Yedo, which was renamed Tokyo, lost little time in setting Japan on her new course. In his charter oath he declared that knowledge would be sought from all over the world in order to strengthen the foundations of imperial policy. His government promptly moved to relax existing restrictions on foreign residents; was shortly to send abroad, to both Europe and the United States, an important, high-ranking mission under Iwakura Tomomi, the new Foreign Minister; and began to invite foreign experts to assist it in every phase of its broadened activities. What in later years might have been termed "an underdeveloped nation" was ready and willing to draw upon all possible foreign aid in making over its archaic institutions and adapting itself to the modern world. The Meiji era—"enlightened rule"—had begun.

Declaring that foolish arguments should be abandoned, an imperial decree now called upon the high officials of the court "to take resolute steps to cast off the stupid opinion of the past to look down on foreigners as dogs, sheep, or barbarians."

9

The Yankee Invasion

"THE YANKEE has invaded the Land of the Gods."

William Elliot Griffis, who came to Japan to teach and was later to write *The Mikado's Kingdom*, was setting out from Yokohama along the ancient Tokaido on January 2, 1871. He was not to meet obsequious villagers bowing to the ground with averted faces as had Townsend Harris along this same highway fourteen years earlier; nor did he, on the contrary, have any reason to fear that swaggering *ronin* might try to cut him down in a frenzy of antiforeign hatred. The times had greatly changed, and the Yankee whom Griffis found invading Japan was matter-of-factly engaged in providing economic transportation between Yokohama and the new capital of Tokyo.

"He jostles the processions of the lords of the land," Griffis wrote. "He runs a coach on the great highway, so sacred to daimios and two-sworded samurai. Here on the Bund stands the stage that will carry a man to the capital for two Mexican dollars."

This shiny new stagecoach ("of regulation Yankee pattern") was a symbol of what was happening in Japan in these opening years of the Meiji era. It was not only that the new government in its complete shift of policy was setting up Western-oriented institutions, building a modern army and navy, embarking upon an ambitious program of industrialization, and acquiring steamships, railways, modern machinery and factories. It was also encouraging the introduction, as rapidly as possible, of everything that was assumed to mark the superiority of Western civilization. The official and educated classes in the major cities and treaty ports were eagerly embracing the technological innovations, the food and clothing, and a bewildering array of the popular fads and fancies of the uncouth foreigners whom they had once thought no more worthy of respect than dogs, sheep or barbarians.

Telegraph poles lined the Tokaido at the beginning of the 1870's in token of Japan's quick adoption of a method of communication which Commodore Perry had first introduced with his gift of a telegraphic apparatus in 1854; more and more urban houses were being lighted by oil lamps—the lamps from Connecticut, the oil from Pennsylvania; the newly imported Singer sewing machines were revolutionizing the making of clothes; barbershops, with the familiar red-and-white-striped poles of every American town and village, were doing a heavy business as the samurai shaved off their topknots in favor of foreign haircuts; and photographic studios represented what was to become (and forever remain) one of the most popular of all Western innovations.

"Condensed milk, Yankee clocks, buttons, petroleum," Griffis would exclaim in amazed surprise on visiting Tokyo, "pictures of Abraham Lincoln, Bismarck, George Washington, Gladstone; English cutlery and umbrellas; and French soap, brandy and wine." The capital's streets were crowded with foreign carriages as well as rickshas, soldiers and police were in regulation Western-style uniform, the shops were full of imported wares and notions, and soon gaslights would illuminate the famous Ginza. Everywhere there were bustle and activity, a sense of restless energy exploding in every direction. "The camp of the chief daimio is no more," wrote its American visitor only four years after the revolution. "Old Yedo has passed away forever. Tokio, the national capital, is a cosmopolis."

The clothing was perhaps the most astonishing illustration of what was taking place. Nothing could have been more incongruous than the bizarre combinations of foreign styles and traditional native dress: the kimono over pantaloons, frock coats and divided silk skirts, bowlers or Homburgs with the old-fashioned *hakama* and wooden *geta*. As early as 1872 the government decreed that all officials should wear foreign clothing, and they blossomed forth, as one contemporary observer reported, in Prussian caps, English jackets and "tight-fitting trousers imitating the full-dress trousers of the American army." There was even encouragement for women to abandon the kimono in favor of Western clothing, the Empress herself approvingly stating that the latter consisted "of an upper and lower garment in accordance with the ancient Japanese system of dress."

"With everyone talking of reforming life, reforming the theater, reforming the novel, reforming races, reforming the sewage system," as one Japanese historian has written, "it would have been strange indeed if no one had tried to reform women and women's clothing."

In the matter of daily living, the Japanese proved more resistant to Western ways than in respect to dress. They did not take to furniture. It made its way into offices, as suggested by the sad comment that government employees were "performing routine official duties by sitting on chairs," but except for one possible "Western room," the Japanese home generally retained its traditional form and style. As for eating, there was no sudden abandonment of native dishes but the gradual adoption of a few foreign foods. They included beef, milk and butter, which the Japanese had not heretofore used; various fruits introduced principally from the United States; and that delectable dessert which the Japanese envoys had so much enjoyed in 1860 and which was now to become popularly known as *aisu-kuriimu*. Needless to say, the Japanese were also importing the champagne, whisky and gin to which Commodore Perry had first introduced them with such enthusiastic results.

These foreign innovations did not immediately affect the people as a whole; they did not reach into the countryside, to the small farming and fishing villages. The Japanese generally were to retain much of their old way of life in spite of the inroads of Western customs. But in sophisticated circles and for the young men-about-town, fashion decreed the adoption of as many foreign ways as possible. Wearing watches, carrying umbrellas (known as "bat shades") and eating beef became conspicuous status symbols among many of the former two-sworded samurai. Children sang the "Civilization Ball Song," as G. B. Sansom has written, and counted the bounces of the ball by naming the ten most popular foreign objects. They were gas lamps, steam engines, horse carriages, cameras, telegrams, lightning conductors, newspapers, schools, the letter post and steamboats!

There was a beginning of Western sports. Japanese boys had taken eagerly to baseball, and it was not long before the game began to rival in popularity the traditional *sumo* that the members of Perry's squadron had watched so wonderingly some twenty years or so earlier. It was in time to become almost as much a national sport as in the country of its origin. Today at professional ball parks, as well in the courtyards of temples and shrines which are the equivalent of America's sandlots, the spectators wrangle over whether the umpire has correctly called the runner *sefu* or *auto*, and happily cheer the occasional *homu-ran* which sails beyond the outfielders. The Japanese were to take up other Western games, but *besu-boru* has always led the field.

The government's vigorous encouragement of these Western innovations, apart from the more important industrial undertakings, reforms in law and administration and virtual revolution in public education, was highlighted by the opening in Tokyo in 1883 of an international social club—the Rokumeikan, or Hall of the Baying Stag. Here the very top officials of the court and members of the new Japanese aristocracy, resplendent in their morning coats and striped trousers, could mingle with the diplomatic corps and other important foreigners; here could be held gala social events with cards, billiards and dancing every Sunday evening to Western music. And shattering all precedent to an even greater degree, the wives and daughters of the aristocracy could attend these functions wearing not the traditional kimono but Paris gowns and imported jewels.

The official blessing granting such revolutionary changes in social life was dramatically emphasized by a magnificent costume ball given by Prime Minister Ito in 1887. It was a formidable affair, closely fashioned after those conspicuous displays of extravagant wealth currently so much the vogue in the society of

New York, Philadelphia and Newport. The Prime Minister himself appeared at the ball as a Venetian nobleman, Prince Arisugawa as a medieval knight, and the chancellor of Tokyo University as a Buddhist pilgrim. The ladies were dressed in the costumes of historic figures from Japanese poetry and legend.

Paralleling such extraordinary encouragement of Western ways, even though there were some critics to suggest they constituted somewhat "unusual behavior," was the official disapproval of certain long-established customs. With the Emperor gravely warning his subjects not to cling to those which might cause foreigners to laugh at Japan and bring ridicule on the nation, officialdom frowned severely upon the traditional topknot, upon samurai wearing swords and upon married women blackening their teeth. New moral codes not only prohibited the sale of young girls to houses of prostitution and banned pornographic literature, but sought in other ways to meet foreign standards of decency. The Japanese having contacts with Westerners had long been embarrassingly aware of the latter's criticism of coolies going about the streets nearly naked and of their shocked disapproval of mixed bathing at the public baths. The government consequently issued strict regulations on both counts. Explaining a new rule requiring the coolies to cover their nakedness, a Tokyo ordinance explicitly stated: "If this ugly practice is left as it is, it will bring shame upon the nation."

These developments, however contrary to Japanese tradition, grew somewhat paradoxically out of that same nationalistic spirit that had characterized Japan when her people had so spiritedly rejected the very idea of any association with the West. The government was not encouraging foreign styles and foreign customs because it had suddenly become convinced of their innate superiority. It simply felt that their adoption was necessary to persuade the West that Japan had become so "civilized" that she could no longer be considered as in any way a backward nation.

The Japanese had smarted under the implications of inferiority implied by extraterritoriality and foreign control over the tariff ever since the Western powers had insisted upon such concessions in the treaties first signed by the Bakufu. The major objective of Japanese foreign policy, once the new imperial government had accepted the permanency of foreign intercourse, was the revision of these early treaties. While it was recognized that reformation of the judicial system and other political reforms were most important in persuading the West to accept Japan on terms of full equality, nothing was to be neglected which might help to demonstrate that Japan had caught up with the spirit of the modern world. If putting trousers on ricksha coolies and dressing up the ladies and gentlemen of the court in medieval costumes were necessary to prove to Western skeptics that Japan had a truly sophisticated culture, Japanese officialdom was quite ready to oblige.

Japan continued throughout these early years of the Meiji era to borrow from both Europe and America wherever it was felt necessary, or desirable, in adapting herself to modern ways and strengthening her world position. She was to build her new navy largely on the model of that of Great Britain, draw heavily upon German institutions in her program of constitutional reform, and look primarily to France for inspiration in art and literature. The pervasive influence of the United States, her first friend and nearest neighbor, was in other areas equally important, reaching out far beyond such obvious American contributions as Singer sewing machines and striped barber poles, ice cream and baseball.

There were many American experts of one sort or another serving as advisers to the new government in the 1870's. George W. Williams, a former banker of Lafayette, Indiana, and a deputy customs commissioner in Washington, was brought to Japan by Ito Hirobumi (who was later as Prime Minister to give the great masquerade ball at the Rokumeikan) for assistance in organizing Japanese finances. He helped to develop along definitely American lines new banking laws, a modern coinage system and an office for the regulation of patents. Two other Americans, Hilliard Miller and Matthew Scott, worked with the Foreign Office in establishing the customs service; Dr. John C. Berry, a medical missionary, played an important role in prison reform, and Samuel Bryan, a young postal clerk from Cadiz, Ohio, developed a program for the Japanese posts, negotiated a series of postal treaties and served for four years as Superintendent of Foreign Mails.

Another interesting foreign expert in this early period was

Erastus Peshine Smith, a graduate of Columbia University and the Harvard Law School, who on the suggestion of Charles E. De Long, the American minister in 1869, was appointed a special adviser to the Foreign Office. During his stay in Tokyo he fell out with De Long, and the latter was soon protesting indignantly to Secretary of State Fish about his behavior. De Long reported that Smith was not only leaking official American secrets to the Japanese but disgracing his country by living with a native concubine and engaging in "perfect orgies" of drinking. The Japanese would not, however, appear to have been greatly perturbed. When Secretary Fish sought to apologize for such reprehensible conduct on the part of an American, the Japanese minister in Washington replied that Smith was serving the government very well. "As long as he does that," the minister added, "we don't mind his private life after office hours."

Smith's legal advice was unquestionably of great value to the Japanese. The historian Chitoshi Yanaga has written that as the first Western adviser to the Foreign Office he "was instrumental in bringing about the end of a humiliating period in Japan's foreign relations by initiating a positive, self-assertive policy."

General Charles LeGendre, a colorful figure on the Far Eastern scene who resigned an American consulship in China to accept employment by the Japanese Government, also served in the Foreign Office. A born adventurer, LeGendre had become greatly interested in Formosa, and his real idea in working with the Japanese was to encourage an imperialistic scheme being hatched in 1873 for Japan's conquest of that island. Visiting Peking with a Japanese mission, he supposedly won the approval of the Chinese Government for a punitive expedition against the Formosan aborigines who had killed a number of Japanese sailors. But when the expedition was about to be launched with LeGendre (together with two other Americans) playing major roles in its organization, the Chinese Government repudiated its alleged approval and prevailed upon American consular authorities in Amoy to arrest LeGendre as having violated American neutrality.

He was soon freed of such a flimsy charge, resumed his services with the Japanese, and while military operations were proceeding in Formosa, returned to Peking as a special commissioner to conclude an agreement whereby China undertook to pay an indemnity for the Formosans' attacks on Japanese citizens. The expedition then withdrew, but here was a first sign of the imperialistic ambitions which would bring Japan back to Formosa some twenty years later. LeGendre handled various other, less dramatic matters for the Japanese Government and on resigning in 1875 he was the first foreigner to be awarded the Order of the Rising Sun.

Even more important in his influence on Japanese policy than the hard-drinking Erastus Peshine Smith or swashbuckling General Charles LeGendre was the contrastingly quiet and self-effacing Henry W. Denison. A Vermont lawyer who had served with the Yokohama consulate, he in turn became a legal adviser to the Foreign Office and continued in this post from his appointment in 1880 until his death in 1912. He was extremely able and played an important role in the negotiatons that ended the Sino-Japanese conflict in 1895 and in those concluding the Russo-Japanese War ten years later. His services in helping Japan to bring about revision of the unequal treaties were also conspicuous, and he repeatedly helped to smooth the path of Japanese-American relations through the confidence he inspired in his integrity and goodwill among both Japanese and Americans.

Over and beyond the role of such experts in the fields of finance, government administration and foreign affairs was that of the pioneer American teachers who came to Japan in the early years of Meiji. In their zeal to "catch up" with the West, the Japanese soon discovered that learning English, that cryptic tongue which has continued to baffle them for a century, was an essential step toward acquiring the new knowledge. Many of them turned at first to the "waterfront professors" of the treaty ports— sailors, clerks, apprentices and ex-bartenders. One description of such characters has them "teaching with pipe in mouth, and punctuating their instructions with oaths, or appearing in the classroom top-heavy." Soon, however, more reputable teachers were available not only in the treaty ports but in a number of small towns and cities in the interior. Young Americans fresh from college began instructing equally young Japanese—a new confrontation of Yankees and samurai—not only in English language studies, but in modern history, economics and the sciences. There were some other Westerners engaged in such tasks, but during the

1870's and 1880's the foreigners teaching in Japan's new colleges and provincial schools came largely from the United States.

Among the hundred or so of such instructors in these days was William Elliot Griffis, who was actually on his way to his post in a provincial school when he first discovered the Yankee who had invaded the land of the gods. A graduate of Rutgers in the class of 1869, an eager, idealistic young man with both a missionary spirit and a keen sense of adventure, he was to present in *The Mikado's Kingdom* a fascinating account of an American teacher in Japan at the opening of the Meiji era.

Griffis had accepted an invitation from Matsudaira Shungaku, the daimio of Echizen, a Western-minded prince whose provincial capital was at Fukui, some two hundred miles west of Tokyo, to organize "a scientific school on the American principle." The man responsible for this unusual invitation being extended to him was the missionary Guido Verbeck. The latter had sent several Japanese students to Rutgers (whom Griffis had known and taught), and he was anxious to have some Rutgers graduates carry on his own pioneer educational work in Japan.

After arriving in Yokohama and taking the stagecoach to Tokyo, Griffis spent some time in the capital making arrangements for his stay at Fukui. Matsudaira undertook to pay him $900 a month, as well as providing him with a Western-style house and a horse, while for his part Griffis agreed to teach physics and chemistry, and pledged himself during his stay neither to trade with the local merchants nor get drunk. This last provision in his contract did not in any way surprise the idealistic young teacher from Rutgers; he had already seen enough of foreigners in the treaty ports to realize that it was "quite justifiable by the bitter experience of the Japanese."

Griffis also secured the services of an interpreter. He first tried to persuade Tateishi Onojiro, the self-same "Tommy" who had so endeared himself to the ladies as a member of the Japanese embassy to the United States in 1860, to accept this assignment. But Tommy, now a major in the army, was unwilling to leave what were already becoming the bright lights of Tokyo. Griffis had to be content with a substitute. His choice fell upon another young samurai, one of the interpreters attached to the new Imperial College. He was a bright, merry lad, forever singing snatches of

American college songs, and was to prove invaluable in every way. Having settled this matter, Griffis then set out with a party of eight, including guards and servants, on the several days' journey to Fukui.

They went first by ship to Kobe, where Griffis stayed with an American missionary, and then on to Osaka ("a gay city with lively people, and plenty of means of amusement") aboard a small steamer flying the Stars and Stripes and commanded by a Yankee captain. The next stage of their journey was overland to Lake Biwa, which they crossed by ferry; and they then continued on through the mountains and valleys of central Japan until on the tenth day after leaving Tokyo they arrived at Fukui. Griffis traveled by norimon, which he found very cramping and uncomfortable, and spent the nights on route at Japanese inns which had never before entertained a foreigner. The young American had to adapt himself to Japanese ways, but there were limits to his tolerance. One night his party was very merry, he recorded, with two geisha being called in "to dispense music, dancing and sake." He conscientiously withdrew and occupied himself "in making notes of the day's trip."

One general observation that Griffis made, priding himself on his realism and honesty, stood in sharp contrast to the views that had been expressed by more restricted foreign travelers. "I began to realize the utter poverty and wretchedness of the people and country," he wrote. "It was not an oriental paradise, such as a reader of some books about it may have supposed." And a few days later on going through a small city he reverted to this theme: "I was amazed at the utter poverty of the people, the contemptible houses, and the tumble-down look of the city, as compared with the trim dwellings of an American town." This was not the Japan that Townsend Harris had described when after his journey from Shimoda to Yedo he had written that the Japanese appeared to be "the best fed, clad and lodged, and the least overworked of any people on earth."

When he arrived at Fukui, Griffis was most hospitably welcomed by the officials of the daimio's court and happily found that the house allotted to him was equipped with a stove, a bedstead, a washstand and other furniture, and that arrangements had been made for preparing his meals Western style. One of the daimio's entourage had actually visited the United States, as he proudly told Griffis, and knew what foreigners wanted. In further offering to help him get a good servant, a horse or anything else he might need, another officer made a suggestion recalling that made to Harris some fourteen years earlier: "The officer said I must have relaxation. He offered to show me the fairest and brightest maiden, whom I might bring to my house, and make my playmate. I thanked him, and accepted all his offers but the last."

Everything about Fukui reflected the mores and customs of the old Japan where Western influence had not yet penetrated. Griffis' home was at least partly foreign style, but he was somewhat dismayed by other circumstances of his isolated life. His household included several officials especially appointed to look after his needs, four armed guards to escort him to and from school, no less than eight gatekeepers, several servants (with their families), and a number of students who wanted to live near their master. Griffis was to have no privacy whatsoever until he so managed things as to be able to get away from Fukui for horseback rides through the surrounding countryside, sometimes staying overnight at village inns.

The school itself had an enrollment of some eight hundred students in five divisions: the English, Chinese, Japanese, medical and military departments. Griffis met his students in an old building that had once been the daimio's residence. They were all young samurai, with shaven heads and topknots, wearing the customary kimono and wooden clogs, and while on coming into the school building they checked their long swords in numbered racks at the entrance, they kept their shorter dirks with them. "They impressed upon my memory," wrote this recent Rutgers graduate, "a picture of feudalism I shall never forget."

The whole account of his life at Fukui makes engrossing reading. A high point, however, was the occasion of the daimio's ceremonial surrender of his hereditary office when under the new imperial regime the feudal fiefs were made over into the modern ken, or local prefectures, and the samurai were stripped of their ancient privileges, sinecure posts and established incomes. These reforms were to cut the number of officials holding government posts in Fukui from five hundred to seventy, including a reduction in Griffis' own attendants ("Hurra for the new Japan," he wrote) from eight to two and the dismissal of all his guards. On the departure of the daimio himself to take a new governmental position in Tokyo, Griffis was invited to attend his last appearance before his followers.

The samurai of the Fukui clan, some three thousand strong, gathered on this epochal occasion in the great assembly hall of the castle to await the appearance of Matsudaira Shungaku, kneeling on the floor with their hands resting on the hilts of their swords, placed upright before them. The daimio appeared, a stern-visaged young man in the full regalia of his feudal state: a purple satin *hakama* with an outer garment of dark silk crepe embroidered with the Tokugawa crest, and a dirk whose carved hilt was of solid gold sticking in his girdle. Quietly walking through the ranks of his retainers, whose every head remained bowed, he took a position in the center of the vast hall and, in a brief and moving address, called upon the samurai loyally to transfer their allegiance to the Mikado. One of them made answer in behalf of the clan, declaring it to be their purpose to become faithful subjects of their new ruler.

As a consequence of the changes taking place at Fukui, Griffis lost many of his pupils. A feeling that the school no longer afforded very worthwhile opportunities for teaching combined with a growing loneliness (he had not seen another person of his own race for six months) to make him increasingly restless. When he shortly afterward received an offer of one of the professorships at the newly established polytechnic school of the Imperial College, he consequently decided to leave Fukui. On January 22, 1872, he said goodbye to his remaining students and, even though it was the dead of winter and travel was very difficult, returned to Tokyo.

Griffis stayed there for three years, teaching at the polytechnic school and watching the growth of the new Japan. He then came back to the United States and entered the ministry. While never again crossing the Pacific, he nonetheless maintained a major interest in Japan for the rest of his life. Through a series of articles for such magazines as *Lippincott's, Appleton's Journal,* the *Overland Monthly* and the *Independent,* and then through *The Mi-*

kado's Kingdom, which quickly went through twelve editions after its original publication in 1876, he became during these years the foremost interpreter of Japan to his fellow countrymen. Perhaps no one exercised a greater influence at this time in encouraging a friendly attitude toward the people about whom he wrote with both authority and a deep appreciation of their native culture.

"Most prominent of American strands in the fabric of the new Japan," the Japanese critic Shigeto Tsuru has written, "was, without a doubt, the educational system which had to be created entirely new." This contribution, over and beyond the role of individual teachers in the provincial academies and the new colleges, was most outstanding in the secondary schools developed in the early years of Meiji. The responsible American was Dr. David Murray, a professor of mathematics at Rutgers, who came to Japan in 1873 as an educational adviser and superintendent in charge of school administration.

He was brought to Japan by Tanaka Fujimaro, the senior secretary of the Ministry of Education and later Vice Minister, who visited the United States in 1871 with the Iwakura mission and was charged with surveying the American school system. The way for this survey had been prepared by Mori Arinori, the first Japanese minister in Washington. He had sought advice from several prominent American educators on "the elevation of the condition of Japan, intellectually, morally, and physically" and had been particularly impressed with a reply from Professor Murray. On Mori's advice, Tanaka consequently sought the assistance of this Rutgers mathematician and then invited him to take over the post in Japan that he was so admirably to fill for some six years.

Although the centralized organization of the French school system was a basic feature of the new Japanese educational program, Murray convinced the authorities that American models should be followed in both the establishment and curricula of elementary schools. As a result of his endeavors American ideas were followed so closely that a Japanese historian has stated that education in this area became for a time substantially identical in every respect with that of the United States. The Japanese not only adopted American methods of instruction, but they took over

American school equipment—the desks, the blackboards, the wall maps, the slates and crayons. Murray opposed a plan suggested by some Japanese educators for making English the actual language of instruction; instead of such a radical departure, he urged the translation into Japanese of American schoolbooks. The *McGuffey Readers*, so universally popular throughout the United States, were among the texts translated, and also *Peter Parley's Universal History* by Samuel G. Goodrich. A whole generation of Japanese children were to become at least vaguely familiar with the democratic principles and moral precepts that these typically American schoolbooks sought to inculcate in the minds of the young.

Murray was also very active in the establishment of normal schools and appointed another American, Marion M. Scott, a former grammar school principal from San Francisco, to head the first institution of this kind in Japan. Many of their graduates (some of them after further study in the United States) became the superintendents of the new public schools being set up throughout the country. In this entire program for training teachers, Murray strongly emphasized the importance of female education and the employment of women as teachers. Indeed, his part in encouraging this unprecedented innovation has often been commended as his most significant contribution to Japanese education.

On first coming to Japan, Murray had felt he had little to do, but his good sense and unfailing tact, his moderation in urging his ideas on his superiors, gradually strengthened his position. He was soon writing home that he had been given far greater responsibilities and a good deal more work. "I am glad and sorry," he said. "It is pleasant to think that my services have secured their confidence and that I can feel that what I do will be appreciated. But I see very well that I will have plenty to do during the rest of my stay."

Few foreigners have been given more appreciative testimonials than those showered on Murray when he left Japan in 1879. The Minister of Education wrote that it was chiefly due to his efficient labors that Japan had been able to make the great improvements that had transformed its whole educational system; Tanaka Fujimaro, the Vice Minister, with whom he worked so closely, paid special tribute to his services in improving school curricula, encouraging female education and founding normal schools; and at a final imperial audience, the Emperor awarded him the Third Order of the Rising Sun. If further evidence of the universal recognition of his work is necessary, the Tokyo *Times* declared that no foreigner of any nationality had had a greater impact on the growth of modern Japan.

After Murray left Tokyo, American influence on Japanese education was notably to decline, with a reorganization of the entire system along German lines and a significant reorientation in objectives. The original Education Act of 1872 had stressed individual values, declaring education to be "the key to success in life . . . no man can afford to neglect it," but eighteen years later a further imperial rescript defined the goals of the school system as "righteousness, loyalty and filial piety." The new education had greatly increased literacy as a democratic goal, ultimately giving Japan in this respect an unrivaled status. In its future development it was to depart from the principles advocated by Murray and instead strongly emphasize the students' duty and obligation to the state.

In the early Meiji period there were many other special areas of study where the services of Americans stand out distinctively. One of unusual interest was the field of music, where Luther Whiting Mason made a unique and lasting contribution. Mason was a good Yankee, born in Turner, Maine, and an entirely self-taught musician who had become a superintendent of music, first in the schools of Cincinnati and then in those of Boston. He knew nothing of Japan, but invited to come there to introduce Western music, in which the Japanese had been greatly interested ever since hearing the bands from Commodore Perry's warships, he eagerly accepted such a challenging opportunity.

Mason performed a memorable job in familiarizing the Japanese with the diatonic scale, organizing bands and choral groups (including one chorus among members of the Ministry of the Imperial Household) and training music supervisors for the schools. Through his efforts Western music (the Japanese called the tunes he popularized "Mason song") was eagerly taken up. The choral singing that remains today a conspicuous feature of university life, so surprising to visitors who had no reason to suspect such familiarity with Western music and even American songs, is a monument to Mason's broad and continuing influence. It has been said, indeed, that while a Japanese called upon to try his hand at painting would inevitably turn out something unmistakably Oriental, "Ask him to sing a tune and he is as likely as not to essay 'Home Sweet Home.'"

Among other teachers there were many American scientists in Japan, and their varied activities have been recently made the subject of a special study by the Japanese scholar, Masao Watanabe. Among them were Frank F. Jewett, a Harvard-trained chemist who lived and taught in Tokyo at the close of the 1870's; Henry M. Paul, an astronomer from the United States Naval Observatory; Thomas C. Mendenhall, a physicist from Ohio State University who, over and beyond his teaching, made very significant contributions to Japanese research through a series of pioneering meteorological reports; and Edward Sylvester Morse, the Harvard zoologist, who taught at Tokyo University from 1877 to 1879 and played an important role in popularizing the Darwinian theories of evolution.[1]

Morse discovered the famous shell mounds at Omori, which helped to inspire Japanese studies in both archaeology and anthropology; maintained a marine laboratory for experimental studies on the island of Enoshima near Kamakura; made extensive collections of Japanese pottery which were ultimately presented to the Boston Museum of Fine Arts; and wrote a unique account of his varied experiences in *Japan Day by Day*. It is again highly interesting to find this close observer of Japanese life emphasizing what so many earlier, and also later, American writers have also especially noted: the rare signs of quarreling among the people, the gaiety of the frequent festivals, the "good babies," the simplicity and frugality of living conditions, the popularity of *sumo* and the ordered, disciplined way of life.

For the most part these scientists all taught at Tokyo University, the outgrowth of the various schools and colleges at which among others Guido Verbeck and William Elliot Griffis had first taught, and in these days it had a distinctly American flavor. When

---

[1] Somewhat later and better known were Ernest Fenollosa and Lafcadio Hearn, to be taken up in Chapter 12.

it attained its official status as Tokyo Imperial University in 1886, there were some thirty Americans teaching in its component departments of law, medicine, engineering, science and literature. "Almost unconsciously," Robert S. Schwantes has written in *Japanese and Americans,* his authoritative study of cultural interaction, "these Americans molded Tokyo University during its formative years, and it set the pattern for the newer universities."

While American educators were playing their part in the creation of the new Japan, the activities of the missionaries, closely linked with education in so many instances, were steadily expanding. It was not until 1873 that the Japanese Government, realizing that it could hardly expect the West to accept it on terms of equality so long as it proscribed Christianity, finally removed the traditional placards outlawing it as an evil sect. But by that time the little band of half a dozen American missionaries had already grown to seventy-five. The American Board of Commissioners for Foreign Missions supported the largest number, some twenty; followed by the Reformed Church, the Episcopalians and the Methodists. Nearly half of them were in Yokohama, with smaller contingents in Tokyo, Osaka, Kobe and Nagasaki, and the missionary total was almost equally divided between men and women.

The missionaries were of course overjoyed to find the way now clear to complete religious toleration. Allowed to preach their faith openly and hold their "Jesus-Way Sermon Meetings" without fear of police intervention, they had renewed confidence in the ultimate success of their campaign to convert all Japan. "It is truly a cause for wonder and thanksgiving," wrote Orramel Gulick, who opened a chapel in Osaka, "to see in this spot, where recently the light of Christianity was so completely excluded, the crowds who passing in the streets, dare to call in, and in numbers seat themselves to hear the words of life." In the reports being sent to mission boards at home, a naïve enthusiasm was the universal keynote. One missionary wrote glowingly of the "constant and cheering progress," and another exuberantly described the zeal of the converts "now flocking in like doves in their windows."

One outstanding figure among the missionaries in these years was Daniel Crosby Greene, a graduate of Dartmouth and the Andover Theological Seminary, who came to Japan in 1869 as a member of the American Board mission, ready to dedicate himself "to a life of happiness in this branch of my Master's service." Staying on in Japan for a full forty-four years until his death in 1913, Greene's conscientious yet broad minded attitude in the promotion of Christian missions and his valuable services in the field of education won for him universal respect and esteem. He was in the tradition of Hepburn and Verbeck and like them one of the few foreigners to whom the Emperor awarded special honors.

Greene was very briefly in Tokyo after first landing in Japan, and went on almost at once to Kobe. There he studied Japanese and taught English in the accepted pattern of missionary work, gradually making friends whom he brought into his home for Bible study and prayer meetings. These activities absorbed him, but at the same time he was deeply troubled by certain aspects of the life he found prevailing in Kobe.

This newly opened port already had a foreign colony of some four hundred persons and was second only to Yokohama as a center for trade and commerce with the outside world. But Greene was shocked to discover how "respectable vice is in this part of the world" and judged Kobe to be a "perfect Sodom." He noted with dismay the sharp cleavage within the foreign colony itself between the easygoing, hard-drinking business and commercial community and the earnest, devout, puritanic missionaries. He grievously felt that many of the Westerners were setting the Japanese the worst possible example of Christian morality.

Greene was to come to like the Japanese immensely, and they in turn liked and respected him. But he was first and foremost a missionary, and in many ways a lot like Guido Verbeck. The faults that he found in Japanese society, especially those relating to standards of sexual morality, could never be eradicated in his opinion until the people accepted Christianity. There could be no compromise in this battle for the Lord. "Our great fight in Japan, it becomes more and more clear every day," he wrote on one occasion, "is with Buddhism." He did not feel that Shintoism was a very important factor in Japanese life, but Buddhism's appeal to the great masses of the people had to be combated with every possible weapon if the saving grace of Christianity were finally to prevail.

Greene stayed in Kobe four years. Once the bans on Christianity were lifted he established a church, beginning with eleven members, and also started work on translating the Bible. The latter task then took him to Yokohama, where he cooperated with Hepburn, and after its completion and a year's leave, he accepted in 1880 the new assignment of teaching at Doshisha College, a school that had been set up at Kyoto by the Japanese Christian leader, Niijima Jo, under the auspices of the American Board. It had at the time Greene began his teaching there some 116 students, of whom thirty were preparing for the Christian ministry.

As the former capital of the empire, the stronghold for the most conservative forces in Japan and the center for so much of her ancient culture, Kyoto had only recently been opened to foreigners. Orramel Gulick had been there in 1872, reporting that with a single exception he was the first missionary to have visited the ancient Japanese city since Francis Xavier 327 years earlier. The next year a number of other foreigners attended the Kyoto Exhibition, which was apparently staged to show the city's varied wares. Gulick had found Kyoto, with a typical missionary reaction to its myriad temples and shrines, "wholly given over to idolatry." He considered its inhabitants to be "as benighted and devoted heathen as any people on earth."

The Greene family, which now included five children, were not so isolated in Kyoto as William Elliot Griffis had been while residing in far-off Fukui. However, there were very few foreigners living there, and the city's conservative character meant that many of the old prejudices against the Western barbarians were still very much alive. But while he felt cut off from the main stream of events in the new Japan, and faced many difficulties in adjusting himself to his new life, Greene was nevertheless greatly to enjoy his work and his contacts with his students.

He found the young men at Doshisha serious-minded, anxious to learn and far more independent in their thinking than those in Kobe or Yokohama. Their background made them less amenable to the strict regulations Doshisha tried to impose on their conduct; they had their own ideas on the curriculum and also on political affairs. On one occasion they set a rather new precedent in Japanese college life by going out on strike against both their native and foreign instructors.

After seven years in Kyoto, Greene made what was to prove his last move in the mission field. He settled down in Tokyo, where his primary function, as the senior member of the American Board mission, was to help and advise the several Japanese churches that had by this time been established in the capital. It was also his hope that, as a result of his long experience in Japan, his knowledge of the language and his wide acquaintanceship, he might be able to play some part in relating the Christian movement within Japan to the country's more general progress and development.

Although the immediate impetus given to missionary activity by the removal of the government bans had definitely slowed down by this time, Greene was never to lose faith in Christianity's ultimate triumph. "The great movement has slackened," he wrote, "but it has not ceased." He was to remain in Tokyo, busy and active in his work, for another twenty-three years.

The services of the early American missionaries in the founding of pioneer schools for both boys and girls, and in generally stimulating the educational revival of the Meiji era, were unquestionably of great benefit to Japan. Edwin O. Reischauer, the son of one of these missionaries, an authority on Japanese history and an American ambassador in Tokyo, has written that it was probably through Christian missions that "the United States exerted its chief influence on Japan."

While the Japanese greatly appreciated the educational phases of missionary activity, as both the official and unofficial tributes to the men engaged in such work abundantly testify, there were occasional flare-ups of antagonism growing out of the missionaries' proselytizing zeal. The mission station in conservative Kyoto, for example, received in 1884 an early Japanese version of the "Yankee Go Home" type of protest. This note read:

You—bad priests, American barbarians, four robbers—have come from a far country with the evil religion . . . but we know your hearts and hence shall soon with Japanese swords inflict the punishment of Heaven upon you. . . . But we do not wish to defile the sacred soil of Japan with your abominable blood—Hence take your families and go quickly.

In spite of such a dire threat, there were no open attacks on the missionaries. The tolerance that even the samurai had come to show toward foreigners generally, after the first flurry of anti-Western feeling in the 1860's, was extended to missionaries as well as other visitors. There was never any equivalent in Japan to the bloody antiforeign Boxer Rebellion that convulsed imperial China in 1900.

However worthwhile their services in education and medicine, certain questions may nevertheless still be raised, from the Western as well as Japanese point of view, as to the missionaries' role in seeking to inculcate the religious and moral ideals of Christianity among a people whom they continued to regard as incorrigible "heathen." Some of the missionaries were all too often narrowly self-righteous, unable to understand or appreciate the real values in Japanese culture, and severely dogmatic in their rejection of any possible good in either Buddhism or Shintoism. In their eyes the Japanese remained sunk in horrid degradation; only the full acceptance of the Christian gospel could redeem them from their evil ways.

This type of missionary was caustically described in a contemporary novel about Japanese life by the American journalist Edward H. House. This well-known member of the Tokyo foreign colony had originally come to Japan when he was twenty-five to teach English literature, and he was also associated with Luther Whiting Mason in the promotion of Western music. He later became the editor of the Tokyo *Times* and vigorously encouraged the efforts of the Japanese Government to revise the unequal treaties. His attitude toward the missionaries (although he recognized that they practiced what they preached) was set forth in his novel *Yone Santo*, first published in the *Atlantic Monthly* in 1888. He has one of his characters describe them as "well intending but curiously unintelligent and illiterate professors of a narrow and microscopic Christianity . . . superficial, one-sided and utterly selfish." Even such a devout Japanese Christian as Nitobe Inazo, writing about this same time, admitted that, in some instances at least, House's critical delineation of the American missionaries was "too well grounded to be denied."

Still, such unhappy characteristics could not be attributed to the missionaries as a whole. The strength of character, nobility of purpose and sense of dedication of the Verbecks, Hepburns, Greenes and many others showed the other side of the coin. Some years later, at the close of the century, Lafcadio Hearn was to express a view that at once recognized the missionaries' own worth and yet still questioned their ultimate goals:

> For myself I could sympathize with the individual,—but never with the missionary cause. Unconsciously, every honest being in the mission-army is a destroyer—and a destroyer only; for nothing can replace what they break down. . . . We are face to face here with the spectacle of a powerful and selfish civilization demoralizing and crushing a weaker and, in many ways, a nobler one.

So far as practical results in the conversion of the Japanese are concerned, the gap between the wildly optimistic hopes of the missionary boards and the actualities of the situation in Japan was never to be closed. "It is not an extravagant anticipation," an editorial in the *Independent* stated on September 6, 1883, "that Japan may become a Christian nation in seventeen years . . . a strong hope that the twentieth century will open upon that island no longer a mission field but predominantly Christian, converted from shadowy paganisms and vague philosophies which now retain but a feeble hold upon the people." But in spite of an increase in the number of American missionaries to nearly 500 (including their wives) and the foundation of some 259 churches and over 100 schools, the number of Japanese converts probably did not exceed 100,000 at the opening of the new century. And eighty-odd years after the *Independent*'s expression of such grandiloquent hopes for the future, the total of Japanese Christians still constituted no more than an approximate one-half of one percent of the country's population.

Although many American writings, beginning with the Constitution, Franklin's aphorisms and the *Federalist*, were early translated into Japanese, the influence of the United States in the field of literature during the Meiji era was in no way comparable to its influence in education or mission work. Japan turned to England and France rather than to America for literary inspiration. The most popular foreign book in Japan during the 1870's should have been written by an American, for its philosophy was so thoroughly that of the contemporary United States, but it was actually the work of an English author. This book was the Rev. Samuel Smiles' *Self-Help,* written very much in the spirit of Horatio Alger, and it had an immense appeal for the Japanese in their zealous efforts to rise in the world by their own efforts, both as individuals and as a nation. Moreover, the popular novels being translated and widely read were not those of American authors but above all others the books of Bulwer-Lytton, Disraeli and Jules Verne. Chitoshi Yanaga has asserted in his *Japan Since Perry* that the publication of Lord Lytton's *Ernest Maltravers* in 1878 created a sensation through its revelation of foreign ways of life in terms of an appealing romance: "It satisfied the craze for Western things . . . set the keynote of the new literature of the Meiji era."

Yet America made at least a minor literary contribution to the desire of educated Japanese to read about the West in foreign books. The translation of Franklin's maxims is reported to have had a very large circulation, and a contemporary poem based on his aphorism, "Eat not to dullness, drink not to elevation," is attributed to the Meiji Empress:

> When flower-viewing in spring,
> And admiring the maples in autumn,
> It is best to drink only in moderation.

Among the few other American writers, Longfellow, Emerson and Whitman have been singled out by the Japanese historian Ki Kimura as having been read by intellectuals and exercising some influence in such rarefied circles. He notes that "The Village Blacksmith" was possibly the first American poem translated into Japanese; that Emerson was one of the authors (the only American) included in a Japanese series of *Twelve Great Men of Letters;* and that before the end of the Meiji era Whitman had become "the most popular poet in Japan." As an offset to such literary figures, it is also recorded that some of the volumes of the Old Sleuth Library, a popular dime-novel detective series, were translated into Japanese and became very popular among students.

An indirect example of American literary influence is found in a Japanese novel of the day, *Kajin no Kigu,* or, as this title has been translated, *Strange Encounters with Elegant Females.* Its author, Shiba Shiro (writing under the pen name of Tokai Sanshi), studied in San Francisco and then at the University of Pennsylvania, returning to Japan in 1884 to set forth the liberal and progressive ideas he had derived from his American experience. The "elegant females" in his dramatic story are of various Western nationalities and engage the Japanese hero, "wanderer of the eastern sea," in a great deal of political discussion. At one point the hero meets Yuran, or Mysterious Orchid, a lovely Spanish girl, at Independence Hall in Philadelphia. After talking for a time about Bunker Hill and Valley Forge, the young lady warmly applauds the progress that Japan has been making:

Now that your country has reformed its government and, by taking from America what is useful and rejecting what is superficial, is increasing month by month in wealth and strength, the eyes of the world are astonished by your success. . . . Thus it is your country and no other that can bring the taste of self-government and independence into the lives of millions for the first time, and so spread the light of civilization.

There was no doubt that this idea of Shiba Shiro was the dream of many Japanese intellectuals: by borrowing primarily from the democratic institutions of the United States and restraining "the rampancy of England and France . . . the designs of Russia," a progressive and benevolent Japan could exercise a salutary influence on the development of all Asia. Other than in such an unusual book as *Strange Encounters with Elegant Females*, however, there is little to be found, according to Japanese scholars, which suggests an American influence on either the literary style or the literary content of the new books being published in Japan during these years. The tone and spirit of the modern Japanese novel may owe a good deal to the West, but to France rather than America.

It remains very difficult to distinguish in any more general way what Japan drew from America and what she drew from Europe in the opening years of foreign intercourse. In the broad area of economic and technological advance, what was taking place was a delayed industrialization that grew out of the circumstances of modern life, and it is easy to overemphasize the contributions of the West, let alone that of any single country. This is even more true in respect to political principles. There was a continuing interest on the part of Japanese progressives in *Minken,* or People's Rights, but the constitution adopted in 1889 grew quite as much out of Japan's own background as from any foreign borrowings (in this case largely from Germany), and it provided for a traditionally authoritarian rather than democratic government. G. B. Sansom has indeed written in *The Western World and Japan* that the nation's future politics were to develop with little reference to the American experience.

Moreoever, the feverish intoxication with the customs and manners of the West that so strikingly characterized the opening years of Meiji was to subside rapidly after its strange and wonderful climax in the social activity of the Rokumeikan and Prime Minister Ito's costume ball in 1887. In many ways this foreign craze had been a momentary aberration. As the Japanese came to realize that such extravagant and foolish aping of the West was not leading to the immediate acceptance of national equality, the attitude of society changed. Such contemporary pamphlets as *Picking Holes in the West* and *Twenty-one Current Evils* graphically disclosed many of the defects in Western culture and the absurdity of the Japanese taking over indiscriminately so many foreign customs. Wearing watches, carrying umbrellas and eating beef, as well as wearing foreign clothes, lost something of their bright glamour as status symbols.

As Japan progressed along her amazing course, making over an ancient civilization along modern lines, she became more and more realistic in her borrowings from the West. She was assimilating what appeared to be beneficial, discarding a good deal that had at first been accepted overenthusiastically, and at the same time resolutely clinging (as she still does today) to many of the basic elements in her own culture. After a period of almost slavish imitation of the West, the Japanese program of modernization became one of careful and critical adaptation.

This is not to say that Japan's emergence as a modern, industrialized state did not continue to owe a great deal to both European and American influence. It most certainly did. Moreover, it may be further added that while the immediate effects of the Yankee invasion were perhaps most apparent on the surface of Japanese life, it continued to have far-reaching consequences in such important areas as education, women's rights, administrative reform and foreign policy. If the United States later lost its predominant role, most Japanese historians would appear to agree with the final judgments expressed by Katsumaro Nakamura and Shigeto Tsuru. "Without the least taint of flattery," the former wrote, "it may be safely asserted that Japan is indebted to no other country so much as the United States," and the latter has stated that the American impact on Japan was "decisively the greatest among all Western nations in the early years of the Restoration."

10

☙

Experiment in Hokkaido

AT THE BEGINNING of the Meiji era, Americans made one unusual and indeed unique contribution to Japan over and beyond their general services to her development. Visiting Hokkaido today and viewing the Ishikari Valley in that most northern of Japan's islands, one can hardly fail to be struck by something quite un-Japanese and vaguely familiar about the landscape. Here are broad fields, sometimes divided by barbed-wire fences, that may be planted to oats and wheat as well as the customary rice. The scattered farms have white frame houses, red dairy barns and brick silos. The scene is reminiscent of the Midwest, except for a background of heavily forested hills. Even the capital city of Sapporo, its streets laid out in a basically rectangular town plan and lined with sidewalks, seems to be more American than Japanese, and the campus of Hokkaido University could easily be that of a New England college. There is evidence on every hand that in Hokkaido, as in no other part of Japan, the foreign influence that has helped to shape the life of its people is distinctively, almost exclusively, that of the United States.

This is primarily the result of the activities and recommendations of an American agricultural mission that worked with the Japanese almost a century ago in developing the island. The Japa-

174

nese Government undertook this novel economic and social experiment in Hokkaido on its own initiative, inviting the American mission to come to Japan and paying all its costs, including the salaries and expenses of personnel. While it was thus not an official project of the United States Government, in almost every other respect the Hokkaido program interestingly foreshadowed the technological aid for underdeveloped countries that has had such a significant role in American foreign policy in the quite different world of the 1950's and 1960's. Moreover, the history of this unusual venture reveals the sometimes wasteful expenditures, the internal squabbling, the friction with local authorities, the criticism abroad and at home, that are not entirely unfamiliar aspects of foreign aid in the twentieth century.

The importance of Hokkaido in the eyes of the whaling industry had led Commodore Perry to single out its port at Hakodate as one of the two places in Japan (the other was Shimoda) to be opened up to Americans. But a century ago this mountainous island, with its deep forests and grassy river bottoms, swept by winter blizzards, was a challenging frontier not unlike America's West. It was not fully explored, in spite of the surveys made by Raphael Pumpelly in 1862, was very sparsely settled, and was generally believed to have great potential resources of minerals as well as valuable timber and rich farm lands. Its shy and primitive indigenes, the "hairy Ainus," numbered no more than about twelve thousand and were described by one visitor as "stupid, gentle, good-natured and submissive."

The objectives of the Japanese Government in deciding almost immediately after the restoration of the Emperor to undertake Hokkaido's development were threefold. Most importantly, there was the need to strengthen the northern defenses of the country against possible aggression by Russia, which had already won a threatening foothold on the nearby Kurile Islands; second was a desire to encourage emigration from the crowded southern Japanese islands to unsettled farm land; and lastly, the hope that exploitation of Hokkaido's resources would strengthen the economy of Japan as a whole. In turning to the United States for help in this ambitious program, the Japanese were influenced not only by the friendly attitude America had consistently shown toward their country but by American experience with large-scale farming and agricultural machinery.

A Colonization Department, the Kaitakushi, was established to carry out the over-all project, and the government appointed as its deputy director, charged with arranging for American aid and overseeing the work in general, a young samurai of the powerful Satsuma clan named Kuroda Kiyotaka. He had fought in the wars against the Shogunate and was destined to make a name for himself in Japanese history, not only as the active head of the Kaitakushi but as a leading statesman of the new regime. He became in time a Prime Minister and one of the Genro, or Elder Statesmen. When he received his appointment to the Kaitakushi, Kuroda was just thirty years old, a keen, intelligent and ambitious young man, open-minded about things of the West and ready to profit from everything he could learn.

On going to the United States toward the close of 1870 to arrange for the aid program, Kuroda saw President Grant and asked his help in securing the services of an outstanding agricultural expert, together with other technical advisers, who would come to Japan for a period of years to work in Hokkaido. The choice finally fell upon the Commissioner of Agriculture in Grant's own administration, General Horace C. Capron. The latter's terms were demanding: a completely free hand except for his responsibility to the director of the Kaitakushi, the right to appoint all his assistants, and a salary at what was then the munificent rate of $10,000 in gold a year, together with full travel expenses, a tax-free house, and payment of such servants, attendants and guards as he might need throughout his stay in Japan. Kuroda accepted these terms, Capron resigned as Commissioner of Agriculture, and President Grant gave the project his blessing.

The American adviser to the Kaitakushi was an arresting personality, an impressive-looking man of sixty-seven with a courtly and distinguished bearing, a firm sense of purpose and a very high opinion of himself. In the minds of many of those who worked with him, he was arrogant and overbearing, but the Japanese appear to have accepted him less critically. He had served with distinction during the Civil War and then devoted himself with great success to various agricultural activities. Before his appointment in Grant's administration, he had developed large-scale farms in both Maryland and Illinois and at one time had been president of the National Agricultural Association. His background and experience appeared to fit him admirably for his unusual post, but his personal egotism and inability to get along with some of his associates made for stormy times during the four years he spent in Japan.

Before leaving America, Kuroda and Capron toured the country together, inspecting farm communities and buying agricultural machinery, livestock, seed and nursery plants. They also purchased two small steamers to provide service between Hokkaido and the main Japanese island of Honshu. Capron then selected his assistants ("God grant that I may find them all that is desired," he wrote), among whom were engineers and geologists as well as agricultural specialists. His original staff was eight men, but some five times this number of Americans were associated with the mission before its operations came to an end.

Capron arrived in Japan on August 22, 1871, and was given a formal reception at Yokohama by the Japanese authorities. An impressive escort of armed samurai then accompanied him on the trip along the old Tokaido to Tokyo, where he was lodged (with "his staff of scientific American gentlemen") in a luxurious former palace furnished completely in Western style. Both the Prime Minister and Foreign Minister called on Capron, somewhat later tendering him an official banquet, and he was also received at court. On the latter occasion the Emperor, who was seated on his throne in his robes of state, said briefly, "I expect you will accomplish a meritorious service." General Capron then withdrew.

While a team of field workers set off to Hokkaido to make a first report on conditions there, the American mission set up three experimental farms in the immediate vicinity of Tokyo. Their dual purpose was to provide a way station for the livestock and nursery plants being imported from the United States and to conduct experiments as to the practicality of introducing them into Japan. Some eight hundred workers cleared the ground for the new farms, and the next spring saw a great area in the countryside miraculously transformed into unfamiliar grain fields and clover pastures, fruit nurseries and vegetable gardens, such as Japan had never before known. It was a formidable achievement. "Notwith-

standing all the croakings and prognostications of not only the
Japanese but foreigners that all would be destroyed by bugs and
vermin of every kind," Capron noted proudly in his journal, "not
a plant has been disturbed so far and the vegetables are progress-
ing with less obstruction than I have ever seen in America."
Moreover, the American minister, Charles De Long (who was to
quarrel so bitterly with Erastus Peshine Smith), was greatly impressed by what Capron had accomplished, reporting to his government the surprised delight of the Japanese over how well things
seemed to be going.

Edward Mason Shelton, a young graduate of the Michigan Agricultural College, was the superintendent of one of the experimental stations. He had helped in the purchase of the livestock
that was to be introduced into Hokkaido, supervised its transpacific passage and unloading in Yokohama, and was then made
responsible for training twenty young Japanese in its care. He was
to remain some eight months in Tokyo, and no small part of his
time, as he recorded in a journal relating his unusual experiences,
was taken up by exhibiting his animals to the countless Japanese
officials and students who inspected the farms. Kuroda Kiyotaka
was a frequent visitor, and on one occasion the Empress made an
unofficial inspection. She was particularly interested in the lambs
and pigs. As they were paraded before her, Shelton wrote, "each
animal was led by its Japanese attendant, wearing the imperial
coat of arms."

On another of the farms Edwin Dun, the son of an Ohio
farmer, had an exciting time when the Emperor himself appeared
on a more formal tour. The young American was called upon to
exhibit the farm machinery. Appropriately dressed for the Emperor (if not for handling machinery) in formal evening clothes
and a top hat, he hitched a team to a mowing machine, a reaper,
and then a wheat drill for a series of demonstrations in American
farming methods. His final performance for the delectation of an
entranced Emperor was the operation of a great steam thresher. "I
believe I am the only man living," Dun was later to recall, "who
has undertaken the job in a dress suit."

The Tokyo farms were kept up even after the American mission
left the country, and their experimental work led to the successful
introduction in Japan of various new fruits and vegetables includ-

ing, ironically enough in this land of cherry blossoms, the first edible cherries. This phase of the American mission's work, however, proved to be immensely expensive. Dun was to remain in Japan long after his co-workers had departed. He set up a stock-breeding farm in Hokkaido, married a Japanese woman, and after a further move to Tokyo and service with the legation, was appointed American minister to Japan by President Cleveland. Looking back on his early experiences in exhibiting agricultural machinery for the Emperor, he seriously questioned in these later years whether the experimental farm project as a whole had been really worth its great cost.

Developments in Hokkaido were, however, the mission's chief concern, and it was at the close of 1871 that the task force that General Capron had sent there on his first arrival made its report. It unhappily revealed a rift among the members of the mission that did not bode too well for the future. Major A. G. Warfield, an official of the Baltimore & Ohio Railroad who was the mission's chief engineer, reported enthusiastically on Hokkaido's resources, but Dr. Thomas Antisell, who had been head of the Agricultural Department's Bureau of Chemistry, returned convinced that the island's cold climate, which he descibed as "Siberian" and "subfrigid," made extensive agricultural development highly impractical.

The controversy within the mission, and then in official circles in Tokyo, was to become greatly embittered, reflecting conflicting ideas about Hokkaido which in some measure still persist. It is the general impression among Japanese in the southern islands that Hokkaido is much too cold for comfortable living. However, inexperience in coping with severe weather rather than really "Siberian" conditions largely accounts for this general prejudice. Hokkaido winters are actually no colder than those of New England or other Northern parts of the United States.

General Capron, in any event, was prepared to accept Major Warfield's more optimistic findings about Hokkaido and to discredit the gloomy forebodings of Dr. Antisell. He officially submitted to the Kaitakushi, in January, 1872, a long list of recommendations for the island's development, including further surveys of its natural resources, establishment of experimental farms and the introduction of wheat and maize as crops that would prove highly productive. Realizing that Japanese settlers might at first experience great difficulties in adjusting themselves to a totally new environment, he at one point suggested that a number of pioneer American farm families might be brought to Hokkaido to help them. However, the expense and legal difficulties of such a plan soon led to its abandonment.

The Kaitakushi accepted these recommendations, and with the approval of the Council of State set in motion an ambitious colonization project. At first the government undertook to give free land and subsidies to prospective settlers from the main islands, and even when this proved too expensive, it remained ready to provide them with housing, loans for seed and fertilizer, and the free use of farm machinery. Settlers were encouraged to plant wheat and maize rather than rice as General Capron recommended, and to use the machinery made available for them.

Somewhat later Kuroda Kiyotaka put into effect a scheme whereby these settlers, for a time restricted to former samurai, would also serve as militiamen, receiving in return for undertaking such service not only free land but general provisions for a three-year period. Operating along these lines the Kaitakushi was to bring some seventy thousand Japanese to Hokkaido from the main islands. Most of them remained in the new agricultural settlements, but a good many were drawn away to take up fishing and trade.

General Capron made his first visit to Hokkaido (together with Mrs. Capron) in the summer of 1872. He felt that in many respects things were going very well, clearly demonstrating that Major Warfield had been right and Dr. Antisell wrong in regard to the climate and the length of the growing season. He spoke rather complacently of "the mistaken judgment of some of my own professors." At the same time, Capron was discouraged by how hard it was to persuade the settlers to change their ways. Undoubtedly he expected too much of them. In spite of the warnings in his original report, he did not ever fully realize the strength of tradition and the virtual impossibility, for example, of entirely convincing the Japanese that they should give over growing rice in favor of wheat.

Capron, indeed, had very mixed feelings about the Japanese

from the moment of his arrival. At one time after glowingly describing a country festival—"There is music, and there are brilliant decorations of flags and lanterns, and there is singing and dancing"—he paid the Japanese farmers high tribute for their garden-like cultivation of the land. "What an instructive lesson for the American farmer," he wrote, "may be gathered from a careful consideration of the agriculture of these people!" Yet on another occasion he confided to his diary with evident exasperation: "Everything in Japan is a mystery to me; how is it that a people naturally so intelligent, appreciative, and so capable of imitating everything they see, should remain so long in a state of semibarbarism, is perfectly incomprehensible."

This first summer in Hokkaido, he could not understand why the new settlers did not take hold as he thought Americans would have. Instead of "villages of pioneers clearing the land," there were only "conglomerations of inept peasants . . . scrabbling for food." Moreover, Capron felt that the Japanese officers of the Kaitakushi were falling down on the job because their "unbounded conceit and confidence in their own ability" led them to reject his advice.

At one large experimental farm Capron found eighteen officials, housed in expensive quarters, overseeing work that was getting almost nowhere. One good American farmer with two sons and a yoke of oxen, he wrote indignantly in his journal, would have produced better results on forty acres. Visiting another settlement, he himself plowed the first furrow in the newly cleared land with a great Illinois plow drawn by a yoke of imported oxen, but when the Japanese tried to take over, they could not control the unfamiliar beasts. Capron felt that it was the men who "required the ring in their noses in place of the bull's." And then he was still more exasperated when, after getting a few farm hands reasonably well trained, an official promptly appeared, with several assistants, to take over a new bureaucratic post as "Master of Bulls."

The letters Capron wrote Kuroda on this and other occasions were one long tirade on how faithfully he was performing his duties and how negligently the Japanese officials were carrying out theirs. He had to grope his way in the dark, Capron said; he was constantly faced with "disagreeable, disheartening and often mortifying circumstances"; and he could make little headway in the face of the "pompous display of subofficials." How he kept on good terms with Kuroda, which he apparently did, is difficult to understand in the light of his petulant, complaining correspondence.

There was also further dissension within the American mission itself. General Capron felt that Antisell had proved a traitor to the whole project because of his discouraging report on Hokkaido's climate, and Antisell in turn considered Capron blundering and inept. Nor were relations between Capron and his younger assistants very friendly. The latter felt that their chief often went off on the wrong track but considered any questioning of his own ideas an impertinence. Edward Shelton, the farm superintendent at Tokyo, was to be most caustic in his criticism. "He knew nothing of agriculture, in any practical sense," Shelton later wrote, "nor, for that matter any other art or science, except possibly the military. As I knew him, he was a fussy old man with extravagant notions as to his own importance."

Many of the internal troubles of the mission appear to have been an outgrowth of the jealousies arising from the great gulf between Capron's position and that of his assistants. As adviser to the Kaitakushi, the General spent most of his time in Tokyo, visiting Hokkaido during the summers and thereby not only escaping the rigors and hardships of the northern winter but enjoying a privileged social life. His journal reveals a smug self-satisfaction with what he describes as his "receipt of various attentions" from Japanese officialdom. One occasion he specially singled out was a formal tiffin at the home of Foreign Minister Iwakura (the other foreign guests included John Bingham, the new American Minister, David Murray and William Elliot Griffis), where in his honor everything was done in the most approved Western style, even to the servants, as Capron proudly reported, wearing swallowtail coats, white vests, cravats and gloves.

The disparity between the social activities of their chief and the hard life in Hokkaido was not, however, as galling to the younger men as the low salaries they received. While Capron was pocketing his $10,000 in gold, they were being paid no more than $1,500 in silver. They perhaps had no complaint in that they had agreed to come to Japan at this low salary, but once there they increasingly resented it.

A general skepticism as to just what the American mission was accomplishing soon found its way into the newspapers both in Japan and America. The English-owned *Japan Mail,* reflecting British antagonism toward the entire project, possibly because it was American-directed, not only attacked General Capron but said the colonization scheme had "no more roots than an artificial flower." In October, 1872, an article in the *Nation,* in New York, found fault with most of the American experts attached to the Kaitakushi, but especially singled out their chief. It stated that he had been no more than a laughingstock while he was with the Department of Agriculture and, quoting a letter from Tokyo, added that in Japan he was proving himself to be "almost useless."

This contemporary criticism, as well as some of the experts' later memories of a "niggling and back-biting feud," exaggerated the general picture. Undoubtedly General Capron put on impossible airs and greatly irritated many of his American colleagues. But he kept things going. Moreover, as already noted, he appears to have stood in very well with the higher Japanese authorities.

Most important, substantial progress was being made in Hokkaido itself. On his later visits to the island, Capron noted a consistent improvement in conditions, in spite of the continuing burden of Japanese bureaucracy, and he found his faith renewed in the over-all program. The farmers were being taught how to develop their farming techniques more efficiently, the native cattle were being bred to imported bulls, merino sheep had been introduced, and many new varieties of both fruit and vegetables were being grown.

The American mission was also proving its usefulness in many other ways, from setting up a canning and fishing industry to supervising the construction of new roads. It also drew up plans for a railroad, which a little later was successfully built under the direction of Colonel Joseph U. Crawford, of the Pennsylvania Railroad, and conducted a number of topographical and geological surveys that were to prove of great value in making known Hokkaido's actual and potential resources in coal and petroleum.

The most valuable survey was one made in 1873 by Benjamin Smith Lyman, a geologist and mining engineer, whom Capron had selected as the mission's chief expert in these fields. A graduate of Harvard, Lyman had studied in both Germany and France, and in addition to previous practical experience in the United States had carried out geological surveys in India. Unlike some members of the mission, he was thoroughly loyal to the Kaitakushi and its objectives, got along well with General Capron, and also both liked and respected the Japanese. He was an outgoing, friendly person who ignored the internal bickerings of the mission, and his correspondence reveals both the warmth of his personality and an appealing sense of humor. In the long report he made after completing his geological survey, Lyman said that he hoped General Capron would not take amiss his inclusion of occasional amusing incidents and even small jokes; they were an attempt to relieve the report's "dreary waste of dryness."

In addition to his careful geological information, Lyman describes the wild, wooded country of Hokkaido's interior and the rough living conditions that the surveying party experienced during its six months of exploratory work. But they found the Ainus, who lived by fishing and hunting, invariably friendly. They welcomed the strange foreigners to their native villages, supplying them with the meat of the deer and bear so plentiful in the forested interior.

Lyman was optimistic about Hokkaido's resources, and also over the future of Japan. It was his sincere purpose, as he wrote Capron, to do everything he could to help the Japanese realize the full potentialities of their country. He wished above all else to be of such service as he could to "the sleeping beauty that the young Prince (America) came to awaken to fresh life and renewed loveliness."

His interest led him to stay on in Japan after completing his work in Hokkaido and for six years he lived in Tokyo, working with his geological students, serving as an adviser to the government and writing learned papers on various aspects of Japanese life. Few foreigners in this period adapted themselves more completely to the ways of the country. Lyman lived in a Japanese house, ate native food and wore the kimono. After his return to the United States, he continued to keep in touch with his students and assistants until his death at the age of eighty-six.

With the redevelopment program in Hokkaido proceeding somewhat haltingly but still commanding government support, General Capron himself returned to the United States in January, 1875. However, before he left, he made a further recommendation to the Kaitakushi that was to have quite as important consequences as anything else he did. This was a proposal that the agricultural school that had been originally set up at Tokyo should be raised to college rank and moved to Sapporo, and that William Smith Clark, the president of the Massachusetts Agricultural College, be invited to undertake its organization and serve as its first president.

Kuroda Kiyotaka acted promptly on this suggestion, and the next year Clark arrived in Japan to carry through what would prove to be one of the most successful ventures that may be attributed to the American mission's over-all program. Today William Smith Clark is better remembered in Japan than Horace Capron. His lasting monument is Hokkaido University, which in 1956, eighty years after his arrival at Sapporo, dedicated in his memory a most impressive William Smith Clark Memorial Student Center.

A graduate of Amherst College in the class of 1848, Clark had studied abroad for a time and then returned to his alma mater as an instructor in chemistry and botany. He fought with the Union Army during the Civil War, once narrowly escaping capture when he found himself trapped behind enemy lines, and was promoted to a colonelcy. At the end of the war he returned again to Amherst to pursue his scientific studies (resulting most notably in a paper on the circulation of sap in sugar maples), and became increasingly interested in agriculture. Made a member of the Massachusetts State Board of Agriculture, he was then instrumental in founding the college of which he was president when he came to Japan.

Nothing in this background foreshadows the amazing success that Clark achieved in Hokkaido. But he was a man of immense enthusiasm, forceful and dynamic, imbued with a deep religious faith, and he somehow managed to communicate this enthusiasm and this faith to the Japanese with whom he came in contact. Inspiring both affection and loyalty, he made an impression that greatly influenced not only the lives of his own students, many of whom were to win later prominence, but even those who came after him.

Clark reached Sapporo on July 31, 1876. He was accompanied by Kuroda Kiyotaka, demonstrating the importance attached to the establishment of the new college, and also by two young American instructors and sixteen Japanese students. "I have very good rooms in a large new government building," Clark wrote his brother-in-law, "including porches, verandahs, bathrooms, etc. etc. For company I have Professors Wheeler, Penhallow and Naito who serves as official interpreter. We keep a cook and two servant boys and live very well." Two weeks after Clark had moved into this building, the college was officially opened. Its president gave an inspirational talk to the "young gentlemen," a local historian has written, that had a profound effect in encouraging their "lofty ambitions."

In organizing the new school, Clark based its curriculum on that of the Massachusetts Agricultural College, set up a model farm to introduce American crops (including beans and tomatoes), established a military unit among the students and hopefully encouraged field sports. As a deeply religious man, he was also prepared to act on the assumption that the moral education of his students was quite as important as, or more important than, their training in agriculture.

The latter question had arisen in discussion with Kuroda when the Japanese official asked Clark how he intended to handle this phase of the school program. Having bought thirty translations of the Bible while in Yokohama, Clark is said to have replied that he intended to teach the Christian gospel. Kuroda promptly objected, "You shall not. Jesus-religion is prohibited by the authorities." But Clark stuck to his guns, and as soon as the opportunity offered, he distributed his Bibles.

As a consequence of this first step in religious training, the students at Sapporo became "believers in Jesus" and adopted a covenant in which they asserted their faith in Christianity and pledged themselves to abstain from any use of opium, tobacco or alcoholic liquors, and to foreswear both gambling and profane language. It was a pledge that has had a lasting influence in what is now Hokkaido University. It is today one of Japan's major governmental institutions, not a Christian college, but the strict

rules governing the Clark Memorial Student Center follow the
pattern of the covenant signed by a handful of Christian students
in 1876.

Clark actually stayed at Sapporo only eight months. When he
left on April 16, 1877, some twenty-five pupils and friends accompanied him part way as he rode to what is now Chitose, the
site of an American air base, on the first stage of his journey
home. After having had lunch with his companions, Clark went on
alone. Mounting his horse he waved farewell and, according to
legend, called back his parting message to the youth of Japan:
"Boys, be ambitious." The glowing exhortation, so much in keep-
ing with the spirit of the new Japan, was to be picked up and
spread throughout the land in the new schoolbooks. Even today
Japanese boys know it well, and an impressive monument marks
the place where Clark gave voice to this popular slogan.

After his return to the United States, Clark resumed the presidency of the Massachusetts Agricultural College, but he shortly
resigned to plan a new enterprise which he called the "Floating
College," in anticipation of several similar projects nearly half a
century later, for the instruction of American students on a round-
the-world voyage visiting the countries of both Europe and Asia.
In an attempt to raise money for this venture, he became involved
in mining operations in Nevada. They were a complete failure and
his scheme for a Floating College never materialized.

His life after his brief stay in Hokkaido may have been an
unhappy anticlimax, but the Japanese did not forget him. On the
fiftieth anniversary of the founding of the agricultural college, its
president, Baron Sato, who had been one of Clark's pupils and
subsequently a classmate of Woodrow Wilson at Johns Hopkins,
stated: "It is fifty years since the departure of President Clark but
our admiration for him has increased with the years, and the words
dropped here and there by our great master seem to guide us till
the ages come."

The over-all results of the American contribution to the Kaitakushi's program in the development of Hokkaido are hard to
evaluate. General Capron was overwhelmed with praise when he
left Japan and the Emperor graciously accorded him the Second
Order of the Rising Sun. Judge Bingham, the American minister,

was also enthusiastic over what he had accomplished for Hokkaido, or, as he called it, Yesso, and wrote Capron a highly eulogistic letter:

When you left it, a State was formed and what is essential . . . the introduction of the industries and the appliances which will secure food, clothing and shelter to a nation. . . . Long after you shall have joined those who have gone before you, when Yesso shall be covered with cattle and sheep and fields of golden wheat and corn, will it be said of you, "this was the work of General Capron."

Such glowing, rhapsodic predictions have not been fully realized, and even in the late 1870's it became clear that Hokkaido's progress was beginning to lose the original momentum imparted to it by the American mission.

One visitor at this time was the English traveler, Isabella L. Bird, an adventurous and intrepid woman who before coming to Japan had ridden and camped, quite by herself, in the Western wilds of America and written of her experiences in A Lady's Life in the Rockies. On visiting Hokkaido in 1878, she again traveled by horseback, living alone among the Ainus except for her Japanese interpreter. Describing these adventures in a further book, Unbeaten Tracks in Japan, she gave a picture of Sapporo which first confirmed the predominant American influence in the establishment of the new capital. Sapporo, Mrs. Bird wrote, was

a town of 3,000 people laid out on the plan of an American city, with wide rectangular streets, lined by low Japanese houses and shops, and tasteless, detached, frame houses. The American idea is further suggested by the Kaitakushi offices with a capitol copied from the capitol at Washington. Besides the Government buildings and those which have been previously mentioned there is a hospital under the charge of an American doctor.

She also singled out the agricultural school ("on the model of the Massachusetts Agricultural College") and wrote approvingly of its American teachers, the model farms and the various projects under way for improving the breed of cattle and horses.

More generally, however, Mrs. Bird was exceedingly skeptical of the Kaitakushi's program. She reported that immense sums were being spent for Hokkaido's improvement but that in many instances the money had been "sunk in unprofitable and costly experiments" or was "eaten up by superfluous officials, who draw salaries and perpetrate 'squeezes,' and do little besides smoke and talk." She also noted particularly that while the climatic conditions in the Ishikari Valley were admirably suited for growing cereal crops, many thousands of acres of good grassland remained completely undeveloped.

The fact was that the Kaitakushi had failed to attract as many settlers to Hokkaido as it had originally hoped to do and its over-ambitious program was grinding to a halt. The government began to lose interest in the whole scheme and cut down appropriations. Finally, in 1881, it abolished the Kaitakushi altogether. By the close of the century, as one contemporary report indicated, the Sapporo Agricultural College appeared to be "the last remnant" of the vast undertaking so hopefully initiated at the opening of the 1870's.

Yet this is not the whole story. Even though it proved to be impossible to transform Hokkaido overnight into a great wheat-growing area comparable to America's own West, the work of the Kaitakushi and the American mission was to have an enduring value. The services of General Capron and his associates pointed the way toward Hokkaido's more effective development and provided a basis for the new reconstruction program, somewhat along the lines of the Kaitakushi's experiment, which has been launched in recent years.

Among other local authorities in Sapporo, the historian Osaka Shingo, who as a graduate of what is now Hokkaido University considers himself "a grandson disciple" of William Smith Clark, has paid warm tribute to the American mission of the 1870's. It was General Capron, he has written, who more than any other single individual may be held responsible for revolutionizing the island's agricultural economy. His work and that of the American specialists enlisted under his banner, in Osaka's words, laid "the cornerstone of the development of Hokkaido" even though nearly a century was to pass before their dream began to be fully realized.

11

The Japanese in America

A GOOD MANY YEARS after Commodore Perry first sailed into the Bay of Yedo, "Mr. Dooley," the irrepressible sage created by Finley Peter Dunne, had occasion to comment on things Japanese. "Whin we rapped on the dure," said Mr. Dooley, "we didn't go in, they came out."

In spite of the Americans living in Japan during the early years of Meiji, there was much truth in this remark. The Japanese did come out, and the greater number of those leaving their own shores came to the United States. There had been in 1860 the first Japanese embassy to travel abroad, parading up Broadway to the admiration of Walt Whitman; within six years, the forerunners of many others, two pioneer Japanese students arrived to study at Rutgers College, and in the early 1870's Kuroda Kiyotaka was only one among the many officials of the new Japanese Government visiting the United States.

"We come to study your strength," the future statesman, Ito Hirobumi, declared at a banquet tendered the Iwakura mission in Sacramento in 1872, "that, by adopting wisely your better ways, we may hereafter be stronger ourselves."

The cultural exchange between America and Japan in the latter half of the nineteenth century was primarily characterized by the westward flow of ideas and institutions across the Pacific. Quite as important as the role of the Americans who went to teach in Japan's new schools or to advise her new government was that of the Japanese who visited and studied in the United States in order to bring back to their own country further Western knowledge.

The intense desire among the educated classes to learn something more of the West than could be discovered through the writings of the "Dutch scholars" was dramatically illustrated as early as the time of Commodore Perry's visit. Two samurai— teachers and scholars—tried to smuggle themselves aboard one of the American ships, in brave defiance of the rigid proscription against any Japanese leaving the country, in order to make their way to the United States.

The attempt was made on the night of April 25, 1854, when the two Japanese pulled alongside the frigate *Mississippi* in a small boat and asked by signs to be taken aboard ship. They were sent off to the flagship. There, after casting off their little boat, they mounted to the gangway and when an interpreter had been summoned, made known their desire to be taken to America. The deck officer consulted Commodore Perry but soon returned to tell the Japanese that however much the commander might like to grant their request, he could not possibly condone what would be a violation of Japanese law. Even when they stated that if returned to the shore they would probably lose their heads, Perry stood firmly by a decision which his official role made inescapable. "A boat was now lowered," the official record states, "and after some mild resistance on their part, they descended the gangway piteously deploring their fate, and were landed at a spot near where it was supposed their boat might have drifted."

The next day Moriyama Einosuke, the Japanese interpreter so friendly with the Americans, came aboard the *Powhatan* to inquire if "last night a couple of Japanese had gone off to one of the American vessels." The flag lieutenant told him that while it was impossible to account for all visitors, he was certain none had committed "a misdemeanor." This was not, however, the end of the affair. A few days later a shore party of naval officers learned that the two Japanese had been found and arrested by the authorities, and on their walk they came upon them confined in "a kind of cage." On the Americans' approach, one of them, Yoshida

Shoin, later to become very well known, handed the officers a message:

When a hero fails in his purpose, his acts are then regarded as those of a villain and a robber. . . . Regarding the liberty of going through the sixty States [of Japan] as not enough for our desires, we wished to make the circuit of the five continents. . . . Suddenly our plans are defeated, and we find ourselves in a half-sized house, where eating, resting, sitting and sleeping are difficult; how can we find our exit from this place? Weeping, we seem as fools; laughing, as rogues. Alas! for us, silent we can only be.

The officers of Perry's squadron never learned of the two men's final fate, but Yoshida's story is well known. He was kept in custody for some time, but after writing a number of pamphlets upholding the Shogunate against its critics, he was released and returned to his teaching. Soon afterward, however, he became convinced that only a unified rule could save Japan. Having turned against the Shogunate for its weakness in the face of foreign threats and called for a revolutionary uprising, he was rearrested, brought to Yedo and there beheaded.

His nationalistic fervor was reflected in a contemporary poem:

Even if the Americans
With the Europeans as allies
Come to invade us,
If our defence is strong,
There is nothing to fear.

Our defence
Is not the warship and the cannon,
But it is our Japanese spirit.

Yoshida's attempt to get abroad had failed, but it was to acquire a symbolic significance with the passing years, repeatedly recounted by Japanese writers and even inspiring a story by Robert Louis Stevenson. The determination of this daring samurai to learn what he could of the West, if only to aid Japan in resisting its encroachments, and his willingness to risk his life in support of his principles, came to be accepted as proof of an ardent patriotism that has made Yoshida an almost legendary hero.[1]

[1] On reading this manuscript the late Kazuo Kawai, an historian of Japanese-American relations in the 1940's, made an interesting comment: "I think you are being overgenerous in your appraisal of Yoshida Shoin. He had

Even before the unsuccessful attempt of the two samurai to board a ship that might take them to the United States, several Japanese had inadvertently—as we have seen—found themselves in America as a consequence of having been shipwrecked and rescued at sea by Yankee whalers. Nakahama Manjiro is the only one of these men whose story is fully known, but there were a number of others of whom at least some record has survived. Commodore Perry had originally planned to return several such castaways, who had been temporary residents of the United States, but they were too fearful of the possible fate awaiting them in Japan to be willing to risk such a venture. One of them nevertheless sailed with the Japan expedition aboard the frigate *Susquehanna* as a common seaman, and another later joined the crew of the *Mississippi*. Both these men subsequently found their way back to their native land.

The first, a fisherman named Senpacki whom the sailors called "Sam Patch," became during the course of his voyage a protégé of Jonathan Goble, the marine who had sailed with the Perry squadron and then returned to Japan as a missionary and invented the jinrikisha. His patron first took Sam Patch home with him to Hamilton, New York, and then brought him back to Yokohama. The young Japanese, however, had neither the education nor the ability to play any such role in his own country as had Manjiro. The early reports of Yokohama occasionally refer to him, and William Elliot Griffis states that he eventually became a cook for an American teacher in Shizuoka. His notoriety as a man who had lived in the United States somewhat "spoiled his pristine virtue," according to Griffis, and his new employer found his head was somewhat turned. He died in 1874, and his grave at Oki, near Tokyo, bore the simple inscription "Sam Patch."

The fate of the second seaman, whose Japanese name was Iwakichi but somehow became in English "Dan Ketch," was rather more dramatic. When he made his way back to Japan in 1859 after visiting the United States aboard the *Mississippi*, he managed to secure a post as an interpreter at the British legation. He now aped Western ways, wore Western clothes, and went about with a Colt revolver on his hip "to swagger and defy his

---

his noble and idealistic side, but he was also an almost comical bungler and crackpot, and he became an inspiration to some of the worst fascistic ultra-nationalists of the 1930's."

countrymen." Their resentment of his behavior mounted until on a day in late January, 1860, a band of *ronin* openly assailed Dan Ketch and slashed him so severely that he died of his wounds.

A far more interesting and better known case of a Japanese returning in these mid-century years from residence in the United States is that of Joseph Heco. His name repeatedly crops up in the annals of Yokohama, where he lived for many years, and he ultimately wrote the story of his life, which was edited and published in 1892 by James Murdoch under the title *Joseph Heco— The Narrative of a Japanese.*

In the summer of 1850, then a boy of fourteen, Heco was on a Japanese junk sailing between Yedo and Osaka. Overtaken by a sudden storm the little craft was completely dismasted, and Heco was to undergo a series of adventures not unlike those which Nakahama Manjiro had experienced nine years earlier. After drifting helplessly for fifty-one days, his junk encountered the American bark *Auckland*. She rescued the starving crew and took them to San Francisco. After spending a year there the Japanese seamen were deported to Hong Kong for possible transshipment to Japan, but Heco (together with two of his companions) came back again to San Francisco. Having learned a good deal of English, the young Japanese now found a job with the customs service, and the Collector of the Port became so interested in him that he promised to provide him an opportunity to get a real education.

The next surprising step in Heco's career was that Senator Gwin of California, whom he seems to have impressed quite as favorably as he had the Collector of the Port, took him east to New York and Washington. After meeting various important political figures, including President Pierce, Heco then entered a Catholic school in Baltimore. He remained in the United States six more years, became converted to Christianity and took out American citizenship. Nonetheless it was always his ambition to return to Japan. Although disappointed in his hope that he might be able to secure some sort of American diplomatic appointment, he sailed for Yokohama in 1859 and there found a job as interpreter at the newly opened American consulate.

Heco recorded many of his impressions of the United States in his *Narrative*. As a young boy he had been both frightened and mystified by this strange new world, never quite knowing what was going to happen to him next. There is one story of how he and his companions, when taken aboard ship for the voyage to Hong Kong, had no idea of what was in store for them and no way even to ask: "We fell on our knees and prayed before the deck officer." On first going ashore at San Francisco, Heco was shocked by the custom of "murdering" cattle, astounded at seeing the men all dressed in dark clothes with "tall black boxes on their heads," and rather fearful of the Negroes on San Francisco's streets with their "black faces and white teeth and huge red lips." After being taken east by Senator Gwin, he saw new marvels, being especially curious about the telegraph and railroad train which "vibrated and undulated like a snake." On meeting President Pierce, he was no more able to believe than were the members of the Japanese embassy a few years later that this gentleman dressed in a plain, dark suit, without either guards or retainers, could possibly be the Chief of the Nation.

Heco remained some two years with the American consulate at Yokohama after his return to Japan. He would have liked to serve as interpreter with the Japanese mission in 1860 (Captain Brooke, sailing aboard the *Kanrin Maru*, speaks of giving him a letter of recommendation), and when this post did not materialize, he left the consulate and in association with a number of American merchants set himself up in business. For a time he was quite successful, but Heco's staying power was never very great. He was soon off again to the United States, hoping this time that he could obtain the appointment of naval storekeeper at Yokohama for such a post "would entitle me," as he wrote in the *Narrative*, "to wear gold bands on my cap and so place me on an equal footing with native officials."

After arriving in Washington on this second visit, Heco managed to see both Secretary Seward and President Lincoln but he did not obtain the post he coveted and so returned to Yokohama to resume his activities as a merchant. He published in 1863 a first account of his travels, two years later set up a Japanese newspaper, and for a time was attached to the Bureau of Currency in Tokyo, which was engaged in establishing a monetary system on the American model. There were often occasions when his unique status as a Japanese-born American citizen enabled him to act as a useful emissary between American and Japanese officials, and he had a wide acquaintance among the government leaders of the day, including such a prominent figure as Ito Hirobumi. Nevertheless Heco remained torn between his two worlds, belonging to neither the one nor the other, and never really distinguished himself as either a Japanese or an American. His account of his life in the United States provides his only distinctive claim to a place in history.

When the Japanese embassy sailed from Yokohama in 1860, there was aboard the *Kanrin Maru* a youthful samurai who had attached himself to the mission in the role of servant to the ship's captain. This young man, driven by the same insatiable curiosity to learn more of the West that had led Yoshida Shoin to try to smuggle himself aboard one of Commodore Perry's ships, was Fukuzawa Yukichi. This first visit to America of the man destined to become Japan's foremost educator during the Meiji era was wholly to convert him to the cause of foreign studies. For the rest of his life Fukuzawa was a determined and zealous exponent of Western learning, exerting an impressive and lasting influence on the whole intellectual climate of the new Japan.

He was the son of a rather unimportant samurai official in Nakatsu, on the island of Kyushu, and while still a boy was consumed by an intellectual curiosity which could not be restrained within the barriers that attempted to seal off all knowledge of the West. His early life, restricted by the traditional conventions of his clan, he was later to write in his famous *Autobiography*, was "like being packed tightly in a lunch box." Three years after the arrival of the Perry expedition, at the age of twenty-one, he broke away from his family and clan to live at Osaka where he could take up the study of Dutch as the best means, so he then thought, of acquiring the golden key to Western knowledge. He was not a pale, retiring, scholarly recluse, but, as he relates with great pride, a vigorous, active, fun-loving young man. He was able to spend prodigiously long hours over his studies, sometimes working right through the night, but he was also "an accomplished drinker" who could happily desert his books for an evening of boisterous fun.

Fukuzawa finally realized that Dutch was not the complete open sesame to knowledge that he had thought, and that he would have to learn English. In 1859 he went to Yedo where there were opportunities for such study and apparently worked even harder than at Osaka. But his ambition went far beyond learning English: he was determined somehow to get abroad. When he heard of the projected mission to America, he succeeded somehow in obtaining his job as a servant to the *Kanrin Maru*'s captain. This first trip overseas was limited to a brief stay in San Francisco, but it gave him a firsthand knowledge of Western civilization. Fukuzawa brought home a copy of Webster's Dictionary. "Once having secured this valuable work," he wrote, "I felt no disappointment on leaving the new world and returning home again."

The antiforeign feeling so rampant in Japan at this time served only to strengthen his determination to encourage Western learning. He was fully convinced that the popular movement to expel the barbarians could only result in impairing Japan's power and prestige, and he made it his goal to do everything he could to change the stubbornly conservative prejudices of his fellow countrymen. There was a good deal of arrogance as well as a sense of dedication in his attitude. This highly intelligent young man, handsome, spirited, with the high forehead that suggested his intellectual force, was never one to suffer fools gladly. His personal conceit as well as his glowing idealism are both reflected in the lively pages of his *Autobiography*.

Fukuzawa was never to be carried away by the extravagant imitation of foreign customs that swept over Japan at the opening of the Meiji era; his interest was in ideas rather than in fashions and manners. He cared very little, as William Elliot Griffis wrote of him, for "the merely external garnish and glitter of civilization." He would continue throughout his life to study, to translate, to write and to teach with the sole purpose of making available to his countrymen the basic sources of Western knowledge, particularly in the fields of science and medicine. His first important book was *The Conditions in the West*, which created a sensation when it was published in 1869. Four years later he brought out an even more popular work, *The Encouragement of Learning*. Its emphasis on equality ("All men are equal, without distinction as to high or low, noble or humble") had an immense appeal. More than

700,000 copies of this book were reported to have been sold, "causing a rise in the price of paper in the capital."

Fukuzawa made several additional trips abroad after his first visit to America in 1860. Two years later he accompanied a Japanese mission to both Europe and the United States, and then in 1867 visited America for a third time, bringing back with him dictionaries, geographies, histories and other books that might be translated and used as school texts. In spite of consistent pressure he refused to enter government service. Education, enlightening his countrymen as to their responsibilities in the new age which Japan was entering, remained his consuming interest. During his life he published something like a hundred books, pamphlets and articles, founded the newspaper *Jiji Shimpo*, and established in Tokyo the school that was to become Keio University. "The final purpose of all my work," Fukuzawa wrote, "was to create in Japan a civilized nation, as well equipped in both the arts of war and peace as those of the Western World."

Neither during Fukuzawa's lifetime nor in later years was Japan ever fully to adopt the the American-inspired democracy, the principles of political and social equality, that this great educator sought to inculcate among his countrymen. Still, Fukuzawa had a great part in the evolution of modern Japan. Inspired by the visions born of his first fleeting visit to the United States, and always greatly influenced by American ideals, no one labored more assiduously to bring Japan in line with Western civilization. Chitoshi Yanaga has written:

His unique role was the liquidation of feudal Japan and its vestiges to build up a new Japan unfettered by the old customs, manners, morality, and old concepts of politics and economics. The realization of equality, freedom and independence was his goal. . . . Fukuzawa contributed immeasurably to the development of Meiji ideas and institutions.

Four years after Fukuzawa's first trip still another young samurai, who escaped Japan by smuggling himself aboard an American schooner, visited the United States. He too was destined in later years to become an important educator, and was even more directly influenced by American ideas and institutions. For Niijima Jo—or, as he was known among foreigners, Joseph Hardy

Neesima—was to stay in the United States some ten years, become converted to Christianity, and on returning to Japan win a place for himself as the foremost native Christian leader of his day.

The backgrounds of Fukuzawa and Niijima were very much alike: both were born of samurai families, were early awakened to an immense curiosity about the West, became avid students first of Dutch and then of English, and were obsessed with the idea of getting to America. While Fukuzawa found his opportunity with a Japanese mission, Niijima had to leave the country by stealth, but both of them served as servant boys in crossing the Pacific. In their later careers they were again alike in abjuring politics and devoting their lives to education.

Niijima's interest in the United States was first aroused by reading about it in an early atlas. "I liked it very much," he later wrote in one of his student essays while in America, "and I thought that a government of every country must be as President of the United States, and murmured myself that, O Governor of Japan! why you keep down us a dog or a pig? We are people of Japan." When his ambition to visit America was finally fulfilled, the twenty-one-year-old youth, sensitive and diffident but with an unwavering singleness of purpose, prepared to get a thorough Western education.

The owner of the ship which Niijima surreptitiously boarded was Alpheus Hardy, a prominent Boston merchant and a member of the governing committee of the American Board of Commissioners for Foreign Missions. He was very much impressed by the ambitious Japanese lad and on reaching the United States undertook to send him through Phillips Andover Academy and Amherst College. Niijima was hard-working and conscientious. Once he had become a devout Christian, there would be no release from his studies in convivial drinking or other college pranks. He graduated from Amherst in 1870 and then went on to study for the ministry at the Andover Theological Seminary.

There was one interruption in this studious career. When the Iwakura mission visited Boston in the course of its American tour in 1872, Niijima served it as an interpreter and then went on with it to Europe. But he returned to complete his theological studies at Andover and on being ordained announced his intention to found a Christian college in Japan. At a meeting of the American Board at Rutland, Vermont, in 1874, he pleaded his cause so eloquently that he won its official support and an initial subscription of $5,000. This step was the genesis of the Doshisha—or "Same Purpose Company"—which three years later was to establish Doshisha College with an entering class of eight students. Associated with Niijima and an early faculty member was the American missionary Jerome D. Davis, and, as we have already seen, Daniel Crosby Greene joined the staff somewhat later.

The college found itself facing tremendous odds in conservative Kyoto because of the violent opposition of the Buddhist priests. But while Niijima had to agree not to teach the Bible to his students, he unabashedly strove to inculcate Christian ethics through courses in moral science. From its foundation Doshisha had a predominantly religious atmosphere. Moreover, its Christian character was greatly strengthened when thirty new students professing the Western faith transferred to Doshisha from a provincial school at Kumamoto, in Kyushu.

This school had been set up by the daimio of Kumamoto, who was primarily interested in the military education of the young samurai of his clan and had appointed as headmaster Captain L. L. Janes, a onetime West Pointer with strong religious convictions. Janes gave his charges a strict, disciplinary training, and under his influence they also adopted Christianity. The attitude of the local officials was decidedly hostile to Christians, however, and the students making up what became known as "the Kumamoto band," including a number of young men who later became very prominent, consequently decided to transfer to Doshisha. They felt they could more successfully continue their education there in dedication to the spiritual reform of their country.

With these and other recruits the enrollment at Doshisha rose in its third year from eight to one hundred. Niijima was encouraged to continue the development of the college along the lines of such American institutions, with which he was fully familiar, as Amherst and Oberlin. He engaged additional American teachers, stressed strongly both morality and science in the curriculum, and declared his purpose to be that of working incessantly for a new Japan. His task was a difficult one: slowly winning the support of the authorities and the Buddhist priests in Kyoto, and struggling always for greater financial support. He made several further trips to the United States in the latter cause, and succeeded gradually in building up through American gifts a substantial endowment.

Before Niijima's death in 1890 at the age of forty-seven (his health had always been precarious), Doshisha had added a girls' school to the original boys' college, developed a full program for Japanese entering the Christian ministry, and attained an enrollment of over a thousand students. The dedicated young man who had smuggled himself aboard a merchant vessel as a first step toward studying in the United States had won wide recognition as a pioneer in Christian education. The school he had founded on such distinctively American lines stood out as one of Japan's leading private colleges, as indeed Doshisha University still does.

While Fukuzawa and Niijima were the most conspicuous pioneers among the young Japanese samurai who sought Western knowledge through direct experience abroad, a number of others were soon eagerly following their example. Even though antiforeign agitation was still a powerful force in the mid-1860's, both officials of the Shogunate and some of the more enlightened daimio were secretly prepared to help such young men get abroad to both Europe and America. However hostile Japan's leaders may have been to the West, they realized that only by learning its science and technology could their country ever hope to resist effectively the danger of further foreign encroachments. The first of these other students to come to the United States appear to have been the two young samurai who began their work at Rutgers in 1866 in accordance with the advice and help of Guido Verbeck. They were immediatley followed by quite a few others, but their number is not known.

The objectives of these students whom either the Shogunate or the daimio sent abroad were under the circumstances more limited than those of Fukuzawa and Niijima. They had a very particular purpose. On being asked about it, the first two going to Rutgers clearly reflected the spirit of the times by answering, according to Nitobe Inazo, that it was to learn how to build "big ships" and make "big guns" to prevent the European powers from taking possession of their country. It was self-defense rather than scientific or industrial progress which justified sending students abroad at a time when the official regulation still proscribed leaving the country.

When Japan's civil war first broke out in 1867, most of these young men were recalled, but they returned to their own country deeply impressed by the superior advantages of foreign institutions. Griffis met a number of them in the early 1870's and spoke of them as "flushed with enthusiastic sympathy with the modern civilization of Christendom." Some of them, as in the better-known cases of Fukuzawa and Niijima, translated Western books or wrote of their own experiences in order to acquaint their countrymen with what was happening in the outside world. They all had a part in instigating the craze for things foreign which was so soon to sweep over the country.

The real impetus for foreign study, however, followed upon the restoration of the Emperor and the pronouncement in his charter oath that "knowledge shall be sought for all over the world." The new government adopted in 1871 an ambitious program to send abroad two carefully selected students from every han in the empire. The greater number of them at this time were destined for America, both because of its relative nearness to Japan and because of the friendly reception accorded those who had already studied there. Griffis wrote in May, 1871, that four hundred Japanese students were slated to leave for the United States within the next two months, and when the Iwakura mission visited Washington the next year, it reported that something like five hundred had at one time or another already been in America.

These figures were greatly exaggerated. From more reliable sources it is estimated that no more than two hundred Japanese students came to the United States under the original government program, and that the over-all total for the entire period 1865 to 1885 probably did not exceed three hundred. Admittedly, there can be no exactness about such statistics. Also, in later years, confusion would be further confounded by the practice of the Japanese Government in giving far more passports for study in the United States than can be accounted for in the American immigration records.

The students in this period were almost invariably the sons of samurai. This was the class, rather than the daimio or court nobles, which was creating, with courage and imagination, the new Japan, and the older generation wished to have their children trained to meet the needs of the modern age. Moreover, it was only samurai, generally speaking, who would have been eligible for the government grants. So it was that these Japanese youth laid aside their swords, shaved off their topknots and abandoned the kimono to take passage across the Pacific and begin their foreign studies at schools or colleges scattered throughout the United States.

Some of them stayed on the West Coast, but the greater number went to Eastern schools. If Rutgers had the earliest associations with Japan, due to Guido Verbeck, Amherst was also popular as a result of Niijima's influence. But a contemporary report by Nitobe Inazo indicates that the Japanese students were everywhere, especially in the technological and law schools. The Polytechnic Institute at Troy, New York, and DePauw University at Greencastle, Indiana, as well as Harvard and Yale, Princeton and Cornell, had their quotas of young men from Japan. During the 1870's there were even twelve Japanese students, by special Congressional permission, at Annapolis.

"Japan, once in the far-off Orient," Griffis wrote in 1876 with his customary enthusiasm, "is now our nearest Western neighbor. Her people walk our streets; her youth sit, peers and rivals of our students, in the classroom; her art adorns our homes, and has opened to us a new Gate Beautiful. . . . We hail the brightness of the rising of this first among Asiatic nations to enter modern life."

As sons of samurai, this first contingent of imperial scholars were youth of good family, carefully chosen from the elite of Japanese society, with ample financial resources. They were also industrious and hard-working. Nitobe, indeed, implies that they worked much too hard. "Physically of feebler calibre," he wrote, "their intense application has carried many bright youths to an untimely grave." As one of them himself, he was either less rigorous in his studies or of stouter constitution: he was to live to seventy-two.

What most distinguished these Japanese students, however, was their sense of national purpose and patriotic dedication. They were in the United States, it may again be noted, to learn whatever would best enable them to serve their country in adapting itself to the modern world.

The Japanese Government was to bring back a number of them, especially those below college rank, before they completed their work. This did not represent any basic change in imperial policy but rather a realization on the part of the officials in Tokyo that many of the students were too ill-prepared to be able to make the most of their opportunities. On the advice of a Japanese Educational Commission set up in Washington, it was to become general policy to have future students learn as much English as possible, and also fundamental science, before going abroad.

The movement for education in the United States drew much of its support from a number of American-oriented Japanese. They included Mori Arinori, the Japanese minister in Washington; Kuroda Kiyotaka, who had been greatly impressed with American education on his trip to recruit advisers for the Kaitakushi; Iwakura Tomomi, head of the mission known by his name, who left his two sons to study at Rutgers; and Fukuzawa Yukichi. Their points of view differed, but each of these men encouraged not only study abroad but particularly study in America.

Mori Arinori, who later became Minister of Education, stands out among all the Japanese leaders of this period for his championship of the United States as the Western country on which Japan might best model her new institutions. He wrote a keen analytical study, *Life and Resources in America*, helped the Japanese students in the United States in every possible way, and on his return to his own country cooperated with Fukuzawa in forming the Meirokusha, an association for study of the West. It provided a forum for the discussion of all the leading issues of the day, including feminism, freedom of the press and representative government. For a time it published a fortnightly magazine, but when the first popular absorption in the ways of the West began to subside, the Meirokusha was dissolved.

Kuroda's role in promoting American studies was related particularly to young women. He had been above all interested in female education when he visited the United States and became convinced that Japanese girls should be given comparable opportunities and also a chance to study abroad. As a result of his urgent advice, the Iwakura mission included among the fifty-four young students it was taking abroad five girls, their ages ranging from eight to fifteen, who were placed in various American schools. The experiment was a success. Two of the girls graduated from Vassar and one from Bryn Mawr; the very youngest of the group, having gone through the entire American school system, had a specially distinguished career. The project gave substantial encouragement to the whole idea of advanced education for Japanese women both at home and abroad.

As for the role of Fukuzawa Yukuchi, no one sponsored American studies more vigorously throughout this entire period. "He preaches through his paper to the young men," wrote Nitobe, "with the authoritative voice of a Horace Greeley, bidding them 'go west.'"

The impressions that the Japanese of this period took home with them were not always completely favorable. In 1872 Charles Lanman, an American serving as secretary to the Japanese legation in Washington, gathered together a little collection of student essays in a book that was first published as *The Japanese in America*, and later reissued as *Leaders of the Meiji Restoration in America*. They reveal that the students could be highly critical of certain aspects of Western civilization as well as appreciative of what America was doing for Japan "in awakening her from a long sleep." They were often skeptical of the "higher morality" that Americans professed. They politely questioned the need for the United States to send its missionaries to "the heathen" in order to teach them to be "good."

Megata Tanetaro, a future director of the Tax Bureau, was one of the early students whose life had many interesting American contacts. He arrived in the United States in 1870 with letters from Guido Verbeck, and after going to a preparatory school, graduated from Harvard with a law degree. He knew well Mori Arinori in Washington, was a friend of Niijima while at Cambridge, and helped to guide the members of the Iwakura mission when it came to Boston. Megata would later recall that at the great banquet given the embassy the final speaker was Ralph Waldo Emerson, who "expressed noble sentiments about Japan and Bushido." Megata was commissioned by his country's Department of Education to collect American textbooks, and he also helped to secure the services of Luther Whiting Mason in introducing Western music to Japan. Some forty years after his student days, he returned to the United States as head of a World War I financial mission.

Even more prominent in later days was Kaneko Kentaro, the young son of a samurai family and one of the students who accompanied the Iwakura mission in 1872. He also went to Harvard, where he came to know Theodore Roosevelt, and under the guidance of Oliver Wendell Holmes took up the study of law. After his return to Japan he became politically active. Kaneko assisted Ito in drawing up the constitution of 1889, was one of the founders of the Seiyukai Party and later served as Minister of Justice. At the time of the Russo-Japanese War his government sent him to the United States to build up popular support for Japan. In Washington he renewed his earlier friendships with Roosevelt and Holmes, now respectively President of the United States and an Associate Justice of the Supreme Court.

The letters in the correspondence Kaneko maintained with both Roosevelt and Holmes offer a great deal of evidence of how he was influenced by American ideals and also of how he influenced his correspondents' ideas about Japan. "It seems to me, my dear Baron," Roosevelt once wrote Kaneko, "that Japan has much to teach the nations of the Occident, just as she has something to learn from them. . . . Certainly I myself hope that I have learned not a little from the fine Samurai spirit, and from the ways in which that spirit has been and is being transformed to meet the needs of modern life." This significant individual link between America and Japan was later broken. After the adoption of the Japanese exclusion law in 1924, Baron Kaneko indignantly resigned from the America-Japan Society which he had been instrumental in forming.

Among the many other students was Nitobe Inazo—so often quoted in this narrative—who came to the United States after studying at the Sapporo Agricultural College. He first went to Allegheny College and then undertook graduate work at Johns Hopkins, where he was a classmate of Woodrow Wilson and John Dewey. His monograph on Japanese-American intercourse, for which he received his Ph.D. in 1891, was only the first of a long series of writings (the most important perhaps was *Bushido, the Soul of Japan*) which made him a foremost interpreter of his country to the American public for some forty-odd years.

Nitobe's life had commenced at a time, as he recalled in his *Reminiscences*, when his countrymen still abhorred the beef-eating, milk-drinking barbarians, and it extended to those years when as a modernized and powerful empire, wholly adapted to the ways of the West, Japan embarked on the imperialist course that was ultimately to lead to war with America. As in the case of Kaneko, intense disappointment at the adoption of the Japanese exclusion law later turned Nitobe against the United States. Moreover, in contradiction of much that he had earlier said and written, he condoned Japan's imperialistic ambitions in the 1930's. Until these unhappy developments, however, no Japanese was more closely associated with the United States or tried in so many ways to build a peaceful bridge across the Pacific.

Just as American influence on educational developments within Japan fell off sharply after the 1870's, so did the role that the United States played as a host to Japanese students. Their actual number may have increased. While available statistics are at once very meager and often conflicting, the total of students coming to the United States in the 1880's has been estimated by Yamato Ichihashi in his studies of Japanese immigration as annually ranging from 196 to 481. What had happened, however, was that the Japanese Government was now limiting its financial support to students going to Europe. As a consequence, the general caliber of those in American schools and colleges was no longer comparable, either intellectually or socially, to that of the early pioneers.

Robert Schwantes has traced in his *Japanese and Americans* the subsequent careers of some 197 of the students in the group visiting the United States between 1865 and 1885. More than half of them came to occupy, he states, "positions of responsibility and influence in government, academic and business life." He lists a large number: ministerial officials, college presidents, outstanding bankers, officers in such important economic combines as the Mitsui and Mitsubishi enterprises. However, their successors did not have comparable potentialities and on their return to their own country had far less distinguished records. The part that the

United States had once played in training the men who were helping to shape the growth of Japan's modern institutions suffered a
significant decline.

The later students often made this country their second choice,
not only in respect to European universities but also in respect to
those in Japan. The competition for entry into the new Japanese
institutions of higher learning had become so intense that a very
considerable number of young men could not win admission and
then turned to the United States. They might not attempt to enter
ranking universities, but under missionary sponsorship enrolled in
small church schools where academic standards were not too
demanding. There were of course many exceptions to any such
generalization, but the fact remained that these young Japanese
simply did not come up to the standards of their forerunners.
Nitobe Inazo himself confessed in the 1890's to the "lowering of
the average intelligence of our students in America."

This shift toward Europe on the part of the better students
going abroad reflected those same forces that were in so many
other ways emphasizing the example of European rather than
American ideas and institutions. The German university was becoming the model in Japan's higher education, German political
principles had been incorporated in the new Japanese constitution,
and it was consequently natural for Germany to have a greater
appeal than the United States for study overseas. And in other
fields than government, economics and science, young Japan was
also turning away from America—to England for studies in literature and to France for studies in art.

Many of the students who did come to the United States had to
work their way through college and took on jobs as household
servants. In these circumstances they spent many years completing
their education, staying on until they were in their late twenties
or early thirties, and sometimes they strung out their studies almost endlessly, or abandoned them altogether to enjoy the economic advantages of American life. These were the students who
were so mercilessly caricatured in Wallace Irwin's somewhat later
stories of Hashimura Togo in *Letters of a Japanese School Boy*.

A few Japanese came to this country in the early days of Meiji
with the idea of settling permanently. At first these immigrants,
like the pioneer students, were from samurai families which had

enjoyed position and status under the Shogunate. Having lost their hereditary stipends and finding it difficult to adjust to the new Japan, they were drawn to America as "a golden country" of greater economic opportunity. Such immigrants totaled only a few hundred a year at the most, and in 1889 it was estimated there were less than fifteen hundred Japanese (including only seventy-seven women) in the United States altogether. About this time, however, the Japanese Government reversed an earlier policy which had withheld passports from "laborers," and the whole character of this immigration began to change. With peasants and fishermen swelling the total, the number of immigrants abruptly rose in the 1890's to an average of about 2,500 a year. By the close of the century, the Japanese population in this country, largely confined to the West Coast and especially California, was an approximate 24,000.

The early immigrants—so many of them samurai—came largely from northern Japan, where the clans had supported the Shogun rather than the Emperor in 1867 and the path to government service was often blocked. They were for the most part young men of education and ability, ambitious to get ahead, who hoped to enter into some sort of commercial activity in the United States. Some of them set up shops and import houses (the Yokohama Specie Bank had branch offices in New York and San Francisco in the 1880's) or developed other small mercantile enterprises. Those with neither funds nor practical experience often found their first jobs in this strange, new land in domestic service —as cooks, houseboys, gardeners—and then, after carefully saving their wages, established themselves in business.

The story of one well-born family making its way in America was told in later years in *A Daughter of the Samurai*, the autobiography of Etsu Inagaki Sugimoto. Her brother had preceded her to this country, and while he had returned to Japan after a rather unsuccessful experience, a family friend had become an art dealer with shops in both Chicago and Cincinnati. The young Etsu Inagaki crossed the Pacific to marry this friend of her brother and then made her new home in Ohio. Life was for a time difficult in these alien surroundings, but the Sugimotos successfully adjusted themselves to their new environment and they became thoroughly American in their outlook.

Upon her husband's death while their children were still very young, Mrs. Sugimoto took her two daughters back to Japan, but six years later returned to New York, where the girls went to school and college. Ultimately they all went back again to their native land; however, their close ties with America were never severed. Interestingly enough, one of the daughters married a grandson of that early pioneer in cementing American-Japanese relations, the famous educator Fukuzawa Yukichi.

In the 1890's the Japanese Government began to encourage emigration to the United States (and also to what was then an independent Hawaii) in view of the pressures exerted by a rapidly rising population and difficult economic conditions at home. An emigration section was set up in the Foreign Ministry and a private organization, the Mutual Association for Emigration Abroad, called for volunteers to establish Japanese communities overseas. The overwhelming number of those now coming to the United States were laborers. While some of them entered domestic service or found jobs in shops or restaurants, most of them became farm hands or took up truck gardening.

The increasing number of Japanese residents in this country by the close of the century and their heavy concentration in California foreshadowed what was soon to become "the Japanese problem." The seeds were being planted for the rabidly intolerant attitude that would in time make the immigration issue such a thorny problem in Japanese-American relations, ultimately leading to the exclusion law that so embittered Kaneko and Nitobe and the whole Japanese people. It was not, however, until after the turn of the century that any significant anti-Japanese feeling developed or the latent racial controversy took on real importance.

The Japanese coming to the United States, as visitors or as residents, quite obviously did not exert any such influence on American institutions as the Americans going to Japan exercised on Japanese life. They were not teachers, technical experts, government advisers or missionaries; on the contrary, they were for the most part students coming to this country to learn the ways of the West. Nonetheless the cultural flow was not entirely in one direction. American life was by no means unaffected, even in these early years, by the contacts that had developed between the United States and its somewhat distant Pacific neighbor.

Ever since the sailors aboard the American ships chartered by the Dutch East India Company for its trade at Nagasaki first brought home their "curios," Americans had continued to have a keen interest in Japanese arts and handicraft. They were soon found in many New England homes (the lacquered furniture Captain Devereux brought back in the *Franklin* is still preserved), and they became greatly prized possessions. This interest was then further stimulated by the gifts which the Japanese sent to the President on the occasion of Commodore Perry's visit and those later presented to the American officials who entertained the Japanese embassy in 1860. After the opening of the trade made possible by Townsend Harris' treaty, the demand grew for such imports as silks and porcelain, lacquerware and cloisonné, screens and paintings.

Japan encouraged this trade not only for its commercial benefit but as a means of demonstrating to the West the artistic values of her highly developed civilization. Her government participated in the Centennial Exhibition held in Philadelphia in 1876, not only with extensive displays of arts and crafts, but by erecting a Japanese "dwelling" which proved to be one of the exhibition's major attractions. It was widely admired—"as nicely put together," one viewer stated, "as a piece of cabinet work"—and inspired a lively interest in Japanese architecture. This was further developed— long before the days of Frank Lloyd Wright—when Edward S. Morse published in 1885 *Japanese Houses and Their Surroundings*, a pioneer study which quickly went through four editions and was hailed by the *American Architect and Building News* as "a noble and unique book."

As for Japanese *objets d'art*, Tiffany and Company was selling them as early as the 1870's, and a little later the Osaka firm of Yamanaka and Company established stores in New York and Boston. A number of wealthy Americans furnished their homes with Japanese-made furniture, wallpaper and screens. William H. Vanderbilt, for instance, had a Japanese room in his Fifth Avenue mansion in New York. Japan again had a pavilion—the *Hoo-den* or Phoenix Villa—at the World's Fair in Chicago in 1893 which was seen by millions of the Americans who crowded that epochal exhibition and in so many ways found their horizons greatly broadened.

About this same time Nitobe Inazo was writing of what he believed to be other areas in which Japan was making an impact on American culture. He spoke—although in this instance without great enthusiasm—of what he described as "Japanese villages" set up in various cities to display his country's wares, singled out the influence of Japanese design on various art forms, and noted the contribution to "the world of female fashion" in the Japanese kimono. He also drew attention to the many ornamental plants— special varieties of wistaria, clematis, magnolia and peonies— which were being introduced from across the Pacific, the pervasive Japanese influence on landscape gardening, and a popular interest in his country's approach to flower arrangements. Several articles on such matters had indeed already appeared in the magazine *House and Garden,* and in 1891 Joseph Conder published *The Flowers of Japan and the Art of Floral Arrangement.* The vogue for things Japanese was so fashionable that a contemporary article in *Harper's* described "Japanism" as "a new word coined to designate a new field of study, artistic, historic, and ethnographic."

Japanese paintings and color prints, including *ukiyo-e,* were to arouse a very special interest in the 1890's, having at first been largely ignored because the Japanese themselves set such little store in this expression of their art. They became a great prize for collectors, as shall subsequently be seen in relating the career of Ernest Fenollosa, the man primarily responsible for their introduction into the United States, and even before this later period they had at least indirectly affected the style of a number of American artists. The prints originally became known to the Western world by way of France, and it was while he was studying in Paris that Whistler fell under their spell and became the first Western artist, E. P. Richardson has written in his *Painting in America,* "to feel the wind from the Orient that was later to blow so strongly." Another leading American artist inspired by Japanese techniques was Mary Cassatt, who also studied in Paris, and in this same period among others the impressionists Childe Hassam and J. Alden Weir.

A Japanese influence was later quite clearly manifest in the literary world, and the whole imagist school of the early twentieth century was deeply indebted to Japanese poetry. Amy Lowell, whose brother Percival Lowell long lived in Japan where he wrote *The Soul of the East,* and Ezra Pound were to become greatly interested in such a poetical form as the *haiku,* the short, epigrammatic, seventeen-syllable verse which the Japanese poet Basho had made famous in the late seventeenth century.

Such contributions to American culture were somewhat more elusive, less tangible, than the far more practical ones Americans were making to the culture of Japan. Nothing could have more clearly demonstrated the difference between the two countries' civilizations than this contrast between America's assistance in helping Japan transform her feudal society into a modern state and Japan's shadowy gifts to America in art and architecture, ceramics, painting and poetry.

12

Love at First Sight

As THE NINETEENTH CENTURY drew to a close, the trans-pacific exchange of American teachers going to Japan and Japanese students coming to America may have lost something of the vigor that characterized it in the days when Japan was first seeking knowledge from all the world. Nevertheless two Americans stand out pre-eminently in the 1880's and the 1890's for the part they played in promoting a greater understanding between the two countries on either side of the Pacific.

Ernest Fenollosa, the art critic, arrived in Japan in 1878 to remain twelve years, and, after living some time in America, returned once again to make his home in Japan from 1897 to 1900. Lafcadio Hearn, the writer, landed in Yokohama the year Fenollosa first left and stayed in Japan until his death in 1904. Among all Americans in any way associated with Japan during the Meiji era, these two men were unique in their deep and sensitive appreciation of their adopted country's ancient culture.

They were in the first instance concerned with their own teaching. As professors at Tokyo University, their primary task was to help the Japanese to assimilate Western philosophy and literature in the tradition of such teachers as Guido Verbeck, William Elliot Griffis and William Clark Smith. But it is as interpreters of Japan that they are today best remembered. As they stayed on in the

214

country, both Fenollosa and Hearn became more and more concerned with discovering for themselves and making better known
to others the artistic values of the civilization which provided the
background for their lives abroad. Having fallen in love with
Japan at first sight (even though experience was to bring some
disillusionment as the new Japan was superimposed on the old),
they were alike in wishing to convey to Americans something of
their own excitement and wonder over what Japan offered the
Western world through her own art, philosophy and folklore.

Ernest Fenollosa, half Spanish from his musician father and
half Yankee through his mother's family, was born in the year
Commodore Perry first visited Japan and grew up in Salem, Massachusetts, with all its long associations with the Far East. A
shy, sensitive boy, attracted to poetry and art, he entered Harvard undecided where his real interests lay but majored, with
brilliant results, in philosophy and political economy. After grad-
uating at twenty-one he turned back for a time to the study of art,
but when in 1878 he accepted the post at Tokyo University,
offered him on the recommendation of the zoologist Edward S.
Morse, it was to teach philosophy.

He lived with his young wife in Tokyo, in a rather luxurious
Western house on the same street as both Morse and the physicist
Thomas Mendenhall, and quickly won a notable success. His
classes were very popular, in great part because of his emphasis
on what were for the Japanese the very congenial doctrines of
Herbert Spencer. Soon, however, his major interest shifted back
from philosophy to art. He had felt from his first arrival in Japan
an instinctive sympathy for the spirit of Japan, and everything
about her traditional civilization—painting, sculpture, No drama,
poetry, the precepts of Buddhism—appealed immensely to his
own artistic nature.

The time, however, was the 1880's. In their almost hysterical
intoxication with everything Western, as symbolized by the social
affairs at the Hall of the Baying Stag, the more cultivated Japanese seemed to have turned their backs on their own heritage. In
seeking to adapt themselves to foreign ways, they felt they had to
discard traditions and customs which were suddenly considered no
more than the relics of a barbarism which was happily being

replaced by the higher civilization of the West. They neglected their ancient shrines and temples, showed little interest in the paintings and sculpture of the past. The possessions of daimio and samurai who had been impoverished by the loss of their estates and special privileges fell into the hands of dealers who had little idea of their real worth. Bronze statues were melted down for their metal and priceless art works carelessly cast aside and forgotten. In later years ancient monuments dating back a thousand years were unearthed from the heaps of rubble piled about abandoned shrines, and Buddhist statuary of inestimable value was only by chance rescued from forgotten dumps.

Shocked by this careless treatment of Japan's historic treasures and also by the slavish imitation of the West which characterized the work of contemporary artists, Fenollosa eagerly threw himself into the study of Japanese painting and sculpture and also began to collect whatever he could find. But he was not content merely to explore for himself this unknown world of Oriental art; he sought to arouse the Japanese themselves to a greater appreciation of their own heritage. Foreigner though he was, Fenollosa was soon exerting an important influence both in encouraging the preservation of all forms of traditional art and in reversing the current trend toward copying Western painting.

In 1882—he had been only four years in Japan—he was invited to give a talk before an aristocratic private audience at the Ueno Education Museum in Tokyo. Taking as his title the phrase "*Bijutsu Shinsetsu*"—or "New Theory of Art"—this earnest young American (he was twenty-nine) called the Japanese to account for so cavalierly casting aside their own artistic inheritance. On the basis of every aesthetic principle, he told his startled audience, the historic painting of Japan was highly superior to the contemporary art of Europe. If modern Japanese artists had courage and imagination in following their own traditions, they could do work far better than European artists seemed capable of producing.

"You Japanese people, therefore," Fenollosa is reported to have said, "must recognize the virtue of your own painting, and do what you can to put new life into it. If only this is done, the value of your Japanese painting will be universally recognized within the next few years."

This talk may be safely characterized as one of the most significant addresses by any foreigner in Japan in the years of Meiji.
Historians of art not only date a modern renaissance in Japanese
painting from 1882, but credit Fenollosa's warnings and advice
with being largely responsible for a reversal in prevailing attitudes
toward Western and Oriental art in general. The perceptive American awoke Japanese artists to a new understanding of what their
own tradition represented and encouraged a more critical approach toward the European models which they had been following so slavishly.

Two years later, having made many friends among the artists
and having been adopted into the famous Kano family, Fenollosa
helped to found the Kankwakai, a club for the appreciation of art,
and also brought together a group of artists into the Shingaku, or
New Painters Group, further to encourage the new art movement.
The latter club gave a series of exhibitions that helped to infuse a
fresh spirit into contemporary painting and also gave additional
impetus to efforts to save the art of the past from loss or destruction.

The Japanese Government itself was stirred to action. It established an art department in the Imperial Museum, appointed a
board of Imperial Commissioners which was to study art education in Europe and America with the ultimate goal of setting up a
modern art school in Tokyo, and also provided for the registration
of all art works throughout Japan as "national treasures" or "important cultural property" which would henceforth be protected
from foreign export. In unexampled recognition of the role of a
foreigner in bringing about these developments, the Government
then appointed Fenollosa as one of the Imperial Art Commissioners, as well as making him a joint manager of the new art museum
and somewhat later a lecturer at the Tokyo Art School.

He went abroad as an Imperial Commissioner in 1886, returning to win new laurels as an art educator, but even before this he
had performed yeoman service in helping the Japanese to preserve
their own artistic treasures. During his summer vacations from his
post at Tokyo University, he had every year traveled widely
throughout Japan seeking out the forgotten relics hidden away
in Buddhist temples and Shinto shrines. Moreover, by purchasing
heirlooms from the old daimio and samurai families that had

fallen into the hands of local dealers, he had himself bought, at amazingly cheap prices, a great collection of paintings, statuary, ceramic sculpture, pottery, screens and painted scrolls. He was later to sell a great many of these art objects—more than one thousand in all—to Dr. Charles G. Weld of Boston to form the Weld-Fenollosa Collection in Boston's Museum of Fine Arts. But even as he was building up this private collection and preparing to send it abroad, Fenollosa realized that what America gained Japan just as surely lost. It was like "the life blood of Japan seeping from a hidden wound." Fenollosa was consequently thoroughly in sympathy with the government program to save Japan from any further despoliation of her antiquities. In company with Okakura Kakuzo, an artist as well as the famed author of *The Book of Tea*, he thereupon undertook as an Imperial Fine Arts Commissioner a further nationwide search to find and secure for Japan the permanent possession of her artistic treasures.

The temples and shrines were again the principal objectives of his quest, and with official authority he was now able to gain access to godowns, or storehouses, which had been virtually sealed away and kept inviolate for generations. Fenollosa discovered examples of Korean art, first introduced into Japan in the ninth century, that had been wholly forgotten, fine pieces of Heian sculpture and elaborate carvings about which even the temple priests knew nothing. On one occasion he happened upon a unique ceramic head of Buddha thrown away in an ash barrel; another time he found an almost priceless Greco-Buddhist statue lying amid a pile of broken mortar.

Fenollosa and Okakura generally encountered a most friendly reception on their travels, but they sometimes had to exercise all their authority to persuade the temple priests to let them see the storehouses which had not only been closed to all visitors but had been completely locked up ever since their guardians could remember. On visiting the great wooden temple of Horyuji, near Nara, they were told that one of the central shrines, dedicated to Prince Shotoku, had been sealed up for two hundred years. They were gravely warned that any such sacrilege as attempting to open it would in all probability cause an earthquake, endangering the entire temple. But Fenollosa insisted that it should be done and with his government credentials finally succeeded in having his way. Describing this experience, he wrote:

I shall never forget our feelings as the long disused key rattled in the rusty lock. Within the shrine appeared a tall mass closely wrapped about in swathing bands of cotton cloth upon which the dust of ages had gathered. . . . But at last the final folds of the coverings fell away, and this marvelous statue came forth to human sight for the first time in centuries. It was a little taller than life, but hollow at the back, carved most carefully from some hard wood which had been covered with gilding, now stained to the yellow brown of bronze. The head was ornamented with a wonderful crown of Korean open-work gilt bronze from which hung long streamers of the same material set with jewels. We saw at once that it was the supreme masterpiece of Korean creation.

Fenollosa also examined on several occasions the rich treasures of the Shosoin. This historic museum of the Todaiji temple, also at Nara, was opened only once a year to air its invaluable contents and was even then accessible only to persons with an imperial rescript authorizing them to see it. Here were collections of palace furniture and royal costumes from the days of the eighth-century Emperor Shomu; banners and screens, musical instruments, swords and other weapons, mirrors, ceremonial masks and rich jewels. They had for the most part been deposited in the Shosoin on the Emperor Shomu's death and been carefully hoarded for a thousand years.

Under Fenollosa's guidance, the Fine Arts Commission officially registered these "important cultural properties" that today constitute an irreplaceable national heritage for the Japanese people. Many of them in temples and shrines, palaces and museums, might well have been lost or dispersed had it not been for the efforts of this imaginative and zealous American in arousing the Japanese to their inestimable value. Fenollosa's services were fully appreciated. The poet Noguchi Yone hailed him as "the very discoverer of Japanese art for Japan," and the Emperor decorated him with the Order of the Sacred Mirror.

Fenollosa was not only interested in the ancient sculptures and paintings of Japan. He became fascinated with the more modern *ukiyo-e*, which had reached their highest artistic excellence in the work of Hiroshige and Hokusai at the close of the Tokugawa era. This style of painting had continued with such cruder color prints as those portraying the coming of Commodore Perry and depicting the foreigners ashore at Shimoda and Yokohama, but the Japanese connoisseurs tended to dismiss all *ukiyo-e* as a cheap and popular art for the common people. Fenollosa, however, believed the earlier artists to have been extremely gifted. Seeking out their work wherever he could find it, he was greatly responsible for introducing *ukiyo-e* to American collectors.

He was also immensely intrigued by No drama, that most ancient of Japanese theatrical forms. Studying it carefully, he became so proficient in both acting and singing that he was able to take part in No performances with his Japanese friends. Under the direction of Okakura Kakuzo, he became highly knowledgeable in all the intricacies of the tea ceremony. There was virtually no aspect of traditional Japanese life that did not awaken Fenollosa's interest and his sympathy, and his acceptance of all that it meant was most significantly demonstrated on his becoming an avowed Buddhist.

When Fenollosa left Japan in 1890, after serving some half dozen years as an Imperial Commissioner of Fine Arts, he entered upon the second phase of his unusual career and the one that is better known in the United States. "You have taught my people to know their own art," the Emperor said to him on the eve of his departure. "In going back to your own country, I charge you, teach them also." And this he did, with conspicuous success.

Returning to Boston, he became the curator of the Japanese holdings of that city's Museum of Fine Arts, and busied himself with cataloguing and further expanding the great collection for which he was himself originally responsible. He lectured widely, awoke a youthful Bernard Berenson to a lasting appreciation of Japanese painting, was instrumental in encouraging the interest of such well-known Oriental collectors as Mrs. Jack Gardner and Charles Lang Freer, and generally played a significant role in making the American art public aware of aspects of Japanese culture of which it had heretofore been almost wholly ignorant. He believed strongly in the possibility of bringing the two civilizations facing the Pacific closer together and in a long Phi Beta Kappa poem, "East and West," delivered at Harvard, he developed his ideas on what Japan could contribute to such a synthesis. Apostrophizing his old friend the painter Kano Hogai, Fenollosa wrote:

> I've flown from my West
> Like a desolate bird from a broken nest
> To learn thy secret of joy and rest.

In 1893, by imperial appointment, he represented Japan at the World's Fair in Chicago and two years later played a major role in staging an epochal exhibition of Japanese painting in New York. It was for this exhibition that he wrote *The Masters of Ukiyoye,* a pioneer descriptive catalogue that served to make known to a far broader artistic public the work of these Japanese painters.

Almost immediately after this event, severing his connection with the Boston Museum of Fine Arts as a consequence of the scandal caused by his divorce and remarriage, Fenollosa embarked on his second trip to Japan, where he would stay with his new wife for another four years. He did some lecturing and teaching, renewed his old studies of No plays and the literature of the East, and made various translations that Ezra Pound was to use as a basis for his own later interpretations of both Chinese and Japanese poetry. He also started on an ambitious project for a history of Oriental art that he was never to complete but which would be published after his death under the title, *Epochs of Chinese and Japanese Art.*

"This is the first time I ever lived," Fenollosa wrote enthusiastically to the editor of *Century Magazine,* for whom he had undertaken to write some articles. "There seems no end to the material that is offering itself to us here." However, this second visit to Japan was not to be as successful as the first. The popular attitude toward foreigners was by no means as cordial as it had been in the 1880's. While Fenollosa could count upon his old friends, most notably Okakura Kakuzo, he no longer had the position or commanded the influence that had once been his as an Imperial Art Commissioner. After three years, he returned once again, and finally, to America.

Whatever his possible disappointments in the Japan of the 1890's, they did not deter him from continuing to write and lecture about that country's art and culture. He not only talked to artist groups and painting schools but joined the Chautauqua circuit, where he became widely known as "the Japanese man" among public lecturers. On one occasion he talked at the White House on the invitation of Theodore Roosevelt. He was recognized as a pioneer breaking new trails in the study of Oriental art and as the foremost authority in America, if not in the world, on Japanese painting.

In 1908—he was only fifty-five—Fenollosa died while on a visit to London. In accordance with his wishes, his body was taken to Japan and interred in a favorite spot on the grounds of the Buddhist temple at Miidera, overlooking the waters of Lake Biwa. It was a symbolic resting place for the enthusiastic young American who while he lived in Japan did more than any other single individual to revive the interest of the Japanese in their own art, and then on his return to the United States played a major part in introducing this art to Americans.

Lafcadio Hearn was just forty when he landed at Yokohama on April 4, 1890, a short, swarthy man, with grizzled hair and mustache, somewhat disfigured as a result of a childhood accident that had blinded him in one eye. He was shy, introspective and reserved. In a continuing search to escape from what he bitterly called the "beastly machinery" of Western civilization, he had come to Japan with a commission to write some descriptive sketches for *Harper's Magazine*. This was the end of his journeyings; he stayed on in Japan the remaining fourteen years of his life.

There were to be disappointments as Hearn came more and more to realize that much of what he loved about Japan—the quiet simplicity of native life, its ever-present beauty and artistry—was being overshadowed by the ugliness of modern industrialism. However, his first impressions of the country were unreservedly ecstatic. Writing his lifelong friend Elizabeth Bisland soon after his arrival, he let himself go completely:

I feel indescribably toward Japan. . . . And I love their gods, their customs, their dress, their bird-like quavering songs, their houses, their superstitions, their faults. And I believe that their art is as far in advance of our art as old Greek art was superior to that of the earliest European art-gropings. . . . We are the barbarians! I do not merely *think* these things: I am as sure of them as death. I only wish I could be reincarnated in some little Japanese baby, so that I could see and feel the world as beautifully as a Japanese brain does.

This exuberant visitor, of whom it has often been said that he became more Japanese than the Japanese themselves, had been born in Santa Maura, a Greek island in the Ionian Sea, of mixed parentage: an Irish father and a Greek mother. Adopted by an aunt after his parents separated, he spent his boyhood in Dublin, and at the age of nineteen he came to America, where he lived for twenty years working as a reporter on a succession of newspapers, first in Cincinnati and then in New Orleans. His discontent with society, born perhaps of his lonely childhood, left him restless and unhappy. A first attempt to discover a freer and more natural life was a two years' stay on the island of Martinique, but this did not prove satisfying. On his return to the United States, the opportunity offered by *Harper's Magazine* to visit Japan appeared to be a godsend.

In his immediate intoxication with everything about this new country, Hearn was persuaded that he must find a way to live there permanently, and he managed to secure a position as an English teacher in the little feudal town of Matsue, on the western coast of Honshu. In its isolation and consequent detachment from the Western influences invading the greater part of Japan, Matsue was very much like the Fukui where twenty years earlier William Elliot Griffis had lived so completely alone, watching with fascination the transfer of feudal power to the Emperor. But Hearn went much further than Griffis in throwing himself completely into native life. He not only lived in a Japanese house, wore Japanese clothes, ate Japanese food and became (like Fenollosa) a Buddhist, but he married the daughter of an old samurai family and in time was to take the final, ultimate step of adopting Japanese citizenship. It is as Koizumi Yakumo that Lafcadio Hearn is today remembered in the country which he made so completely his own.

Yet for all his apparent acceptance of everything Japanese and his romantic absorption in the ways of a people whom he found so lovable, Hearn still remained bound to many of the ways of the West. He was unable completely to submerge his own identity in the strange and unfamiliar life of the Orient. He could not adjust himself to winters at Matsue with only a *hibachi* and *kotatsu* (however romantic he first found these Japanese equivalents of Western stoves) to warm his house; he did not really enjoy native food and finally gave it up (except once a day) for more accept-able beefsteaks, bread and Bass's Ale. Nor did Hearn ever really learn Japanese, speaking what he himself characterized as a sort of "Hearnian dialect." On becoming a Japanese citizen, he illogi-cally resented the consequent reduction in the salary he had en-joyed as a foreigner. "The Government told me," he complained, "that I ought to be satisfied to live on rice like a Japanese."

There were always inexplicable contradictions in Hearn's out-look, and much of what he wrote about Japan (in private corre-spondence rather than published articles) reflected his own difficult and mercurial character. He was impulsive, often torn by doubts and indecision, easily offended. He was a visionary con-stantly facing disillusionment. Noguchi Yone (the friend also of Ernest Fenollosa) was to write that while Japan appeared to Hearn to be the most magical of lands, his dreams were them-selves ghosts "under whose spell he wove the silvery threads of the ideal." His wife, writing after his death, explained him rather more simply: "He put too much importance to Beauty and Nicety perhaps."

The ecstatic visions of his first days in Japan, in any event, were never entirely recaptured. After a long winter at Matsue, he sought out a warmer climate and took another teaching post at Kumamoto, the town in Kyushu where Captain L. L. Janes had taught in 1870 and formed the "Kumamoto Band" of Christian students. The onetime feudal stronghold had become in 1892 a bustling modern city ("devilishly ugly and commonplace"), and after his quiet life in Matsue, Hearn realized more than ever that, through her expanded intercourse with the West, Japan could not hope to escape "the sorrows of the nineteenth century." "With what hideous rapidity Japan is modernizing, after all!—not in costume, or architecture, or habit, but in heart and manner. . . . We bombarded unhappiness into the country—beyond any doubt. Force sowed the seed; the future will gather the black crop." He began to feel, as he so repeatedly expressed it in his letters, that all that was good and noble and true belonged to the old Japan, wishing that he could somehow "fly out of Meiji forever."

Yet his next move, for after two years' teaching at Kumamoto he spent a year in Kobe working on an English-language newspaper, the *Chronicle*, would again bring out the contradictions that bedeviled his attitude toward the whole of life. "What a joy to feel the West!" we surprisingly find him describing the modern treaty port Kobe had become. "What a great thing is the West." Feeling that his illusions about Japan had been forever shattered, he wrote unhappily of what he felt to be wrong with Japan and of "how thoroughly detestable Japanese can be."

Then his mood would again change and he would recall nostalgically "the old first love of Japan and things Japanese," alternating querulous outbursts against frock coats and loud neckties with recalled memories of the "moral beauty" that he had once felt pervaded Japanese society. Setting this old Japan against Western modernity, he said: "Carpets,—dirty shoes,—absurd fashions, —wickedly expensive living,—airs,—vanities,—gossip: how much sweeter the Japanese life on the soft mats,—with its ever dearer courtesy and pretty, pure simplicity."

It was now, in 1894, that he was offered and accepted an appointment at what had become Tokyo Imperial University and started on the teaching of literature that for the next decade was to have such a lasting effect on successive classes of Japanese students. Some of these young men who fell under his influence have left their impressions of their *sensei*—or honorable teacher. His appearance—a clumsy, almost misshapen man with the cruel disfigurement of his early accident—was never prepossessing, but the kimono hid some of the awkwardness. In class he invariably held his audience's rapt attention, reading slowly from his carefully prepared lectures, and his eccentricities of manner awoke sympathy rather than criticism. He soon inspired a deep affection on the part of his students. "It was their delight," Noguchi was to write in describing the familiar figure of this foreign teacher, "to see his somewhat bending body, under an old, large-rimmed soft hat like that of a Korean, carrying his heavy books, wrapped in a purple *furoshiki*."

When difficulties developed with the university authorities, who not only reduced his salary but refused him a leave of absence, Hearn felt he had no alternative other than to resign his position. His students met in protest, as described in the diary of one of them, Osanai Kaoru, and declared that Tokyo University was best known abroad because of Lafcadio Hearn—"What had the university to be proud of, if he goes?" But Hearn discouraged any action in his behalf, and after a time which he spent wholly on his own writing, he was invited to lecture by Waseda University and in 1904 found himself on its more congenial campus.

During these years in the capital, even though in typical fashion he often exclaimed in his letters about "this horrid Tokyo . . . I am caged and can't sing," Hearn appears to have been happier than he had been at either Kumamoto or Kobe. Although he grew more and more absorbed in his teaching and writing, there was one exception to his withdrawal from social life. He had come to know Fenollosa when the latter returned to Japan in 1896, and for a time there was a close friendship and frequent exchanges of visits between the two families.

On one occasion, in the spring of 1898, Mrs. Fenollosa enthusiastically described her own first meeting with Hearn. He had been talking for a time with her husband when the latter burst upstairs to cry out: "Oh, he is splendid, I love him as I do Okakura. He will see you. He *wants* to see you. It is a delight to see such a man!" Going down, she found "a small man of grey tone with delicate, slightly distorted features and with his personality warped, twisted a little to the right. . . . But his beautiful voice—sweet, vibrating—never loud nor piercing—has an irresistible charm. . . . As he stayed on," Mrs. Fenollosa continued, "he became more confidential, charming, and close. . . . It was a wonderful afternoon."

Another time her daughter was rather less sympathetic in describing Hearn as a luncheon guest: "But Mr. Lafcadio Hearn was repulsive to look at; he had a wonderful voice, to be sure, and he talked well; but he was totally blind, and his food landed in strange places, much to my delight."

Soon, however, he was foregoing even such associations and wrote Fenollosa, "Alas! I can afford friends only on paper. Visiting is out of the possible." He had come to consider complete isolation indispensable for his work, and in another letter said that he had happily given the Fenollosas more time than any other persons in Tokyo: "But now—I must again disappear."

Throughout the fourteen years of his life in Japan, Hearn had been pursuing, as had Fenollosa, two distinct and separate goals. Through his teaching Hearn hoped to give his students a greater knowledge and understanding of the West, but in his writing he explored and sought to make better known, both to the Japanese themselves and to Americans, the wellsprings of Japanese culture. Fenollosa's major interest had been art; Hearn's was folklore and mythology. Each was intensely interested in preserving something that in the last quarter of the nineteenth century appeared to be in imminent danger of being forever lost. They were both conservators in a time of destruction.

Hearn had set himself on his first arrival in Japan to learn all that he could of the simple, daily life of the people still untouched by Western influences, and to collect from every possible source the myths, the legends, the superstitions that were a part of the ancient folklore. He called upon his Japanese friends for help; put his students to work gathering and translating material; corresponded with such authorities as the Englishman Basil Hall Chamberlain, who was the author of, among many translations and other books, *Things Japanese;* and followed every possible lead with insatiable curiosity. His letters are full of questions: "Whether the ancestors are ever worshipped before the *kamidana* in the same way as they are worshipped before the *butsudan?*" "Are any particular *family*-prayers said by Buddhists when praying before the *kaimyo?*" And there are notes expressing appreciation for the help received: "Many thanks for your very valuable notes about the January customs. You told me quite a number of things I did not know before."

In spite of the language barrier, Hearn came to know more of Japan in many ways than any other foreigner in the country, and what he wanted to do was to preserve all this by getting it down on paper, into print, before the memory of it was lost. Just as Fenollosa was safeguarding the sculpture and paintings of the ancient shrines and temples by having them officially registered and protected by the government, so Hearn was trying to save the myth and folklore by making a permanent written record of it.

The descriptive sketches, the popular legends and the poetic fantasies went into the articles that he was writing for *Harper's,* and they were also the stuff of his varied books. Their titles show what he was doing. His first book, *Glimpses of Unfamiliar Japan,* was largely a personal record of his own experiences while living in Matsue. Among the later volumes were *Japanese Fairy Tales,* originally printed from Japanese wood blocks; a collection of supernatural stories published under the title *In Ghostly Japan*; and two books whose subtitles are even more revealing: *Kotto: Being Japanese Curios, with Sundry Cobwebs* and *Kwaidan: Stories and Studies of Strange Things*. Hearn's approach was always highly romantic. Some critics have found his sensitivity no more than sentimentality ("embarrassing psuedo-mystical gush" is one rather unenthusiastic comment), and certainly he has never been accused of an unwarranted realism in his writings. None of the diatribes against the new Japan ever found its way into his published works. But while his idealization of an irrecoverable past may have borne little resemblance to the actualities of the present, no one has ever written of the old Japan with more imaginative insight or more sympathetic understanding.

He was of course writing in English, and for the most part publishing in the United States. His discovery of the wonders of Japanese mythology and folklore was nonetheless to have its impact in Japan itself for many of his sketches and fantasies were translated and found their way into Japanese literature. The fairy stories and ghostly tales he resurrected still appear in schoolbooks, and they are familiar to generations of Japanese children through having been saved from possible oblivion by the interest of this American writer. Hearn has for more than half a century been almost a cult among those Japanese who seek to keep alive their country's legendary past. Writing in 1911, Noguchi Yone rhapsodically recognized what he felt was the debt Japan owed Hearn:

We Japanese have been regenerated by his sudden magic and baptized afresh under his transcendental rapture; in fact, the old romances which we had forgotten ages ago were brought again to quiver in the air, and the ancient beauty which we buried under the dust rose again with a strong yet new splendor.

A more important consequence of his writings than suggested by this poetic effusion was their influence on the American public. Again as in the case of Fenollosa, but even more significantly, the role of this romantic writer in painting a portrait of Japan that emphasized so strongly her art and literature, her religious beliefs and her "moral beauty" helped to create in the United States a new popular image of that country. "He has caught the dying strains of an epoch's swan song," said a writer in the *Atlantic Monthly* for June, 1895. His vision affected American ideas and concepts for many years after an industrialized, militaristic empire had in so many ways supplanted the old Japan of which he had written with such deep sympathy.

A later book than these early descriptive sketches, *Japan: An Attempt at Interpretation*, first published in 1904, had an even greater impact than its predecessors. It was accepted by no small part of the reading public in America as the final word on that still mysterious empire which Commodore Perry had opened up to the West just a half century earlier. Lafcadio Hearn and Japan, Japan and Lafcadio Hearn, became almost inseparably associated in the popular mind.

This final study dealt not only with the old Japan but with the new Japan; it was history and politics, as well as art, religion and folklore. It sought to explain the Japan that had evolved out of the interaction of her own past and the modernity of the West, discussing political institutions, industry, armaments, even the possibilities of war, in present-day terms. With his emphasis on the continuing influence of religion and ancestor worship, and on the inherent gentleness and simplicity of Japanese life, Hearn was nevertheless still giving, with consummate literary skill, a rose-tinted picture of Japan that once again reflected his own idealistic visions. It was a book well received—"The subtlest and most searching analysis of Japan and the Japanese ever published," wrote one critic—and it served to strengthen the friendly feelings that Americans had had for Japan ever since the days of Commodore Perry and Townsend Harris. It was not a book, however, to prepare them for the realities of the twentieth century; it was still a highly romanticized Japan that emerged from Hearn's impressionistic attempt at interpretation.

The very year of the publicaton of this last book, its author died suddenly. The final days of the idealistic, restless, paradoxical teacher and writer had been unhappily shadowed by dark clouds—ill-health, a growing discontent, a sense almost of persecution. He lived entirely unto himself, hardly emerging from the study of his Tokyo home except, almost reluctantly, to have meals with his Japanese wife and children. His funeral at the Buddhist temple of Kobudera, associated with one of the Zen sects, was attended by three foreigners, forty Japanese professors and a hundred students.

There are various monuments to the memory of Lafcadio Hearn. The most significant among them is not anywhere in Tokyo; it is the memorial hall standing near his first home in Matsue. This was where he knew and deeply experienced the old Japan that he loved so well.

13

❧

Globe-Trotters

IN THE LATTER HALF of the nineteenth century the descriptive term for round-the-world travelers was "globe-trotters." No sooner had Commodore Perry persuaded a reluctant Shogunate to open Japan's door to foreigners than such peripatetic Englishmen and Americans sought to include this still secluded and feudalistic empire on their tourist itineraries. Margaret Ballagh, a missionary wife, noted as early as 1861 that globe-trotters were stopping off in Yokohama; William Elliot Griffis wrote a decade later that they were such frequent visitors to Japan as to be recognized as a distinct class, and Basil Hall Chamberlain, discussing them at some length in *Things Japanese*, first published in 1890, singled out as their distinctive characteristics sun helmets, blue glasses, scant luggage and celluloid collars. Even though Griffis' enthusiastic prediction that "the coming orthodox bridal tour and round-the-world trip will soon be made *via* Japan first, then Asia, Europe and America," was somewhat fanciful, a gradually increasing number of tourists were invading Japan well before the century's close and "doing" its sights with conscientious industry.

A majority of them were still perhaps empire-conscious Englishmen, but their ranks were swelled by Americans who were caught up by the fascination of the Far East. Here was a confron-

231

tation of a new breed of Yankees and quite modernized samurai
under circumstances that could hardly have differed more from
those marking the original contacts between Americans and Japanese a century earlier. Their hosts nevertheless welcomed these
transpacific guests with the cordiality, tempered by a sense of
baffled puzzlement, which the people of Japan had shown toward
Americans even in the days when the policy of their government
was still so antiforeign.

In a lively and colorful account of tourist travel published in
1891, *Jinrikisha Days in Japan*, the American writer Eliza R.
Skidmore reproduced a contemporary poem that reflects something of the perplexity with which the Japanese (themselves the
most assiduous of tourists in their own country) viewed their
wandering visitors:

> What are these strangely-clad beings
> Who move quickly from one spot of interest to another
> Like butterflies flitting from flower to flower?
>
> These are Americans.
> They are as restless as the ocean,
> In one day they will learn more of a city
> Than an inhabitant will learn in a year,
> Are they not extraordinary persons?

A pioneer globe-trotter visiting Japan was William H. Seward,
the former Senator and Lincoln's Secretary of State. After his
retirement, at the age of sixty-nine, he embarked with a party of
seven friends and members of his family on an ambitious round-
the-world tour that brought him to Japan a scant two years after
the restoration of the Emperor, a time when "the swaggering two-
sworded samurai" might still be seen in the streets of Tokyo. His
adopted daughter, Olive Risley Seward, kept a faithful account
of this unusual journey and, on publishing "these notes" shortly
after the party's return to America, stated that she had recorded
Seward's "political, social, moral and philosophical reflections in
his own words."

The Seward party arrived in Yokohama on September 25,
1870, after a twenty-day passage from San Francisco aboard the
4,300-ton *China*, one of the little side-wheeler steamships that the

Pacific Mail Line had this early placed on the transpacific run. She carried sixty-six cabin passengers, including fifteen missionaries bound either for Japan or China, and in her steerage some five hundred Chinese coolies. The latter were returning from work on the Central Pacific Railroad, which only the year before had been linked with the Union Pacific when Leland Stanford drove the golden spike at Ogden, Utah, that marked completion of the country's first transcontinental railway system. The *China* had a good voyage, and when she steamed into Yokohama's harbor, the cabin passengers waited expectantly, as have all later arrivals at that port by sea or air, to get their first view of Fujiyama. But alas, wrote Olive Seward, the sacred mountain "veils his head."

The party stayed for a time in Yokohama, its sights and scenes seeming less strange than might have been expected because of the visitors' familiarity with Japanese designs on porcelain and lacquerware, and they made what was already the customary side trip to see the Daibutsu at Kamakura. To Olive Seward at least the expression on the great Buddha's face seemed "dull and meaningless." As the railroad linking Yokohama and Tokyo had not yet been built, they took a small boat to the capital and, after experiencing a terrific typhoon, arrived there safely and took up quarters in its one foreign-style hotel.

Seward had no official status, but as a former Secretary of State (he had also met the members of the Japanese embassy in 1860) he promptly called on the Foreign Minister. Defying the usual custom, he took the ladies of his party with him. The Japanese officials were somewhat startled but received them cordially, serving tea and cakes as well as champagne and cigars. The Foreign Minister tactfully commented in conversation with his distinguished visitor, "I see that you are very old and very handsome."

There was also to be an audience with the Emperor Meiji. Before that took place, however, Seward and his companions played the role of ordinary tourists and sight-seers—perhaps the first Americans in such a commonplace category to see Japan. They drove about Tokyo in newly imported carriages, with especially assigned guards protecting them from the "intrusive curiosity" which their presence invariably provoked. They visited palaces, temples and parks, including the always popular Asakusa district (still a tourist Mecca) with its myriad shops and places of amusement as well as famous temple. They drove out along the old Tokaido, where the crowds were "labyrinthian" and the grooms running at their horses' heads could hardly make headway through the dense throng. One final day they went shopping for souvenirs, visited a teahouse where they were served raw fish and sake, and only after the streets had been gaily lighted with paper lanterns, returned weariedly to their hotel.

The Emperor's reception took the form of a private audience in a special lodge of the garden of the imperial palace. The rage for things foreign had not yet engulfed the court, and the ceremony brought out dramatically the differences between East and West. The Americans appeared in swallowtailed dress coats, with tight pantaloons and stiff, black boots; the Emperor, sword at his side, was formally gowned in a voluminous robe of saffron.

After their Tokyo visit, the Seward party went on to Kobe and Osaka, and through the Inland Sea to Nagasaki. They were as impressed as its earliest visitors had been by the beauty of Nagasaki's harbor and were especially interested to see the island of Deshima ("the mart and the prison" of the Dutch), which Miss Seward described as hardly broader than a flatboat. They found the people friendly wherever they went, and in remarking on their invariable courtesy, Miss Seward made a further comment which almost paraphrases that of the youthful George Cleveland who had visited Nagasaki some seventy years earlier. He had spoken of having never seen a person "that appeared to be angry with another, but the most perfect harmony prevailed among them"; Miss Seward wrote that "we saw not one act of rudeness, and heard not one word of ill-temper."

Seward himself, as quoted by his adopted daughter, was on many points quite critical of the Japanese. He felt that beneath the façade of their courtesy and polite manners there was a measure of cunning and even possible cruelty ("the chrysanthemum and the sword," as a much later writer would phrase it), and he strongly censured their want of modesty and their treatment of women. He was impressed by the progress the country was already making in adapting itself to Western ways but convinced it needed a further period of "American tutelage." He wished above all friendship between the two peoples. The policy of the United States, Seward urged after this firsthand view of Japan, should be one based on the broad principles of magnanimity, moderation and humanity. America should send to Japan not armies and navies but teachers and instructors.

Nine years after Seward's visit, an even more celebrated American globe-trotter visited Japan. Former President Grant made a sight-seeing trip around the world that after stopovers in India and China brought him to Japan for a six weeks' visit in the early summer of 1879. It still has its mementos. Two trees, a cypress and a magnolia, in the popular Ueno Park in Tokyo bear small plaques noting that they were planted by General and Mrs. Grant when inspecting the park with the Emperor; and every visitor to Nikko is today shown the house where they stayed while viewing the shrines of the Tokugawa Shoguns.

It was both a more interesting and more important visit than that of Seward, for never had Japan had the opportunity to entertain so distinguished a guest as this great military hero and former President of the United States. There were special trains, guards of honor and military parades with bands playing "Hail Columbia"; elaborate banquets and colorful receptions; displays of spectacular fireworks. The Emperor not only received Grant in formal state but broke all precedent by coming to call on him personally in the detached Shiba palace placed at the former President's disposal for his stay in Tokyo. Grant was to give the Emperor candid and frank advice on Japanese policy, and the friendliness that he made manifest throughout his visit contributed immensely to the goodwill between America and Japan.

At one great official dinner, the Emperor escorted Mrs. Grant to the table, and General Grant escorted the Empress. Never before had anything quite like this taken place. Contemporary accounts state that several of the court officials, disturbed and worried over such flouting of tradition, carried concealed daggers, ready at once to stab the General should he so much as touch the Empress' hand. Their precautions were unnecessary. "Grant was . . . quite circumspect," the Japanese source for this story states, "walking a discreet distance from the Empress, much to the relief of all concerned."

There were meetings with Japanese statesmen—Iwakura Tomomi, who had led the second mission to the United States in

1872; Mori Arinori, the first minister in Washington; and Kuroda Kiyotaka, who had brought General Capron to Hokkaido—but most important were Grant's private and completely informal conversations with the Emperor. A transcript of a conference at the Hamarikyu, or "Seaside Palace," which has been preserved under the title *Grant Shogun to no Gotaiwa Hikki*, strikingly reveals the sympathy with which Grant viewed Japan's problems at home and abroad.

He warned the Emperor against the hazards of Japan becoming involved in the European political system and urged upon him the paramount importance of a policy of complete independence. Economic penetration could be as dangerous as military intervention, Grant declared, and Japan should endeavor to pay off her foreign indebtedness as quickly as possible. "You are doubtless aware," he said, "that some nations are very desirous to loan money to weaker nations whereby they might establish their supremacy and exercise an undue influence over them. They lend money to establish political power." On an immediate issue of unusual interest from an American point of view, that is, a threatened conflict between Japan and China over ownership of the Ryukyu Islands, the former President was even more explicit in his advice against any move that might invite European intervention.

Commodore Perry had visited these islands—they were then known as the Lew Chews—and had urged the establishment there of an American naval base "for the accommodation of our ships of war." A century later as a consequence of hostilities hardly foreseen in 1879, they were indeed occupied by the United States, and it still retains a great air and naval base at Okinawa. Nothing of all this of course entered into Grant's thinking, and there is a certain irony, in the light of such developments, in the advice he gave Japan:

In your discussions with China on Lew Chew, and on all matters at issue, do not invite or permit so far as you can avoid it, the intervention of a foreign power. European powers have no interest in Asia, so far as I can judge from their diplomacy, that do not involve the humiliation and subjugation of the Asiatic people. Their diplomacy is always selfish, and a quarrel between China and Japan would be regarded by them as a quarrel that might ensue to their own advantage.

Grant, however, convinced the Emperor, whatever might lie in the more distant future, that the United States did not have any imperialistic designs in Asia, was fully committed to friendly relations with Japan, and was prepared to take her side and offer its good services in the event that she became involved in any controversy or conflict with the European powers. His statements on American policy were accepted as convincing proof that Japan had nothing to fear from the Pacific neighbor which was doing so much to help her adjust her ancient ways to the exigencies and the dangers of the modern world.

For all his official receptions and informal talks with the Emperor, General Grant still found time to be a tourist. Sight-seeing was the real purpose of his globe-trotting journey, and he availed himself of every opportunity to see as much of Japan as possible. He had first visited Nagasaki, but on voyaging through the Inland Sea had been discouraged by the prevalence of cholera from making any further landings until his ship reached Yokohama. He then saw the sights of Tokyo, and made visits to both Nikko and Hakone. He also inspected schools and universities, collected souvenirs (especially the famed Japanese swords, one of which Townsend Harris had given him so many years before), and as often as he could went about as an ordinary, nonofficial traveler.

On the eve of his departure, Grant issued a final parting message to the people of Japan in which he observed that he had experienced no discourtesy and no unpleasantness throughout his entire stay. He declared that it was his own firm hope that Japan would be able to realize her full strength and greatness wholly independent of dictation by any Western power. And in expressing such a hope, he further told his hosts, he believed he was reflecting the sentiment of the great majority of his own countrymen. When he sailed from Yokohama, the entire Japanese cabinet attended his departure; cheering, flag-waving crowds were at the dock, and his ship sailed amid the thunderous salutes of the harbor batteries. General Grant's visit had been a rousing success.

Although perhaps not globe-trotters, for they traveled no farther on their eastward voyage, two interesting visitors in the next decade were Henry Adams and John La Farge. Historian and artist, they spent some five months in Japan in 1886, and apart from La

Farge's special interest in painting, their activities also conformed
to what was already becoming the accepted pattern of Japanese
tourism. They of course visited Yokohama and Tokyo, went on to
Osaka and Kyoto, and stayed for a time in Nikko. They conscientiously went through temples and shrines, palaces and museums,
parks and gardens; they saw No plays and curiously watched the
popular *sumo* bouts. Adams at least photographed madly (he
relates standing on his head "at an angle of impossibility" to get a
picture of the Daibutsu at Kamakura). They bought what their
letters home suggest were almost tons of curios.

On landing in Yokohama the two travelers met William Sturgis
Bigelow, the Bostonian Orientalist who was then living in Japan,
and through him they soon came to know Ernest Fenollosa. These
earlier arrivals in Japan were to act as guides and couriers for
Adams and La Farge, advising them on where to go, what to see
and how to buy. "Fenollosa and Bigelow are stern with us,"
Adams wrote. "It seems we are to be taken to Nikko shortly, and
permitted to admire some temples there." They rented a small
house near where both Bigelow and Fenollosa had summer
homes, and remained in Nikko a full month. While La Farge
painted, Adams walked about the wooded hills, visited the Tokugawa shrines and read. Tokyo had been very hot, with the threat
of cholera, and Nikko was a wonderful relief. Their little house
was close by a waterfall, with its own garden and view of a nearby
Buddhist temple, and their friends generously helped them to re-
solve the problems of living for a time somewhat off the tourist
track. "Mrs. Fenollosa has rescued us from our trials," was
Adams' grateful comment in one letter. "I cannot imagine what
we should have done without her."

The two men became badly infected by the collecting mania to
which Fenollosa and Bigelow were addicted, both for themselves
and, in Adams' case, for his close friend in Washington, John
Hay. In a letter to the latter he gives a graphic account of their
purchases at Nikko:

Every day new bales of rubbish come up from Tokyo or elsewhere,
mounds of books, tons of bad bronze, holocausts of lacquer. I buy
literally everything that is merely possible. . . . I am trying to spend
your money. It is hard work, but I will do it, or succumb. . . . A man
at Osaka has sent up some 250 dollars' worth of lacquers, sword-hilts,

inlaid work and such stuff. As he has the best shop in Japan, we took the whole lot and have sent for more.

In spite of his frivolous tone Adams was a careful buyer, following the advice of Fenollosa and Bigelow, and grew especially interested in Hokusai prints, *kakemono*, porcelain and, for his friends at home, silk gowns.

La Farge enjoyed and appreciated Japan immensely, as clearly shown in *An Artist's Letters from Japan*, published some eleven years after his visit. He vividly describes his first impressions of the landscape: the steep mountains, the curious shapes of the pine trees, the little temples hidden away on the hillsides and (in a familiar phrase) the land everywhere cultivated like a garden. With the enthusiasm of every American traveler in Japan, beginning with Townsend Harris, he also tells of how one gray, overcast day he first glimpsed through the clouds "a pale, clear blue opening in which was an outline more distinct—the cone of Fusiyama."

La Farge was intrigued and amused by the jinrikisha, now in universal use, the little trains on the new railroad lines, the popularity of spectacles and frock coats. But what appealed to him most as an artist, apart from the beauty of the land itself, was the quiet, unadorned simplicity of Japanese homes, with their sliding panels, *tatami* mats and the *tokonoma* framing its single scroll. La Farge was certain that when he returned to the United States he would have an intensified distaste "for the barbarous accumulations" that crowded American houses and would recall nostalgically "the far more civilized emptiness persisted in by the more aesthetic race." His approach to Japan was very much like that of Lafcadio Hearn—sensitive, artistic, romantic. "Where else," La Farge asked, "do the newspapers announce the spring openings of the blossoms?" It was a question modern tourists have put in various forms: where else would a taxi driver have a bouquet of flowers attached to the dashboard of his car or a policeman keep a vase of chrysanthemums on the island from which he directs the city traffic?

Adams was also deeply affected by the beauty of Japan, by its art and literature, but his mood was a more somber one than that of La Farge. His wife had died the year before, and it was largely to assuage his loneliness that he had embarked on his Japanese tour. His letters are often characterized by what a recent biographer has called a "desperate flippancy." One to John Hay seeks to describe the country, but perhaps reflects quite as much his own unhappy state of mind:

Positively everything in Japan laughs. The jinrickshaw men laugh while running at full speed five miles with a sun that visibly sizzles their drenched clothes. The women all laugh, but they are obviously wooden dolls, badly made, and can only cackle, clatter in pattens over asphalt pavements in railway stations, and hop or slide in heelless straw sandals across floors. I have not yet seen a woman with any better mechanism than that of a five-dollar wax doll; but the amount of oil used in fixing and oiling and arranging their hair is worth the money alone. They can all laugh, so far. The shopkeepers laugh to excess when you say their goods are forgeries and worthless. I believe the Mikado laughs when his ministers have a cabinet council. The gilt dragon-heads on the temples are in a broad grin. Everything laughs, until I expect to see even the severe bronze doors of the tombs, the finest serious work I know, open themselves with the same eternal and meaningless laughter, as though death were the pleasantest jest of all.

There are other comments in his letters stressing his impression of Japan as a doll's country. "All is toy," he once wrote, and another time after describing life as a dream, he said that in Japan "one dreams of the nursery." In another critical letter he told his correspondent that the Japanese were badly made and awkward, "suggestive of monkeys," and that the countryside as viewed from a train window presented only a "ridiculous landscape." He apparently did not really like to travel. He was uncomfortable even in his foreign hotel in Tokyo and when staying at native inns would not eat Japanese food.

Nevertheless La Farge and Adams returned home after their five months' stay (Fenollosa was on the same ship, starting on his tour to study art education in behalf of the Japanese Government) with deep and lasting impressions of Japan. La Farge was to make immediate use of them in his painting, and while Adams was not so directly affected, something of the East had also entered into his thinking and would significantly influence his later philosophy.

During these years many other tourists visited Japan, especially members of the ubiquitous fraternity of journalistic globe-trotters. Even before Seward's visit, Richard Henry Dana, the author of *Two Years Before the Mast,* made a trip around the world and sent back letters to the New York *Tribune.* In one of them describing Yokohama, he commented in familiar vein on such aspects of Japanese life as the perennial happiness of the children, the blackened teeth of the married women and the mixed public baths. "All foreigners here agree in their testimony," Dana wrote in introducing the latter topic, "that, in one respect, the Japanese are the most shamelessly immoral people on earth."

Bayard Taylor was to return after that first trip as a master's mate with Commodore Perry's squadron, publishing still another book on his experiences; and William Eleroy Curtis, also a well-known professional travel writer, wrote the popular *Yankees of the East* after making the tourist rounds from Tokyo to Nagasaki. Edward Greey reflected the general interest in the island kingdom by compiling two children's books: *Young Americans in Japan* and *The Wonderful City of Tokio,* while in somewhat the same vein, Mabel Gillette wrote her *Jingles from Japan.*

A quite different visitor was Percival Lowell, whose influence was so important in directing his sister Amy Lowell toward Japanese poetry. Best known as an astronomer and the founder of the Lowell Observatory at Flagstaff, Arizona, he lived and traveled in Japan in the 1880's, and his fascination with that country not only led him to write *The Soul of the Far East* (it was largely responsible for Lafcadio Hearn's great venture) but to explore many parts of Japan where few if any Westerners had ever been. His travel book *Noto* beautifully describes the wild and picturesque scenery of that little-known peninsula jutting out from Ishikawa into the Japan Sea.

Another American who was to color the popular image of Japan more than any of these travel writers, having an influence perhaps only comparable to Gilbert and Sullivan with *The Mikado,* was the author of *Madame Butterfly.* But ironically enough John Luther Long, whose first telling of the romantic affair of Lieutenant Pinkerton and Cho-Cho-San appeared as a short story in *Century Magazine* in January, 1898, was never actually in Japan. He obtained his material from a missionary sister living in

Yokohama. After its magazine publication David Belasco made the story over into a play, but it only won its lasting popularity when Puccini set it to music in 1906 and *Madame Butterfly* opened as an opera at New York's Garden Theatre.

Contemporary records and guidebooks suggest that for most of the American travelers who managed to include Japan in their foreign tours in the late nineteenth century—their total number was of course very small in the light of distance and expense— popular itineraries were very much the same as those still recommended by the official guidebook of the Japan Tourist Bureau. The cities generally visited lay along the old Tokaido and on the shore of the Inland Sea—Tokyo and Yokohama; the closely grouped Kyoto, Osaka and Kobe, and the historic port of Nagasaki, with side trips to Kamakura, Nikko and Hakone.

It is hardly surprising that tourists still follow this well-beaten path. What does seem astounding, however, is that the pioneer globe-trotters should have been casually marking it out within so brief a time of that period when Japan (except for the few Dutch at Deshima) admitted no Westerners whatsoever. In the 1840's those unfortunate Americans who might find themselves shipwrecked on the Japanese coast were welcomed, as John Sewall had once phrased it, "to a dungeon or a cage." Thirty years later William Elliot Griffis described how foreigners hardly dared go abroad without a Smith and Wesson revolver at hand to guard against the reckless attacks of antiforeign *ronin*. But once the Emperor Meiji had set forth the change in Japan's policies toward the West, it was within no time at all that the government was warmly greeting foreign travelers. It progressively liberalized the restrictions on visiting the interior (though passports remained necessary to go outside the cities specifically open to foreign residence), and began in every way to provide the facilities and comforts of modern tourism.

A first edition of *Murray's Handbook for Travellers* was published in Tokyo as early as 1881 (there would be five editions before the end of the century), and it engrossingly told in the most up-to-date terms how to sight-see in Japan. Perhaps nothing demonstrates more clearly, more dramatically, the spectacular progress Japan was making in adjusting herself to the modern world than this ready encouragement of tourist travel so soon after the first assaults on her historic seclusion.

Steamship service had become available for Americans going to Japan in 1867, less than a decade after the opening of the country to trade, when the Pacific Mail Company placed in operation between San Francisco and Yokohama the four-thousand-ton steamship *Colorado*, described as a fast and "palatial" vessel that could make the transpacific passage in twenty-two days. Other ships, such as the *China* on which William H. Seward crossed, were soon added to the company's fleet and sailed on a regular schedule. English and French lines—the Peninsular and Oriental and the Messageries Maritimes—also linked Japan with the outside world in the 1870's, and Yokohama, Kobe and Nagasaki could be made ports of call on any world tour.

Among the steamships under Japanese registry linking Nagasaki and Shanghai as early as the late 1870's was one named the *Hiroshima Maru*. In the light of later associations with the city from which this vessel derived her name, it is somewhat ironic to note that as described by one traveler, she was "a large American sidewheel, deck-over-deck, unrigged steamer . . . she was the Golden Age on the old Panama route, and, in the palmy days of California, used to carry 1,000 passengers at a time to the golden land."

Beginning also in the 1870's, a Japan Guides' Association was prepared to offer the services of licensed, English-speaking guides who were guaranteed to be "competent, trustworthy and well-informed," the ubiquitous Thomas Cook and Son was arranging special tours for hurried travelers, and soon not only *Murray's Handbook*, (which advised the globe-trotter that in visiting Japan at least a week was necessary "to form an adequate idea of its magnificent beauties") but a rival *Tourist's Guide and Interpreter* was providing discursive information on everything the traveler might wish to know—passport regulations, travel itineraries, hotels and the best shops.

By the 1890's the tourist landing in Yokohama found himself in a thriving modern city that had grown incredibly since the Shogunate had first made provision for a handful of foreigners in 1859. Its total population was some 150,000, and the Americans and Europeans, still living for the most part in bungalows on the

Bluff, now numbered about 1,600. Their social life continued, as in the 1860's, to be largely dominated by the English. It still centered about the foreign clubs (to which Japanese were not admitted), and for the most part consisted of formal dinners, dances, amateur theatricals and sporting events.

The offices of the international steamship lines, the foreign banks, three English-language newspapers, the several modern hotels (among which the Grand, "modelled on the American fashion," was the most luxurious) and the countless curio shops underscored the dramatic transformation Yokohama had undergone in a brief thirty years. Here the visitor had his first chance to shop for screens, cloisonné, *kakemono*, ivory carvings and silks, while the local newspapers also advertised the availability of riding horses, patent medicines, Pear's soap and photographic supplies. "I have a Camera," one notice stated, displaying a picture of tourists grouped about the base of Kamakura's famed Daibutsu.

The trip to Tokyo was easily made by the magnificent train service which had been instituted at the opening of the 1870's (it was no longer considered necessary, as earlier advertisements had advised, to secure "treasure pills" to combat possible dizziness), but should the traveler take the old Tokaido, he found it rather changed since the days of Townsend Harris. In one of his letters Lafcadio Hearn appended a little sketch which he titled "Beauties of the landscape-scenery between Tokyo and Yokohama." It shows a row of great signboards along the Tokaido with such glaring labels as Shirts, Highland Whisky, Curios, Gin, Bootmaker, Jim's Grog for Sailors.

Tokyo had become a great, sprawling city with a strange intermingling of native and foreign buildings. Its streets were lined with water pipes and telegraph poles, crowded with the hurrying traffic of omnibuses and rickshas. One English visitor was appalled by the extent to which the public buildings had been "Americanized" and also described the new wooden houses as "illustrations of ideas imported from Denver or Virginia City," the family dwellings all too often combining "the cold and discomfort of Japanese houses with the ugliness and discomfort of third-rate suburban villas in America." The Ginza had a double line of tram cars, and at night was a dazzling show with its flaring gaslights. Off rather to itself, the legation quarter looked for all the world, as another traveler reported, "like a well-painted American suburb." The old Yedo whose passing William Elliot Griffis mourned even in 1871 had receded ever more deeply into the dim recesses of an irrecoverable past.

The accommodations for foreigners had considerably improved since this same early visitor had described "the huge caravansary, which the Japanese . . . fondly believe to be a comfortable hotel." The Tokyo Hotel itself advertised "nice clean rooms," a parlor for ladies and that most universal token of Yankee intrusions—an American bar. Among other hostelries was the Imperial—"one of the finest hotels in the world"—which, some thirty-five years before its modern successor designed by Frank Lloyd Wright, advertised the special safeguards that had been taken in its construction against earthquakes. *The Tourist's Guide and Interpreter*, recommended these hotels and also listed the five largest houses in the Yoshiwara pleasure quarter!

The accounts of traveling Americans in the 1890's indicate that they almost universally followed the example first set by General Grant in visiting the shrines of the Tokugawa Shoguns at Nikko, and most of them also went to Miyanoshita and Lake Hakone. A few climbed Fujiyama (Lafcadio Hearn did so with his family, and also Eliza Skidmore), or if not that venturesome, they at least visited the lakes that ring its base. The Fujiya Hotel at Miyanoshita, modeled on the large, sprawling hotels of American watering places, opened before the close of the 1880's. Along the wall of one of its long corridors may still be seen photographs of its distinguished foreign guests in these early days. As another link with the present, *Murray's Handbook* recommended the Minakuchi-ya at Okitsu, on the old Tokaido, the hotel which was to become well known to Americans some seventy years later through Oliver Statler's account in *The Japanese Inn*.

Perhaps no other city had changed more in its attitude toward foreigners than the former imperial capital at Kyoto. When Daniel Crosby Greene moved there in 1881 to teach at Doshisha College, it was almost completely untouched by Western influences. Foreigners could stay in Kyoto only by reluctant official permission, and the old antagonism toward the barbarians generally prevailed. A decade later Kyoto still represented more of the old Japan with its historic palaces, its innumerable Buddhist temples and Shinto shrines than any other city in the land, but perhaps for that very reason it now cordially welcomed tourists. Attracted by the wealth of artistic treasures that Ernest Fenollosa was doing so much to preserve, even the most harried globe-trotters were making it a sight-seeing "must" as they traveled overland between Tokyo and Kobe. A three-story Hotel Kyoto was advertising in 1890 that it was "thoroughly European," that all rooms were equipped with an "Edison Incandescent Electric System," and that "the cuisine is controlled."

As a port second only to Yokohama, one where all steamships crossing the Pacific necessarily called, Kobe had, at least on the surface, grown up as a predominantly Westernized city. It had little to offer the sight-seer, and most of its visitors found "the sensation of foreign life very unpleasant." Rudyard Kipling, writing of his travels in Japan in letters sent back to an Indian newspaper in 1888 and later published in *From Sea to Sea*, described Kobe as "a raw American town . . . hideously American in externals."

There was little travel off the beaten paths. The contemporary guidebooks, warning far more gravely against the hazards of native inns and native food than would such books today, gave very careful instructions for anyone so daring as to break away from the foreign-style hotels. They advised tourists to carry their own supplies of Western food—sausage, corned beef, biscuits, cheese, tea and sugar—but also noted more cheerfully that at the *tobutsuya*, or foreign goods stores which were to be found in many of the small towns, they could at least be assured of getting beer, claret and spirits. *Murray's Handbook* was particularly explicit on the need to have special food supplies, and also Western knives, forks and spoons. It also suggested that on stopping at a native inn the traveler insist on being provided with chairs and tables for they could easily be obtained from the local school or police station. For all Japan's proverbial reputation for cleanliness, the guidebooks also stressed the imperative need to be equipped with insect powder and carbolic acid whenever traveling in the interior.

William Eleroy Curtis, urging prospective travelers in his *Yankees of the East* to hurry to "the land of fans and flowers" before it was too late, had much advice for tourists in his book's opening chapter, "A Word to the Wise." He said that in contrast to the many excellent foreign hotels the Japanese inns were far from comfortable and their food would hardly satisfy North American appetites. If in spite of such inconveniences the foreigner nevertheless wished to attempt travel in the interior, he should put everything in the hands of a competent guide or courier. Special passports were necessary, he further wrote, in which the tourist agreed in return for his special privileges not to break windows, scribble on temple walls, travel at night without a light or attend a fire on horseback!

There were some few Americans who from the first days of the opening of the country had been easily able to adapt themselves to Japanese ways: Raphael Pumpelly cheerfully eating with chopsticks and enjoying raw fish, Benjamin Smith Lyman taking a Japanese house and wearing Japanese clothes, William Elliot Griffis living happily in isolated Fukui. For the most part, however, the visitors from the United States found such adjustments very difficult, especially in the matter of food. As we have seen, Townsend Harris had felt obliged to bring his own foreign-trained cook with him on his journey from Shimoda to Yedo, Henry Adams resorted to mulligatawny soup from a tin can, and Lafcadio Hearn returned after his early experiences with a Japanese diet to beefsteak and Bass's Ale.

The gap between the everyday living customs of Japan and those of the West would appear to have been less easily closed in the nineteenth century than is presently the case when so many American visitors delight in staying at Japanese inns. The globe-trotters of the earlier period were very cautious about exposing themselves to the unfamiliar. *Murray's Handbook* warned ominously of "spirits sunk and tempers embittered" when tourists found themselves faced by what it termed the discomforts of native life and inadequacies of native food.

The Americans who briefly visited Japan under these circumstances in the 1880's and 1890's, especially those staying no more than the week or two allowed them by round-the-world tours, neither contributed anything to Japan (except their tourist dollars) nor learned very much about the country. They cannot be compared to those earlier visitors who came to teach, to advise, to aid the government or seriously to study Japanese culture. Yet they provided a further link in the close relationship that was gradually developing between Japan and America.

Eliza Skidmore's contemporary quotation touching on American tourists, "Are they not extraordinary persons?" perhaps reflected a general sense of bewilderment on the part of the Japanese as to the nature of this particular breed of foreigners. She may also have spoken for most of her fellow countrymen in reflecting the double image they had always had of the Japanese when she wrote that they "were the enigma of this century; the most inscrutable, the most paradoxical of races." But even though Americans and Japanese could never fully understand each other, they generally maintained in the 1890's that cordial association which had marked their first mid-century contacts.

Unhappily this friendly era was now drawing to a close. On either side of the Pacific, political and economic circumstances were soon to bring about a sharp change in the feelings of mutual trust and confidence that had heretofore characterized Japanese-American relations. And what was soon to become a threatening political rivalry was reflected in more limited cultural associations, and less frequent personal intercourse, than had generally prevailed in the previous period of goodwill.

14

❧

End of an Era

THE BREAKDOWN in the close friendship between Japan and America, with a consequent decline in their cultural ties, cannot be given a precise date. It was not clearly apparent until after the Russo-Japanese War of 1904-5. Following that conflict, in which Theodore Roosevelt had sought to exercise a moderating influence on a spectacularly victorious Japan, the expansion of Japanese power to the Asiatic mainland appeared to threaten American interests in eastern Asia, while at the same time the measures being taken in the United States to restrict Japanese immigration aroused deep and abiding resentment throughout Japan. As a result of the mounting antagonism inspired by these controversial issues, the relations between the two Pacific powers became increasingly strained, and there was already foreshadowed the possible war that was so tragically to break out in 1941.

Even before these somber developments, however, there had been a weakening in Japanese-American bonds. The friendly and cordial ties of the nineteenth century had grown out of a relationship in which the United States played a foremost role as Japan's defender among the nations of the West and in which Japan had freely acknowledged the debt she owed America for her aid and support. But the rising tide of nationalism in Japan and a latent imperialism in America suggested even in the late 1890's that this

249

relationship, almost that of guardian and ward, could not endure permanently. The later political controversies centering about Manchuria and the immigration issue served only to deepen a cleavage that was already becoming manifest with the gradual growth of expansionist ambitions in both nations.

Japan had not fully accepted the inescapable necessity of meeting the West on its own terms until after the restoration of the Emperor in 1868. Her government had then encouraged the adoption of Western ways—from battleships to foreign haircuts—in order to attain full equality among the powers. In foreign policy its major aim was to revise those provisions of the early treaties forced upon the Shogunate which so humiliatingly impinged upon Japanese sovereignty by granting the Western powers their special extraterritorial rights. Once this objective had been achieved with revision of the treaties in 1894, Japan felt free of any further need to conciliate the foreigners and strong enough to assert her own independent position in the world.

While the United States shared the special privileges enjoyed by all the powers in Japan, it had been prepared from the very first to relinquish them as soon as the European nations would do so and consistently sought to hasten treaty revision. The further promotion of trade and commerce, which had provided the underlying motive in seeking to open up Japan, was always a primary objective of American policy. Over and beyond such practicalities, however, the United States remained deeply concerned in helping the Japanese to help themselves in their adjustments to the modern world. This had been the persistent aim of Townsend Harris, as so clearly indicated on innumerable occasions, and in spite of the flirtation with a "cooperative" policy bringing forceful pressure on Japan in the 1860's, it was an important consideration in every stage of America's Far Eastern diplomacy. General Grant had explicitly set forth this point of view when he urged Japan to seek above everything else to establish her full independence of any sort of foreign control, political or economic, and many other instances might be cited in which American officials proffered comparable advice.

The activities of those individual Americans who went to Japan during the early years of Meiji were directed toward this same end. As government advisers, as educators, as missionaries and as students of Japanese culture, they were consciously or unconsciously playing their part in helping to create the new Japan that between 1854 and 1900 made such spectacular progress in the modernization of her institutions and of her whole way of life.

Even though in many cases the Japanese turned to European models in shaping their new institutions, they nonetheless continued to recognize a special indebtedness to America and to Americans. And their feeling of gratitude was repeatedly expressed in official documents and private writings. One significant and perhaps representative statement was made by Fukuzawa Yukichi in an editorial this foremost proponent of Japan's westernization wrote for the *Jiji Shimpo* in January, 1886: "When we remember that it is to the United States of America that we owe our success and our advancement to our present proud position, we cannot help entertaining for them sentiments of peculiarly deep respect and esteem."

He then went on to say that Americans above all foreigners had proved themselves to be leaders and guides in the transformation of Japan, and that in no instance had they shown "an unreasonable spirit in dealing with this country." On another occasion, he made an even more revealing comment on the Japanese reaction to individual Americans. "It is literally true," Fukuzawa wrote, "that the name of 'American citizen' is an invincible passport in any part of Japan."

Some years later Count Hirokichi Mutsu reflected very much the same sense of appreciation in respect to what he called the "deep-rooted and sincere" feeling of friendship the Japanese had for Americans. "It is a natural result," he wrote, "of that helpful and fairminded policy which has ever been pursued by the United States toward Japan since her emergence from the isolation of the past down to the present time."

Nevertheless Americans were Westerners. They were not exempt from the revived antiforeign feeling among the Japanese that one contemporary writer in the 1890's called their "impulsive patriotism." This changed attitude, accompanying somewhat ironically but quite naturally the final revision of the unequal treaties, swept widely over a country sensing a new-found power in its spectacular material growth.

It was manifest in the return to native dress, at least a partial repudiation of the foreign manners and customs once embraced so indiscriminately, and in a new spirit of independence in many other phases of Japanese life. It found even more concrete expression, so far as the United States was concerned, in a virtual end to the government's employment of American advisers (except for Henry Willard Denison in the Foreign Office), a sharp reduction in the number of American teachers at schools and universities, and the withdrawal of government support for students going to the United States. America was still held in deep respect and until after the close of the century continued to be regarded as the most friendly of the foreign powers. Nevertheless Japan was clearly breaking away from any idea of the "tutelage" that William Seward had advocated in the 1870's.

Lafcadio Hearn emphasized this new attitude on the part of the Japanese. "I think we are secretly despised or hated, or both," he said in 1893. "This by the new Japan, of course." He felt that in reaction to what had always been the somewhat condescending or supercilious attitude on the part of Westerners generally, Japan was bound in time to seek retaliation. With the outbreak of hostilities between China and Japan in 1894, he became even more convinced of the ominous outlook for the future. In a long letter to Basil Hall Chamberlain, he wrote:

After the war there will be a strong anti-foreign reaction—outrages —police repressions—temporary stillness and peace; then a new crusade. Life will be made wretched for Occidentals—in business—just as it is now being made in the schools. . . . The nation will show its ugly side to us—after a manner unexpected but irresistible.

Nothing of the sort happened quite so soon. During the Sino-Japanese conflict the United States maintained a neutrality that generally favored Japan (it gave friendly warning of the later intervention of the European powers which forced Japan to relinquish her major wartime gains), and the Japanese Government was fully appreciative of this sympathetic attitude. American policy during the war, the Emperor Meiji wrote President Cleveland in 1895, had "served to draw still closer the bonds of friendship which happily unite our two countries."

But the future was clouded. There were soon to be Japanese attacks on American policy in Hawaii as endangering the peace of the Pacific, and sharp American questioning of Japanese ambitions on the Asiatic mainland. In the United States a youthful Senator from Massachusetts, Henry Cabot Lodge, would declare that the Japanese "have just whipped somebody and they are in a state of mind when they think they can whip anybody." Even though it may not have been fully realized on either side of the Pacific, a measure of mutual distrust was already exercising its corrosive influence.

It would be a happy conclusion to this chronicle of the contacts between individual Americans and Japanese, Yankees and samurai, during the nineteenth century to be able to record that the friendly personal associations established in these years withstood the rise of nationalism and mounting political rivalry in the aims of foreign policy. This of course was not to be. There was no staying the growth of new suspicions, new antagonisms and new conflicts, gradually separating the peoples of the two countries, as Japan and the United States followed their inexorable course to the final breaking point of actual war.

What may be said, however, is that the bonds established between Americans and Japanese in the latter half of the nineteenth century have helped to point the way, after the tragic interlude of war, to a revival of the two nations' historic friendship. The services once performed by Commodore Perry and Townsend Harris, by Horace Capron and William Clark Smith, by Ernest Fenollosa and Lafcadio Hearn, in the creation of modern Japan, and the roles played by such Japanese as Kuroda Kiyotaka and Mori Arinori, Kaneko Kentaro and Nitobe Inazo, in seeking to strengthen their country's ties with the United States, have today a new significance. They have provided a basis for the renewal of those constantly broadening cultural exchanges which ever since the war have once again been drawing Japan and America together.

It may be hoped that this promising new *rapprochement*, rebuilt on the foundations of the past, will this time endure.

Bibliographical Notes

THE SOURCES drawn upon for this account of Japanese-American relations are almost entirely documents, records, contemporary writings and monographs in English. A great part of my research, however, was carried on during a six months' stay in Tokyo and I had some access to Japanese materials which were translated for me by Thomas Shimizu and Kay Nakada, students at the University of Tokyo, and (after my return to this country) by Masaya Yamamoto, a graduate student at The Ohio State University.

This material included Ryuko Kawaji's *Kurofune-ki* (*The Black Ships*) published in Tokyo, 1953; *Harris*, by Seiichi Sakata (Tokyo, 1961); *Man-en-Gannen Kenbei-Shisetsu-Shiryo Shusei* (*Collected Documents of the Japanese Mission to America, 1860*), published in Tokyo (7 vols., 1961); and sections of the still untranslated volumes in the two Centenary Culture Council Series: A *Cultural History of the Meiji Era* and A *History of Japanese-American Cultural Relations* (Tokyo, 1957-58).

The following bibliographical notes give my major sources on a chapter-by-chapter basis, but there should first be noted a number of more general books dealing in whole or in part with the period in Japanese-American relations covered in this volume.

On the history of Japan: Hugh Borton, *Japan's Modern Century* (New York, 1955); Chitoshi Yanaga, *Japan Since Perry* (New York, 1949); E. H. Norman, *Japan's Emergence as a Modern State* (New York, 1940); and W. G. Beasley, *The Modern History of Japan* (New York, 1963).

On political relations between the United States and Japan: John W. Foster, *American Diplomacy in the Orient* (Boston, 1903); Tyler

Dennett, *Americans in Eastern Asia* (New York, 1922); Payson J. Treat, *Diplomatic Relations Between the United States and Japan* (3 vols., Stanford, 1932-38); Edwin O. Reischauer, *The United States and Japan* (rev. ed., Cambridge, 1957); and William L. Neumann, *America Encounters Japan* (Baltimore, 1963).

More directly dealing with the topic of this book: Inazo Nitobe, *The Intercourse Between the United States and Japan* (Baltimore, 1891); Harry Emerson Wildes, *Aliens in the East* (Philadelphia, 1937); George Sansom, *The Western World and Japan* (New York, 1950); and Robert S. Schwantes, *Japanese and Americans, a Century of Cultural Relations* (New York, 1955).

1. "Red Hairs from America"

The basic material from Japanese sources on the early visits of American ships to Japan has been brought together by Shunzo Sakamaki in "Japan and the United States, 1790-1853," *Transactions of the Asiatic Society of Japan*, Sec. Ser., Vol. XVIII (Tokyo, 1933). It is largely based on the records compiled in Makoto Horiuchi, ed., *Nan-ki Tokugawa Shi* (18 vols., Wakayama, 1930-33), and *Tsuko Ichiran* (8 vols., Tokyo, 1912-13). This study may be supplemented by J. Feenestra Kuiper, "Some Notes on the Foreign Relations of Japan in the Early Napoleonic Period," also in *Transactions of the Asiatic Society of Japan*, Sec. Ser., Vol. 1 (Tokyo, 1923-24), which draws upon material from the archives of the Dutch East India Company, and Richard Hildreth, *Japan As It Was and Is* (New York, 1855), which is in turn (in its discussion of the visiting American ships) based on Hendrick Doeff, *Herinnerigen uit Japan* (Haarlem, 1833). Another but less detailed pioneer monograph by a Japanese historian is the previously noted Inazo Nitobe, *The Intercourse Between the United States and Japan*.

The source references in American writings for the early voyages are found in "John Hoskins' Narrative of the Second Voyage of the 'Columbia'" and "Robert Haswell's Log of the Second Voyage of the 'Columbia'" reproduced in Frederic Howay, *Voyages of the "Columbia"* (Boston, 1941); Amasa Delano, *Narrative of Voyages and Travels* (Boston, 1817); Archibald Campbell, *A Voyage Round the World, from 1806 to 1812* (Edinburgh, 1818); the Devereux papers (log of the ship *Franklin*) and Derby papers (journal of George Cleveland) in the Essex Institute and the William Cleveland journal in the Peabody Museum. Extracts from the Devereux and Derby papers have been reprinted in E.S.W., "The First Voyage to Japan," *Historical Collections of the Essex Institute*, Vol. II (June, 1860), and J. F. Allen, "The First Voyage to Japan," the same publication, Vol. II (December, 1860); in the appendix to Arthur B. Christy, *The Asian Legacy and American Life* (New York, 1945); in Ralph D. Paine, "The First American Voyagers to Japan," *Outing*, Vol. 1 (August, 1908); and the same author's *The Ships and Sailors of Old Japan* (New York, 1909). There is also some material from the William Cleveland journal in the introduction of Henry Graff, *Bluejackets with Perry in Japan* (New York Public Library, New York, 1952).

Among the secondary sources that might be cited are Frederic W. Howay, "John Kendrick and His Sons," *Quarterly of the Oregon Historical Society*, Vol. XXXIII (1922); Samuel Eliot Morison, *The Maritime History of Massachusetts* (Boston, 1921); and the previously noted Dennett, *Americans in Eastern Asia*, and Wildes, *Aliens in the East*.

The material on David Porter and John Quincy Adams is taken from the *North American Review*, Vol. XXXXVIII (1856), and Allan B. Cole, "Captain David Porter's Proposed Expedition to the Pacific and Japan, 1815," *Pacific Historical Review*, Vol. IX (1940).

The voyage of the ship *Morrison* is described (apart from the Japanese material in Sakamaki, "Japan and the United States") in S. Wells Williams, "Narrative of a Voyage of the Ship Morrison . . . July and August, 1837," the *Chinese Repository*, Vol. VI (Canton, 1837); Peter Parker, *Journal of an Expedition from Singapore to Japan* (London, 1838); and C. M. King and C. T. Lay, *The Claims of Japan and Malaysia upon Christendom* (2 vols., New York, 1839). There is also some additional material in the letters printed in Frederick W. Williams, *The Life and Letters of S. Wells Williams* (New York, 1889), and George B. Stevens, *Life and Letters and Journals of the Rev. and Hon. Peter Parker, M.D.* (Boston, 1896).

2. Whalers, Shipwrecks and Iron Cages

The greater part of the material on Americans in Japan in the decade or so before the Perry expedition is drawn from *House Executive Document 84* (31st Cong., 1st Sess.) and *Senate Executive Document 59* (32nd Cong., 1st Sess.), with their official reports from naval officers and the depositions of the repatriated seamen; from contemporary magazine and newspaper articles, many of which were reprinted in *Littell's Living Age*; and once again from the Japanese records in Sakamaki, "Japan and the United States."

The story of the *Manhattan* first appeared on February 2, 1846, as written by C. F. Winslow for *The Friend*, published in Honolulu, under the title "Some Account of Captain Mercator Cooper's Visit to Japan in the Whaleship *Manhattan* of Sag Harbor." This article was reprinted some two months later in the *Chinese Repository* and then appeared in *Living Age*, Vol. X (1846). An account of the seamen rescued by Commander Glynn of the *Preble* made its first appearance in the *Chinese Repository* under the heading "Cruise of the U. S. Sloop-of-War Preble . . . to Napa and Nagasaki." Proof sheets were sent to the Providence *Journal*, it was again reprinted in the New York *Courier and Journal*, and then came out in the *Living Age*, Vol. XXIII (October 27, 1849).

The principal source for the adventures of Ranald MacDonald is his own narrative as later published in William S. Lewis and Naojiro Murakami, *Ranald MacDonald* (Spokane, 1923). This account may be supplemented by Herbert H. Gowen, "An American Pioneer in Japan," the *Washington Historical Quarterly*, Vol. XX (1929), and the same author's sketch in *Five Foreigners in Japan* (New York, 1936).

Among the secondary sources dealing with this period, in addition to those generally cited for Chapter 1, are James Morton Callahan, *American Relations in the Pacific and Far East, 1784-1900* (Baltimore, 1901); Charles Oscar Paullin, *Diplomatic Negotiations of American Naval Officers, 1778-1883* (Baltimore, 1912); James Murdoch, *A History of Japan: The Tokugawa Period* (New York, 1926); and Teijuhn Wada, *American Foreign Policy Toward Japan During the Nineteenth Century* (Tokyo, 1928).

3. The Discovery of America

The reports on American impressions of the Japanese in 1853 are taken from John S. Sewall, "With Perry in Japan," *Century Magazine*, Vol. LXX (July, 1905), and the official report of the mission by Francis L. Hawks, *Narrative of the Expedition of an American Squadron to the China Seas and Japan* (3 vols., Washington, 1856). The material on the Dutch scholars is derived from S. Ballard, "A Sketch of the Life of Noboru Watanabe," *Transactions of the Asiatic Society of Japan*, Vol. XXXII (1905); Herbert H. Gowen, *A Precursor of Perry*, University of Washington Chap Book (Seattle, 1928); and Marius B. Jansen, *Sakamoto Ryoma and the Meiji Restoration* (Princeton, 1961).

The accounts of Japanese books on the United States are taken in their entirety from Sakamaki's invaluable "Japan and the United States." He has three chapters: "Early Maps and Knowledge of America," "American Notices in Dutch Reports" and "Japanese Accounts of the United States."

The story of Nakahama Manjiro has in recent years been retold in both Japan and in the United States. The basic source, still untranslated, is Nakahama Toichiro, *Nakahama Manjiro-den* (Tokyo, 1936), but two biographies in English by Japanese writers are Masuji Ibuse, *John Manjiro: The Castaway* (Tokyo, 1941), and Hisakazu Kaneko, *Manjiro, the Man Who Discovered America* (Boston, 1956). Another and more substantial American account is Emily V. Warinner, *Voyager to Destiny* (Indianapolis, 1956). A condensation of Kaneko's book, with Miss Warinner's illustrations, was published in *The American Heritage*, Vol. VIII (December, 1956). The quotations in the text are taken from the sometimes differing translations in these biographies of *The Narratives of the Castaways*, the report made by Manjiro to the Japanese officials at Nagasaki. The comments of Captain John Mercer Brooke are taken from his diary as published in the *Documents of the Japanese Mission to America* (see Chapter 7 for full citation), and the references to Viscount Ishii and Franklin D. Roosevelt are from Kaneko's biography.

4 and 5. A *Treaty Is Signed* and
"Nippon and America, All the Same Heart"

The basic primary sources for Commodore Perry's visits to Japan and the treaty negotiations are the previously cited Francis Hawks, *Narrative of the Expedition . . . to Japan* (available also in one volume, Washington, 1856), and the highly interesting Japanese account, "Diary of an Official of the Bakufu," *Transactions of the Asiatic Society of Japan*, Ser. II, Vol. VII (December, 1930). Moreover, in spite of the Commodore's decree that none of the members of the expedition should publish their own journals, a number of them did so; and also in more recent years, several heretofore unprinted accounts have been discovered and published.

Two accounts which appeared at the time (although very brief) may be found in Bayard Taylor, *A Visit to India, China and Japan in the Year 1853* (New York, 1855), and J. W. Spalding, *Japan and Around the World* (New York, 1855), while John S. Sewall later recalled his experiences with the expedition in "With Perry in Japan," *Century Magazine*, Vol. LXX (July, 1905).

The records published later include S. Wells Williams, "A Journal of the Perry Expedition to Japan," *Transactions of the Asiatic Society of Japan*, Ser. I, Vol. XXXVII, Part II (1910); Shio Sakanishi, ed., "A Private Journal of John Glendy Sproston," *Monumenta Nipponica Monographs* (Sophia University, Tokyo, 1940); the diary of Lieutenant George Henry Preble, which has been published by Boleslaw Szczesniak under the title *The Opening of Japan—A Diary of Discovery in the Far East* (Norman, Okla., 1963); the diaries of two seamen edited by Henry F. Graff in *Bluejackets with Perry in Japan* (New York, 1952); and two accounts edited by Allan B. Cole: *A Scientist with Perry in Japan: The Journal of Dr. James Morrow* (Chapel Hill, N. C., 1947) and *With Perry in Japan—The Diary of Edward Yorke McCauley* (Princeton, 1942). Further contemporary records, one published at the time and the other later, which deal with naval visits immediately following that of the Perry squadron itself, are Alexander W. Habersham, *The North Pacific Surveying and Exploring Expedition; or, My Last Cruise* (Philadelphia, 1857), and Allan B. Cole, ed., *Yankee Surveyors in the Shogun's Seas* (Princeton, 1947).

These firsthand reports, as indicated in the text itself, have all been drawn upon in describing the experiences of the squadron's members afloat and ashore. They have been supplemented in Chapter 4 by Japanese material in Nitobe, *The Intercourse Between the United States and Japan*; quotations from Masaaki Kosaka, *Japanese Thought in the Meiji-Taisho Era* (Tokyo, 1958); a translation of *Kurofune-ki* (*The Black Ships*) by Ryuko Kawaji (Tokyo, 1953), as well as the important "Diary of an Official of the Bakufu." On the reaction of Japanese officials to the squadron's arrival, as reflected in the replies made by the daimio to the Shogunate's circular, I have relied on W. G. Beasley, ed.,

Select Documents on Japanese Foreign Policy, 1853-68 (London, 1955).

For Chapter 5 there is the further firsthand record of a Japanese resident in Hakodate, made available by Matajiro Kojima in *Commodore Perry's Expedition to Hakodate, May, 1854* (Hakodate, 1953), and a series of fascinating prints of the first landings of the Americans at Shimoda reproduced in *The Black Ship Scroll,* published with an introduction by Oliver Statler for the Japan Societies of San Francisco and New York (Tokyo, 1963).

The best secondary account of the opening of Japan, lively and well written, is Arthur Walworth's *Black Ships Off Japan: The Story of Commodore Perry's Expedition* (New York, 1946). Nearly ninety years ago, William Elliot Griffis wrote a pioneer and still very useful biography of its leader, *Matthew Calbraith Perry* (Boston, 1877). Two interesting articles of recent vintage by Japanese writers appeared in the Perry Centennial Edition of *Contemporary Japan,* Vol. XXII (1953): Ryuko Kawaji, "Negotiations with Commodore Perry," and Ki Kimura, "The Significance of Commodore Perry's Expedition." *American Heritage* published in its Junior Library, in 1963, a booklet with excellent illustrations, *Commodore Perry in Japan.*

6. Envoy Extraordinary

Although it does not fully cover his stay in Japan, the material on Townsend Harris is for the most part drawn from *The Complete Journal of Townsend Harris,* edited by Mario Emilio Cosenza. It was first published in New York, 1930, and then a second edition (including a preface by Douglas MacArthur II) was brought out in 1959 in Tokyo and Rutland, Vt. It is supplemented by a number of surviving letters, several of which first appeared in *Littell's Living Age* in 1858 and 1859 while others have been brought together in Shio Sakanishi, ed., *Some Unpublished Letters of Townsend Harris* (New York, 1941). And there has recently been published, in English, the valuable *Japan Journal, 1855-1861* of Henry Heusken (Harris' interpreter), translated and edited by Jeannette C. van der Corput and Robert A. Wilson (New Brunswick, 1964).

Further information may be found in the contemporary accounts of visitors to Japan. They include Lawrence Oliphant, *Narrative of the Earl of Elgin's Mission to China and Japan* (2 vols., New York, 1860); Rutherford Alcock, *The Capital of the Tycoon* (2 vols., London, 1863); William Maxwell Wood, *Fankwei, or the San Jacinto in the Seas of India, China and Japan* (New York, 1859); James D. Johnston, *China and Japan: A Narrative of the Cruise of the Steam Frigate Powhatan* (Philadelphia, 1861); Margaret T. Ballagh, *Glimpse of Old Japan, 1861-66* (Tokyo, 1908); and several anonymous magazine articles: "An American in Japan in 1858," *Harper's,* Vol. XVIII (1858); "Mr. Harris' Progress with the Japanese," *Living Age,* Vol. LIX

(1858); and "Consul Harris in Japan," *Living Age*, Vol. LX (1859).

Additional material is also available in the diplomatic correspondence of this period and in the later report by David Murray on the preparations made in Yedo for receiving Harris which is found in *Papers Relating to the Foreign Relations of the United States, 1879* (Washington, 1879).

A short contemporary article, "Hon. Townsend Harris, America's Minister to Japan," appeared in *Frank Leslie's Illustrated Newspaper*, Vol. X (June 30, 1860). Two subsequent American biographies are William Elliot Griffis, *Townsend Harris: First American Envoy to Japan* (Boston, 1895), which has much interesting material, and Carl Crow, *He Opened the Door of Japan* (New York, 1939), which adds nothing to the record. Herbert H. Gowen has a chapter on Harris in *Five Foreigners in Japan*; Roland S. Morris published a brief pamphlet, *Townsend Harris* (New York, 1921); an article entitled "A Salute to Townsend Harris" appeared in the *Japan Quarterly*, Vol. V (1948); and most recently there is Emily Hahn, "A Yankee Barbarian at the Shogun's Court," *American Heritage*, XV (June, 1964).

A modern and very sympathetic Japanese biography (still untranslated) is Seiichi Sakata's previously noted *Harris*. There have been earlier studies, however, and the legend of Townsend Harris and Okichi-san has always intrigued Japanese writers. One account is an amusing play, *Amerika no Tsukai*, translated into English by Kido Okamoto under the title *The American Envoy* (Kobe, 1931). More recently a number of articles discussing the legend have appeared in the *Asahi Evening News* (May, 1961) and *Japan Queries and Answers* (Tokyo, February, 1962).

The treaty negotiations are fully covered in Treat, *Diplomatic Relations Between the United States and Japan*, and in a number of histories of Japan, including Joseph H. Longford, *The Story of Old Japan* (London, 1910), from which the tribute to Harris is taken, and John R. Black, *Young Japan, Yokohama and Yedo* (2 vols., Yokohama, 1880). See also Henry Satoh, *Lord Hotta* (Tokyo, 1908).

The political background in Japan for these years is discussed in three absorbing Japanese histories which have fortunately been translated: Ernest M. Satow, *Kinsei Shiriaku: A History of Japan* (Yokohama, 1876); Henry Satoh, *Agitated Japan. The Life of Baron Ii Kamon-no-Kami Naosuke* (based on the *Kaikoku Shimatsu* by Shimada Saburo), which was published in Tokyo, 1896; and (with its special references to Harris) Shunkichi Akimoto, *Lord Ii Naosuke and New Japan* (based on *Ii Tairo To Kaiko* by Katsumaro Nakamura), published in Tokyo, 1909.

7. *"Hither from Niphon"*

The progress of the Japanese embassy in the United States in 1860 was extensively covered by reports in contemporary American newspapers and magazines (especially in the illustrated articles in *Harper's Weekly* and *Frank Leslie's Illustrated Newspaper*), and described in the diaries of members of the mission which have in recent years been published in Japan.

The most important collection of the diaries, assembled in connection with the centennial celebration of the embassy, is the previously listed *Man-en-Gannen Kenbei-Shisetsu-Shiryo Shusei* (*Collected Documents of the Japanese Mission to America, 1860*). They include the diary of Captain John Mercer Brooke, the American naval officer aboard the *Kanrin Maru*, and a volume of of extracts from the newspapers in every city the embassy visited. The rest of the material is in Japanese. Together with nine major diaries, one of which is in *waka* (Japanese verse) and another inscribed from an oral record, there are also full accounts of the embassy's personnel, its purchases and expenses, and other official data.

I am indebted for translations from this invaluable source, as already noted, to Miss Kay Nakada and Masaya Yamamoto.

Two highly interesting Japanese diaries were previously published in English. The first is that of Muragaki Awaji-no-Kami, the Vice Ambassador, which originally appeared under the title *The First Japanese Embassy to the United States of America* (Tokyo, 1920) but was more fully reproduced in *Kokai Nikki, The Diary of the First Japanese Embassy to the United States of America* (Tokyo, 1958). The second is that of Yanagawa Masakiyo, the chief retainer of another of the envoys, which was edited and published by Junichi Fukuyama and Roderick H. Jackson in *The First Japanese Mission to the United States* (Kobe, 1937).

Further firsthand accounts by Americans are found in Allan B. Cole, ed., "The Private Journal of Henry A. Wise, U.S.N.," *Pacific Historical Review*, Vol. XI (September, 1942), and Patterson Du Bois, "The Great Japanese Embassy of 1860," *Proceedings of the American Philosophical Society*, Vol. XLIX (1910).

Among the secondary accounts are Chitoshi Yanaga, "The First Japanese Embassy to the United States," *Pacific Historical Review*, Vol. IX (June, 1940); Allan B. Cole, ed., "Japan's First Embassy to the United States, 1860," *Pacific Northwest Quarterly Review*, Vol. XXXIII (April, 1941); "The First Japanese Mission to America," *Life*, Vol. XII (February, 1942); and E. Taylor Parks, "The First Japanese Diplomatic Mission to the United States—1860," *U.S. State Department Bulletin*, Vol. XLII (May 9, 1960).

8. A Time of Turbulence

The background for these days of turbulence is best described in a number of contemporary accounts which include the already cited Ernest M. Satow, *Kinsei Shiriaku*, Black, *Young Japan*, and Alcock, *The Capital of the Tycoon*, together with William Elliot Griffis' colorful *The Mikado's Kingdom* (New York, 1876) and Ernest Satow, *A Diplomat in Japan* (London, 1921). Among subsequent studies of the period are M. Paske-Smith, *Western Barbarians in Japan and Formosa in Tokugawa Days, 1603-1868* (Kobe, 1930); Nitobe Inazo, ed., *Western Influences in Modern Japan* (Chicago, 1931); and Sansom, *The Western World and Japan*. See also Borton, *Japan's Modern Century*, Yanaga, *Japan Since Perry*, and Beasley, *The Modern History of Japan*.

The material on the early trade and growth of Yokohama has been taken from Townsend Harris' *Journal*, contemporary consular reports in successive volumes of the *Commercial Relations of the United States with Foreign Nations*, and the accounts of a number of early residents. The latter include Robert Fortune, *Yedo and Peking* (London, 1863); Ernest Satow, *A Diplomat in Japan* (London, 1921); Margaret T. Ballagh, *Glimpses of Old Japan, 1861-66* (Tokyo, 1908); D. B. Simmons, "Five Years in Japan," *Galaxy*, Vol. X (May, 1868); and William Elliot Griffis, "Inside Japan," *Lippincott's Magazine*, Vol. XII (August, 1873), together with other material by the latter writer in *The Mikado's Kingdom*.

The contemporary life of Yokohama is graphically portrayed in the fascinating selections from two collections of Japanese prints and paintings which have been recently published: *Reflections of the Culture of Yokohama in the Days of the Port's Opening* (Yokohama, 1962) and Carl H. Boehringer, "Meeting with the West," *American Heritage*, Vol. XIV (August, 1963).

The account of Jonathan Goble is derived from material in the *Narrative of the Expedition . . . to Japan*; Black, *Young Japan*; Basil Hall Chamberlain, *Things Japanese* (Tokyo, 1890); and Otis Cary, *A History of Christianity in Japan—Protestant Missions* (New York, 1909). Raphael Pumpelly has recounted his Japanese experiences in *Across America and Asia* (New York, 1871). The stories of Hepburn and Verbeck are fully recorded in *A History of Christianity in Japan*, but William Elliot Griffis has also written a biography of the latter missionary, *Verbeck of Japan* (Chicago, 1900).

The quotation from the poem attacking the Shogun is translated by Burton Watson and taken from Donald Keene, *Modern Japanese Literature, An Anthology* (Grove Press, Inc., New York, 1956).

9. The Yankee Invasion

The greater part of the material in this chapter is derived from the records of Americans living in Japan, as subsequently noted, but important secondary sources bring together much otherwise unavailable Japanese material. The most satisfactory account of the general impact of the West remains Sansom, *The Western World and Japan* (from which, for example, the "Civilization Ball Song" is taken); Robert S. Schwantes has a great deal of interesting information in his *Japanese and Americans*, and there are also, as again previously noted, the two series of books dealing with Japanese culture and Japanese-American relations during the Meiji era, published by the Centenary Culture Council. The latter have not all been translated, are extremely uneven and often poorly organized, but they have many scattered references to the effect of American influences in Japan.

The most interesting or helpful of these Japanese-written books are Ki Kimura, ed., *Japanese Literature: Manners and Customs in the Meiji-Taisho Era*; Keizo Shibusawa, ed., *Japanese Life and Culture in the Meiji Era*; Kunio Yanagida, ed., *Japanese Manners and Customs in the Meiji Era*; Masaaki Kosaka, ed., *Japanese Thought in the Meiji-Taisho Era*; Keizo Shibusawa, ed., *Japanese Society in the Meiji Era*; Yoshie Okazaki, *Japanese Literature in the Meiji Era*; and among the volumes on Japanese-American relations, Hikomatsu Kamikawa, ed., *Japan-American Diplomatic Relations*; Hideo Kishimoto, ed., *Religion and Education*; Ki Kimura, *Science and Literature*; *Customs and Manners*; and Keishi Ohara, *Trade and Industry*.

In more specific terms, the experiences of William Elliot Griffis are taken from the autobiographical sections of *The Mikado's Kingdom*; the account of David Crosby Greene and his associates from the biography by Evarts Boutell Green, *A New Englander in Japan* (Boston, 1927), and Katherine Fiske Berry, *A Pioneer Doctor of Old Japan* (New York, 1940). Further material on missionary activity has been derived from the *Missionary Herald* (incorporating the annual *Proceedings of the American Board of Commissioners for Foreign Missions*) and the previously cited *History of Christianity in Japan* by Otis Cary.

A further important source for these days is Edward S. Morse, *Japan Day by Day* (2 vols., Boston, 1917), and there is also a biography of this well-known scientist, *Edward Sylvester Morse*, by Dorothy G. Wayman (Cambridge, 1942).

On the secondary source level there are also the well-researched account of American experts in Japan in the chapter "Missions to Japan" in Merle Curti and Kendall Birr, *Prelude to Point Four* (Madison, Wis., 1954), and some further material in an undated but recent Japanese pamphlet (with summary in English) by Masao Watanabe which is entitled *The Influence of American Science in Early Meiji Japan*.

The final quotations in this chapter are taken from Satoh, *Agitated Japan*, quoting Shimada Saburo; Hirokichi Mutsu, "A Japanese View of Certain Japanese-American Relations," *Overland Monthly*, Vol. 32 (November, 1898); and Shigeto Tsuru, "Japanese Images of America," in Arthur M. Schlesinger, Jr. and Morton White, eds., *Paths of American Thought* (Boston, 1963). For further Japanese evaluations of American aid see also (as noted above) Keizo Shibusawa, *Japanese Life and Culture in the Meiji Era*; Ki Kimura, *Science and Literature*; and also Toyokichi Iyenaga, *Japan's Real Attitude Toward America* (New York, 1916).

10. *Experiment in Hokkaido*

The story of American aid in the development of Hokkaido is most fully told in II. Capron and His Assistants, *Reports and Official Letters to the Kaitakushi* (Tokyo, 1875), but this account may be supplemented by the article, "Agriculture in Japan," in *Report of the Commission of Agriculture* (Washington, 1874), further letters of members of the mission, and other manuscript material in the library of the Department of Agriculture, Washington. A scholarly account of the venture by John A. Harrison, "The Capron Mission and the Colonization of Hokkaido," appeared in *Agricultural History*, Vol. XXV (1951), and a biographical sketch of its leader by Merritt Starr, titled "General Capron, 1804-1885," has been published in the *Journal of the Illinois State Historical Society*, Vol. XXIII, Part 1 (1925). There is further material in the chapter, "Mission to Japan," in Curti and Birr, *Prelude to Point Four*, and Louisa Kerwin Thiers, "An Advisor to the Japanese Government," *Journal of American History*, Vol. VII (October, 1913).

Herbert H. Gowen has written an account of the activities of Edward Shelton, one of Capron's assistants, in "An American Pioneer in Japan," *Washington Historical Quarterly*, Vol. XX (1929), and Gonpei Kuwada has recounted the life of the mission's geological expert in *The Biography of Benjamin Smith Lyman* (Tokyo, 1937).

Two contemporary accounts of Hokkaido are Benjamin S. Lyman, *Geological Survey of Hokkaido* (Tokyo, 1875), and the interesting travel record of Isabella L. Bird, *Unbeaten Tracks in Japan* (New York, 1880). For more general studies, see John A. Harrison, *Japan's Northern Frontier* (Gainesville, 1953), and F. C. Jones, *Hokkaido* (London, 1958).

There is very little material on William Smith Clark. His contributions to Hokkaido are noted in every account of that island, however, and there is a brief biographical chapter on his career in Herbert Welch, *Men of the Outposts* (Cincinnati, 1937).

On a visit to Sapporo, I was given two relevant pamphlets by a local historian, Shingo Osaka, which throw considerable light on how Hokkaido looks back upon events nearly a century ago. They are entitled "Memoir of Horace Capron" (Sapporo, 1960) and "On Our Own Dr. William Clark Smith" (Sapporo, 1960).

11. *The Japanese in America*

Two quite different books provide the basic material for any account of Japanese in America. The first account, by Charles Lanman, who was attached to the Japanese legation in Washington, was originally published in New York, 1872, as *The Japanese in America*, reissued in Tokyo some fifty-four years later, and then once again published, with added material by Y. Okamura, under the new title *Leaders of the Meiji Resoration in America* (Tokyo, 1931). The second study, carrying the story into the period of steadily increasing immigration in the twentieth century, is Yamato Ichihashi, *Japanese in the United States* (Stanford, 1932). I have also drawn upon translations (by Masaya Yamamato) of sections from *Nichibei Bunka Koshoshi* (*A History of Japanese-American Cultural Relations*), Vol. 5., *Immigration*, edited by Matsuzo Nagai (Tokyo, 1955).

The account of the attempted journey to the United States by Yoshida Shoin is largely taken from Francis Hawks, *Narrative of the Expedition to Japan*, and J. W. Spalding, *Japan and Around the World*, while the quoted poem is taken from H. Van Straelen, *Yoshida Shoin* (Leiden, 1952). The Robert Louis Stevenson essay is "Yoshida-Torajiro," included in *Familiar Stories of Men and Books*.

The records of "Sam Patch" and "Dan Ketch" are very fragmentary (references in Hawks' *Narrative* and early accounts of Yokohama), but Joseph Heco wrote the story of his adventures, which was edited and published by James Murdoch, under the title *Joseph Heco—The Narrative of a Japanese* (2 vols., Yokohama, 1892).

Fukuzawa Yukichi's *Autobiography*, translated by Eiichi Kiyooka (Tokyo, 1948), is one of the best sources for early developments in the Meiji era. Arthur S. Hardy has written *Life and Letters of Joseph Hardy Neesima* (Boston, 1891), and another briefer biography of this religious leader is Jerome D. Davis, *A Sketch of the Life of the Rev. Joseph Hardy Neesima* (New York, 1894). Nitobe Inazo has recalled his early days in *Reminiscences of Childhood* (Tokyo, 1934), and there is a short biography by Sukeo Kitasawa titled *The Life of Dr. Nitobe* (Tokyo, 1933). Information on other Japanese studying in the United States has been taken from the *Japan Biographical Encyclopedia and Who's Who*.

Further information on the students in general may be found in Charles F. Thwing, "Japanese and Chinese Students in America," *Scribner's Monthly*, Vol. XX (July, 1880), and in a much later study, primarily concerned with recent students but at least touching on the historical background, John W. Bennett, *et al.*, *In Search of Identity— The Japanese Overseas Scholar in America and Japan* (Minneapolis, 1953).

On the influence of Japan on America, Nitobe, *The Intercourse Between the United States and Japan* is interesting; there is some material in Shigeto Tsuru, "Japanese Images of America," and Earl Miner, *The Japanese Tradition in British and American Literature* (Princeton, 1958); once again Schwantes, *Japanese and Americans* is very helpful, and most important is Clay Lancaster's beautifully illustrated *The Japanese Influence in America* (New York, 1963).

12. *Love at First Sight*

Ernest Fenollosa wrote two important books: *The Masters of Ukiyoye* (New York, 1896) and *Epochs of Chinese and Japanese Art* (New York, 1921). While they throw little light on his career, there is a brief biographical sketch by his wife in the latter book's introduction. A general account may be found in the opening chapter of Van Wyck Brooks' *Fenollosa and His Circle* (New York, 1962), and there has more recently been published *Fenollosa: The Far East and American Culture*, by Lawrence W. Chisolm (New Haven, 1963). A review of the latter book by Hisatomi Mitsuya (a foremost Japanese authority on Fenollosa) appeared in the *Japan Quarterly*, Vol. XI (1964), under the title "Fenollosa and the American Dream," while another earlier article by the same writer is "Ernest F. Fenollosa and Japan Art," again in the *Japan Quarterly*, Vol. V (1958). There is some discussion of Fenollosa's contributions to Japan in Keizo Shibusawa, *Japanese Society in the Meiji Era*, and of his role in introducing Japanese art to America in Aline B. Saarinen, *The Proud Possessors* (New York, 1958).

His own books and letters, together with several biographical studies, provide the material for Lafcadio Hearn. *Glimpses of Unfamiliar Japan* (New York, 1894) and *Japan, An Attempt at Interpretation* (New York, 1904) are highly interesting, but they give a quite different picture of the country of his adoption than Hearn's more frank and candid personal letters. The latter are available in Elizabeth Bisland, *The Life and Letters of Lafcadio Hearn* (2 vols., New York, 1906), and the same author's *The Japanese Letters of Lafcadio Hearn* (New York, 1910). A readable biography—the best of those published—is Elizabeth Stevenson, *Lafcadio Hearn* (New York, 1961).

Among many interesting articles may be noted Albert Mordell, "Lafcadio Hearn's Love for Old Japan," *Today's Japan*, Vol. V (1960); Marcel Robert, "Lafcadio Hearn," *Transactions of the Asiatic Society of Japan*, Ser. III, Vol. I (1948); and John T. Espey, "The Two Japans of Lafcadio Hearn," *Pacific Spectator*, Vol. IV (1950).

Hearn's popularity in Japan is attested by the publication in 1920-23 of a nine-volume edition of his writings: the *Hearn Memorial Translations*.

13. *Globe-Trotters*

This chapter's opening material on tourism is taken from such previously noted books as Ballagh, *Glimpses of Old Japan*; Griffis, *The Mikado's Kingdom*; and Chamberlain, *Things Japanese*. The poem is quoted from Eliza R. Skidmore, *Jinrikisha Days in Japan* (New York, 1891).

The information on Seward is primarily derived from Olive Risley Seward, ed., *William H. Seward's Travels Around the World* (New York, 1873) and that on Grant from John Russell Young, *Around the*

World with General Grant (2 vols., New York, 1879). There is also further information on these two important visits in State Department correspondence utilized by Treat, *Diplomatic Relations of the United States and Japan*, and in Yanaga, *Japan Since Perry*.

The Japanese visit of Henry Adams and John La Farge is described in their letters, those of the former available in Worthington C. Ford, ed., *Letters of Henry Adams* (2 vols., Boston, 1930), while the latter's have been separately published as *An Artist's Letters from Japan* (New York, 1897). There is further material in Brooks, *Fenollosa and His Circle*, Elizabeth Stevenson, *Henry Adams* (New York, 1955), and Ernest Samuels, *Henry Adams, the Middle Years* (Cambridge, 1958).

The information on travel in the 1890's is taken from contemorary sources already cited (including Lafcadio Hearn's letters), together with *Murray's Handbook for Travellers in Japan*, 3rd ed. (Tokyo, 1891), and *The Tourist Guide and Interpreter* (Yokohama, 1891). One among several contemporary magazine articles is Eustace B. Rogers, "Life in the Foreign Settlements of Japan," *Harper's Weekly*, Vol. 38 (December 29, 1894).

14. *End of an Era*

For the over-all story of the diplomatic relations between the United States and Japan, reference may again be made to Treat, *Diplomatic Relations Between the United States and Japan*, while the changing attitudes of the peoples of the two nations are revealed in contemporary magazine articles and newspaper reports. The specific quotations in the text are taken from Fukuzawa's *Autobiography*; Bisland, *The Japanese Letters of Lafcadio Hearn*; "The Reaction in Japan," *Nation*, Vol. 52 (March 9, 1891); Hirokichi Mutsu, "A Japanese View of Certain Japanese-American Relations," *Overland Monthly*, Vol. 32 (November, 1898).

Index

Adams, Commander H. A., 54, 65, 81
Adams, Henry, 237-40, 247
Adams, John Quincy, 17-8, 22
Advisers, to Japanese Government, 153-5
Akimoto, Shunkichi, *quoted*, 104
Alcock, Sir Rutherford, 102, 129
American Whig Review, 39
Amerika Soki, 45
Antiforeign sentiment, in Japan, 103-104, 126-32, 143-4, 167-8, 251-3
Antisell, Dr. Thomas, 179, 180, 182
Arisugawa, Prince, 152
Armstrong, Commodore James, 85, 86

Bakufu, as administrative arm of Shogunate, 13; measures against stranded seamen, 25, 33; policy toward Commodore Perry, 52, 58-60; toward Townsend Harris, 85, 99, 100-1; dealings with foreigners, 128, 131; *see also* Shogunate
Ballagh, Margaret, 231
Berry, Dr. John C., 153
Biddle, Commodore James, 29-30, 33
Bigelow, William Sturges, 238, 239
Bingham, John, American Minister, 182, 187-8
Bird, Isabella L., 188-9

Bisland, Elizabeth, 222
Black, John R., *quoted*, 141
Blake, William P., 137, 138
Bridgman, Dr. Elijah Coleman, 45
Brooke, Captain John Mercer, 50, 107, 195
Bryan, Samuel, 153
Buchanan, Commander Franklin, 54
Buchanan, President James, 102, 107, 117, 118, 124
Bulwer Lytton (Lord Lytton), 170
Burrows, Silas E., 132

Campell, Archibald, 12
Canton, American trade at, 4, 18, 19
Capron, General Horace C., 176-85, 187, 189
Caroline E. Foote, 133
Cass, Secretary of State Lewis, 117
Cassatt, Mary, 212
Castaways, Japanese, 19, 45, 56, 63, 193; *see also* Manjiro; Heco, Joseph
Century Magazine, 221, 241
Chamberlain, Basil Hall, 227, 231
China, American trade with, 4; missionaries in, 19; treaty of 1844, 64; Harris consular appointment, 84; Anglo-French intervention, 100, 101
Chinese Repository (Canton), 24

Choshu, 130-1, 144
Christian Remembrancer, 39
Christianity, in Japan, 2, 19, 25-6, 139, 164, 169; *see also* Missionaries
Clark, William Smith, 185-87
Cleveland, George, 8, 9-10, 116, 234
Cleveland, President Grover, 179, 252
Cleveland William 8-9, 26, 72
Columbia, 3-5
Columbus, U.S.S., 29-30
Conder, Joseph, 212
Cooper, Captain Mercator, 26-8, 61
Crawford, Colonel Joseph U., 183
Curtis, William Eleroy, 241, 246-7

Dana, Richard Henry, 241
Davidson, Captain J., 6
Davis, Captain Ira, 47
Davis, Jerome D., 200
Davis, John W., 33
Deal, Captain James, 6
Delano, Captain Amasa, 4, 11
Delano, Warren, 51
De Long, Charles E., American Minister, 154, 178
Democratic Review, 39, 57
Denison, Henry Willard, 155, 252
Derby, Captain Samuel, 8, 10
Deshima, Dutch trading factory, 2; visited by Americans, 7, 9, 17, 24, 38; visited by William Seward, 234
Devereux, Captain James, 7, 211
Dewey, John, 206
Disraeli, Benjamin, 170
Doshisha College, 166, 200-1
Dougherty, T. T., 133
Douglas, Captain James, 4
Dun, Edward, 178-9
Dunne, Finley Peter, *quoted*, 190
Du Pont, Captain Samuel F., 107
Dutch, in Japan, 2, 7, 11, 24, 31, 34, 43, 45; *see also* Holland
Dutch East India Company, 6, 7, 10-11, 26, 31
"Dutch scholars, 41-2

Edwards, Captain Lawrence B., 36
Eclipse, 11-12

Education, American contribution in Japan, 160-2, 172-3; *see also* Griffis, Fenollosa, Hearn
Elgin, Earl of, 88
Eliza, 6, 10
Emerson, Ralph Waldo, 205
England, *see* Great Britain
Exclusion edicts, Japanese, 2, 12, 22, 23, 29
Exclusion law, American, 206, 207, 210
Extraterritoriality, 64, 152, 250, 251

Fenollosa, Ernest, 212, 246; life in Japan, 214-20; meets Hearn, 226; meets Henry Adams, 238-9, 240
Fillmore, President Millard, 53, 54, 56, 57, 61, 62
Finch, Captain John, 34
Fish, Secretary of State Hamilton, 154
Formosa, Japanese expedition (1873), 154-5
Foster, John W., *quoted*, 82
France, signs treaty with China, 100; with Japan, 102, 133; cooperative policy, 144; influence in Japan, 153, 169, 208
Frank Leslie's Illustrated Newspaper, 83, 105, 108, 109, 118, 123
Franklin, Benjamin, 169-70
Franklin, ship, 7, 8
Franklin, whaleship, 47
Freer, Charles Lang, 220
Friend, The (Honolulu), 24, 28
Fukui, visited by William E. Griffis, 156, 157-9
Fukushima Yoshikoto, 114, 116, 117
Fukuzawa Yukichi, 201, 202, 204, 205, 210; visit to America and influence on Japanese education, 196-8; *quoted*, 131-2, 251
Fumi-ye, 25, 37, 139

Gardner, Mrs. Jack, 220
Geisinger, Commodore, 33
General Palmer, 19
Germany, influence on Japan, 153, 208
Gillette, Mabel, 241

Globe-trotters, 231-2; *see* Seward, Grant, Adams, La Farge, *and* tourists
Glynn, Commander James, 33-34, 55, 61
Goble, Jonathan, 136-7, 193
Godey's Lady's Book, 137
Grace, 4, 5
Grant, General U. S., 83, 176, 245, 250; visit to Japan, 235-7
Gray, Captain Robert, 3
Great Britain, early contacts with Japan, 2; imperialism, 17; treaties with Japan, 87-8, 102, 133; with China, 100; cooperative policy, 144; influence on Japan, 153, 169, 200
Greeley, Horace, 121
Greene, Daniel Crosby, 164-7, 200, 245
Greey, Edward, 241
Griffis, William Elliot, 182, 193, 223, 231, 242, 245, 247; in Japan, 148-149; 150-60; *quoted*, 197, 202, 203
Gulick, Orramel, 164, 166
Gwin, Senator William K., 194

Hakodate, opened as treaty port, 64; visited by Perry squadron, 67, 68, 77, 78-9; visited by *Caroline E. Foote*, 133
Hardy, Alpheus, 199
Harper's New Monthly Magazine, 39, 212, 222, 223, 227
Harper's Weekly, 108, 109, 123
Harris, Townsend, 106, 111, 125, 126, 128, 129, 132, 133, 157, 237, 250; arrival in Japan, 82; background and character, 83-5; life at Shimoda, 85-92; visit to Yedo, 92-100; illness, 100; final treaty negotiations, 100-3; signature of treaty, 101-2; last days in Japan, 103-5; death, 105
Hassam, Childe, 212
Haswell, Robert, 5
Hawaiian Islands, 4, 28, 252
Hawks, Francis L., 40, 54n, 69, 72, 74, 77
Hawthorne, Nathaniel, 54n
Hay, John, 238, 240

Hayashi, Count, 140
Hayashi Daigaku-no-Kami, 62, 63, 64, 77
Hearn, Lafcadio, 245, 247; arrival in Japan, 214, 222; life in Japan, 222-230; *quoted*, 73, 169, 252
Heco, Joseph, 194-6
Hepburn, James, 140-1, 142, 143
Heusken, Henry, arrival in Japan, 85-86; quotations from journal, 87, 90n, 93, 96, 99, 100; assassination, 103-4, 125, 126
Hiroshige, 16, 93, 219
Hokkaido, 24, 34, 36, 64, 137-9, 174-189
Hokusai, 16, 219
Holland, treaties with Japan, 87, 102, 133; *see* Dutch, in Japan
Holmes, Oliver Wendell, 206
Honolulu, 46, 47
Hoskins, John, 5
Hotta Bitchu-no-Kami Masayoshi, 95, 97, 98, 101
House, Edward H., 168
Howe, George, 31-2
Howel, John, 4
Huston, John, 92n
Hutchings, Captain W. V., 8

Ichihashi, Yamato, *quoted*, 207
Ii Kamon-no-Kami-Naosuke, 101, 126-127
Immigration, of Japanese, 209-10; *see also* students
Ingersoll, Captain David, 19
Inouye Shinano-no-Kami, 90, 95, 96, 97, 98
Irwin, Wallace, 208
Ishii, Viscount Kikujiro, 51
Ito Hirobumi, 151, 153, 172, 190, 196, 206
Iwakichi, see Ketch, Dan
Iwakura mission, 147, 160, 190, 199, 204, 205
Iwakura Tomomi, 147, 182, 204, 235
Iwasa Higo-no-Kami, 98
Iyeyasu, 13, 145

Janes, Captain, L. L., 200, 224

Japan, at close of eighteenth century, 12-6; political disturbances, 143-7; restoration of Emperor, 146-7; modernization program, 148-53; 171-3; foreign polciy, 152-3, 249-250; influence on United States, 210-13

Japan Expedition, rumors of coming, 51-2; background, 55-7; first visit, 53-5; second visit, and treaty, 60-4

Japan Express, 134

Japan Mail, 183

Japanese, Americans' ideas of, 8-10, 39, 68-74, 87-9, 157, 222, 229, 239-40, 248

Japanese Embassy (1860), experiences in America, 106-10; impressions of America, 110-17; visit in Washington, 117-9; visit in Baltimore, 119-20; visit in Philadelphia, 120-21; visit in New York, 121-3; final consequences, 123-5

Jewett, Frank F., 163

Jiji Shimpo, 198, 251

Jinrikisha, invented, 137

John Howland, 46

Johnston, Lieutenant James D., 84-85

Joy, A. O., 134

Kabuki, 16, 120

Kaempfer, Engelbrecht, 17

Kagoshima, visit of *Morrison*, 21, 22, scene of Manjiro trials, 47, 48; British attack on, 130, 143

Kaitakushi, 176, 181, 183, 184, 188, 189; *see also* Capron, General Horace *Kajin no Kigu* (*Strange Encounters with Elegant Females*), 171

Kaneko Kentaro, 206

Kano Hogai, 220

Kanrin Maru, 50, 106, 107, 195-6

Kashinoura, 1, 2, 5

Kato Somo, 113-4, 115

Katsu Rintaro, 106-7

Kawai, Kazuo, *quoted*, 192-3n

Kendrick, Captain John, 11, 25; **visit** to Japan, 1, 3-6

Ketch, Dan, 193-4

King, Charles W., 18-22, 26, 55

Kipling, Rudyard, *quoted*, 246

Kobe, as treaty port, 102, 136; visited by Greene, 165; in 1890's, 245-6

Koizumi Yakumo, *see* Hearn, Lafcadio

"Kumamoto Band," 200, 224

Kuroda Kiyotaka, 190, 204-5; as director of Kaitakushi, 176, 177, 178, 180, 181, 185

Kyoto, imperial capital, 65, 101; missionary enterprise in, 166-7, 200; in 1890's, 245-6

Lady Pierce, 132

Lady Washington, 3, 4, 5

La Farge, John, 237-40

Lagoda, 34-5, 36, 38

Lanman, Charles, 205

Lawrence, 30-1, 32, 33, 34, 36, 38

Le Gendre, General Charles, 154-5

Lewis, John R. C., 71-2

Lincoln, President Abraham, 104, 110, 124, 195

Lodge, Henry Cabot, 253

Long, John Luther, 241

Longford, Joseph H., *quoted*, 102

Lowell, Amy, 213, 241

Lowell, Percival, 213, 241

Lyman, Benjamin Smith, 183-4, 247

MacArthur, General Douglas, 58

McCauley, Lieutenant Edward Yorke, 68, 73-4, 75

MacDonald, Ranald, 35-8, 61

Macao, 18, 20, 21, 45

Madame Butterfly, 241-2

Madison, President James, 17

Manhattan, 26-8, 37, 45

Manifest Destiny, 56

Manjiro, 52, 73, 107, 193, 194; visit to the United States, 46-7; return to Japan, 47; reports on United States, 48-9; later career, 49-51

Marcy, Secretary of State William L., 84, 102

Margaret, 8, 9

Mason, Luther Whiting, 162-3, 168, 206

Massachusetts, 8

Matsudaira Shungaku, 156, 159
Matsue, visited by Lafcadio Hearn, 223-4
Matsusaki Michitaro, 77
Megata Tanetaro, 205-6
Meiji Emperor, 178, 242, 252; restoration, 145-7; receives Capron, 177; receives Seward, 233, 234; receives Grant, 235, 236-7
Melville, Herman, *quoted*, 23-4, 56
Mendenhall, Thomas C., 163, 215
Meriken Shinsi, 44, 45
Miller, Hilliard, 153
Minstrel show, 76-7
Missionaries, in Japan, 139-43, 164-9
Mori Arinori, 160, 204, 205, 236
Moriyama Einosuki, 27, 28, 37, 61, 63, 73, 89, 191
Morrison, 19, 20-2, 41, 55
Morrow, Dr. James, 70, 72, 74
Morse, Edward Sylvester, 163, 211, 215
Morton, Dr. W.T.G., 120
Mount Vernon, 6
Mung, John, *see* Manjiro
Muragaki Awaji-no-Kami, as Vice Ambassador of Japanese embassy, 107; diary comments, 111, 113, 114, 115, 116, 117, 119, 121, 123; after return to Japan, 125n
Murdoch, James, *quoted*, 194
Murray, Dr. David, 96, 160-2, 182
Murray's Handbook for Travellers, 242, 243, 245, 246, 247
Mutsu, Hirokichi, *quoted*, 251

Nagasaki, Dutch at, 2; early American visits, 6-11; seamen detained in port, 24, 25, 31-2, 34; visited by Commander Glynn, 33-4; by Ranald MacDonald, 36-7; by Manjiro, 47-8; as treaty port, 136
Nagasaki Maru, 11, 12
Nakahama Manjiro, *see* Manjiro
Nakahama Toichiro, 51
Nakamura, Katsumaro, *quoted*, 173
Narratives of the Castaways, The, 46, 48
Nation, 183

Neesima, Joseph Hardy, *see* Niijima Jo
New York Herald, 34, 123
New York Illustrated News, 106
New York Tribune, 121, 123, 141
Niijima Jo, 166, 198-201, 203, 205
Nitobe Inazo, as student in the United States, 206-7; *quoted*, 20, 127, 168, 203, 205, 208, 212
Noguchi, Yone, *quoted*, 219, 224, 225, 228
Nonomura Chujitsu, 116
Northwest coast, 1, 4, 5, 11-2, 18-9

O'Cain, Captain Joseph, 11-2
Oguri Bungo-no-Kami, 107, 125n
Okada Bingo-no-Kami, 90
Okakura Kakuzo, 218, 220, 221
Okichi-san, 90-1
Okinawa, 236
Oliphant, Lawrence, 88
Oliphant and Company, 18
Omura, Lord of, 11
Osaka, 144, 157, 242
Osanai Kaoru, 225

Palmer, Aaron H., 55
Parker, Dr. Peter, 19, 21
Patch, Sam, 193
Paul, Henry M., 163
Perry, Commodore Matthew Calbraith, 2, 19, 20, 25, 30, 49, 50, 87, 125, 132, 138, 149, 150; arrival in Bay of Yedo, 40, 51-2, 53-55; character, 57-8; negotiations with Japanese, 60-4, 65; relations with Japanese, 68, 74, 76-78; *see also* Japan Expedition
Philadelphia Inquirer, 120
Pierce, President Franklin, 83, 84, 95, 194, 195
Plymouth, 36
Porter, Captain David, 17, 22, 55
Portuguese, in Japan, 2
Pound, Ezra, 213, 221
Powhatan, U.S.S., flagship of Perry expedition, 61, 70, 76, 77; return to Japan (1858), 100, 101; and Japanese embassy (1860), 106, 107

Preble, Lieutenant George Henry, 63-4, 71, 72, 76n, 77, 79-80
Preble, U.S.S., 33-4, 35-8
Pruyn, Robert H., American Minister, 128, 132, 144
Pumpelly, Raphael, 137-9, 175, 247

Reed, W. C., 133
Reischauer, Edwin O., *quoted*, 167
"Richardson affair," 129
Richardson, C. L., 129
Richardson, E. P., *quoted*, 212
Roberts, Edmund, 18
Rokumeikan, 151, 172
Roosevelt, President Franklin D., *quoted*, 51
Roosevelt, Theodore, 206, 221, 249
Russia, threats to Japan, 17, 175; treaties with Japan, 87, 102, 133
Russian-American Company, 12
Russo-Japanese war, 249
Ryukyu Islands, 47, 236

Sakamaki, Shunzo, *quoted*, 42, 44, 48
Sansom, George B., *quoted*, 16, 151, 172
Sarah Boyd, 47
Saris, Captain John, 92
Satsuma, clash with British, 129-30
Schwantes, Robert S., *quoted*, 164, 207
Scott, Marion M., 161
Scott, Matthew, 153
Seamen, shipwrecked in Japan, 24-6, 30-5, 55, 63
Senpacki, *see* Patch, Sam
Sewall, John, 40, 45, 75, 242
Seward, Olive Risley, 232, 233, 234
Seward, Secretary of State William H., 104, 144, 145, 195, 252; visits Japan, 232-5
Shelton, Edward Mason, 178, 182
Shiba Shiro, 170-1
Shimazu Nariakira, 47
Shimmi Buzen-no-Kami, 107, 114, 125n
Shimoda, opened as treaty port, 64; visited by Perry squadron, 67, 68, 72, 77-8, 80, 81; residence of Townsend Harris, 82, 85, 86, 88, 100; visited by *Caroline E. Foote*, 133

Shimonoseki, Straits of, battle, 130-1, 143
Shingo, Osaka, 189
Shogunate, as governing agency in Japan, 13, 15; faces crisis (1853), 58-60; sends mission to United States, 106; employs Raphael Pumpelly, 137-8; rivalry with imperial party, 126, 131-2, 143-5; final collapse, 145-6; *see also* Bakufu
Shoyer, Ralph, 134
Sino-Japanese war, 252
Skidmore, Eliza R., 232, 245, 248
Smiles, Samuel, 170
Smith, Erastus Peshine, 154, 155, 178
Spalding, J. W., 72-3
Spencer, Henry, 215
Sproston, Midshipman John G., 76, 77, 81
Statler, Oliver, 245
Stevenson, Robert Louis, 192
Stewart, Captain William Robert, 6, 10-1
Straits Times (Singapore), 24, 31, 32
Students, Japanese, in America, 202-9
Sugimoto, Etsu Inagaki, 209-10

Takano Nagahide, 41-2
Tanaka Fujimaro, 160, 161-2
Tateishi Onojiro ("Tommy"), 108-9, 156
Taylor, Bayard, 58, 68, 71, 241
Tokaido, 93-4, 129, 148-9, 234, 244
Tokugawa Shogunate, *see* Shogunate
Tokyo, renamed from Yedo, 146; described by Griffis, 149-50; in 1890's, 244-5
Tokyo (Imperial) University, 50, 142, 163-4, 215, 225
Tosa, Lord of, 59
Tourists, in 1890's, 241-8
Trade, American, with Japan, under Dutch flag, 7-10; popular interest in, 17-18, 55-6; at Yokohama, 133-134; later promotion of, 211
Treaty, commercial (1858), 133, 139, 211; negotiations by Townsend Harris, 98-101; final provisions, 101-2; exchange ratifications, 106, 107, 118

Treaty of Kanagawa (1854), 66, 80, 92, 132; negotiations by Commodore Perry, 62-4; final provisions, 64
Tsuru, Shigeto, *quoted,* 160, 173

Ukiyo-e, 135, 212, 219-20, 221
United States, early Japanese ideas of, 42-45, 51; developing interest in Japan, 16-8, 23-6, 39, 55-7; first treaty with Japan, 60-4; commercial treaty, 98-9, 101; trade with Japan, 132-4; aid and assistance to Japan, 153-5, 160-3, 172-3
Uraga, 20, 22, 27, 28, 37, 54

Vanderbilt, William H., 211
Van Valkenburgh, R. B., American Minister, 144, 145
Verbeck, Guido, 140, 141-3, 163, 165, 201, 203
Verne, Jules, 170
Vincennes, U.S.S., 29

Wada, Teijuhn, *quoted,* 34
Walsh, Hall and Company, 133
Warfield, Major A. G., 179, 180
Washington, George, 43, 44, 49
Watanabe, Masao, *quoted,* 163
Watanabe Noboru, 41-2
Weir, J. Alden, 212
Weld, Dr. Charles G., 218

Whaling, 23-4; issue of shipwrecked seamen, 24-6, 30-5, 55, 63
Whistler, James A. M., 212
Whitfield, Captain William H., 46-7
Whitman, Walt, 122-3, 170, 190
Whitmore, Captain, 47
Williams, George W., 153
Williams, S. Wells, 19, 63, 67, 68, 80, 84
Wilmington, 133
Wilson, Woodrow, 187, 206
World's Fair (1893), 211-2, 221
Worth, Captain A. J., 133
Wright, Frank Lloyd, 211, 245

Yamanaka and Company, 211
Yanaga, Chitoshi, *quoted,* 154, 170, 198
Yanagawa Masakiyo, 112-3, 115-6, 118, 119
Yedo, as Shogun's capital, 13, 65; visit of Townsend Harris, 92, 94-100; right of foreign residence, 102; Harris establishes legation, 102-3; becomes Tokyo, 146
Yedo, Bay of, 2, 20, 27, 40, 53, 58, 60
Yezo, *see* Hokkaido
Yokohama, 60, 102, 128, 140, 141, 148, 164; establishment of treaty port, 133-6; in 1890's, 243-4
Yoshida Shoin, 191-2, 196